ENGLISH REVIEW MANUAL

A program for self-instruction

ENGLISH REVIEW MANUAL SECOND EDITION
A program for self-instruction

JAMES A. GOWEN
UNIVERSITY OF KANSAS

McGRAW-HILL BOOK COMPANY

New York	Düsseldorf	Panama
St. Louis	London	Sydney
San Francisco	Mexico	Toronto

ENGLISH
REVIEW
MANUAL
A program for self-instruction

Library of Congress Catalog Card Number 71-116665

1 2 3 4 5 6 7 8 9 0 Q B B P 7 9 8 7 6 5 4 3 2 1 0

This book was set in Helvetica by B. Handelman Associates, Inc., printed on permanent paper by Quinn & Boden Company, Inc., and bound by The Book Press, Inc. The designer was Edward Zytko. The editors were Robert Fry, Cheryl Kupper, and Timothy Yohn. Adam Jacobs supervised the production.

PREFACE

This book offers the advanced student a thorough review of the principles of written English. Its plan allows the student to study independently, using the text according to his particular needs. Primarily designed to help composition teachers minimize the expense of classroom time on the principles of grammatical usage, the book is also suited to courses dealing exclusively with usage problems. In addition, students not enrolled in English courses will find it a convenient guide for independent study.

This book is a proved equivalent of intensive initial units dealing with usage problems in college composition courses. By assigning it for parallel study to replace such units, a teacher can concentrate from the beginning of the course on the more important aspects of composition—organization, paragraphing, diction, tone, style, and the rest. The theme-correction symbols at the front of the book make the text a reference guide useful during the remainder of the course and during related courses.

The plan of this book makes it readily adaptable to courses concerned primarily with usage problems. The teacher need assign only the first six parts in the order in which they appear; he can then assign without loss of continuity the other nineteen parts in the order he has found to be the most satisfactory for his course. He can also omit any part if the emphasis of instruction and exercises in his course makes such an omission desirable.

An instructor's manual is available on request. It contains a detailed explanation of the book's structure and suggestions for using the text in different kinds of courses. Also available from the publishers are individual test booklets designed for use with the text both for additional exercise and progress measurement. The test booklet contains comprehensive diagnostic and final examinations as well as quizzes for each of the text's twenty-five chapters.

I would like to thank the following teachers whose criticism was extremely helpful in the revision of the text for its second edition: Dr. Eileen Lothamer, California State College, Mrs. Violet Skorina, Western Connecticut State Colege, and Miss Renate Lepehne, Northeastern University.

An early version of the present text was tested among students in the United States and Canada. The results, together with the comments of those who participated, were invaluable during subsequent revisions of the text. I would like to acknowledge my gratitude, therefore, to the following teachers and their students: Dean James Lawrence Billwiller, City College of San Francisco; Dr. Richard M. Diamond, University of Miami; Mrs. Evelyn Gray, Eastern Nazarene College; Dr. Harry Huffman, Virginia Polytechnic Institute; Self-development Center, Metropolitan Life Insurance Company; Miss Ruth Jackson, University of Oregon; Dr. Ralph Martin, Knoxville College; Mr. Raeburn Miller and Dr. George F. Reinecke, Louisiana State University; Dr. Bernard O'Donnell, Ball State Teachers College; Mr. Howard Richmond and Mr. Edward F. Warner, Asbury Park High School; Miss Mildred Sic, Midland Lutheran College; Dr. E. J. Tyler, Brandon College; and Dr. Melvin Wolf, University of Massachusetts.

Particularly helpful in the final revision of the text were the suggestions and criticisms kindly offered by Dr. William F. Irmscher, University of Washington, and Dr. J. William Moore and Dr. Wendell I. Smith, Bucknell University. For her editorial work on the earliest version of the text, I am grateful to Mary Lyle Rempel.

To my wife Marianne, whose help and advice I depended upon constantly during all stages of the text's preparation, I owe my greatest debt of gratitude.

JAMES A. GOWEN

TO THE STUDENT

This book offers you a way to review selectively the principles of written English. Its programmed form of presentation enables you to learn efficiently with or without the direct supervision of an instructor.

The design of the text arises from the particular needs of advanced students who have studied grammar and usage in elementary and high schools. If you have had such training, you probably do not need another exhaustive course in English. Yet writing clear and effective prose for college courses and for a profession normally requires some additional study. This book accordingly provides a system which permits you to identify your individual deficiencies; in this way you can study as much or as little as you need, concentrating on those problems with which you have difficulty.

Since this is a programmed text, you should acquaint yourself with its organization before you begin to study.

First, glance through the book briefly. Notice that it is divided into individual paragraphs called *frames*. Notice also that certain frames, called *express frames*, are set apart in boxes. Each frame calls for one or more responses; the correct responses are in the margin beside the frames.

As you will see, a blank space may represent one missing word, or it may represent several missing words.

The express frames—those set off in boxes—are at the beginning of each short sequence of frames dealing with a particular subject. When you begin study, cover the answer column with an envelope or a folded piece of paper and read the first express frame. If you can complete it without difficulty, skip over the intervening frames to the next express frame. Your ability to complete an express frame indicates that you do not need to study the frames of the sequence which directly follows it.

Be sure to use wisely your option of skipping sequences. When completing an express frame, do not guess. Be sure you have a reason for your response. Any difficulty you encounter in completing an express frame is simply a signal that you need to study the following sequence of frames.

Be sure also to complete all the short review sequences. These are identified in the same way that the express frames are, by a box. If you do poorly on a review sequence, go over the preceding frames and identify the source of your difficulty before you proceed.

Students who used a preliminary version of this text discovered that they studied most efficiently during short periods—twenty minutes to a half-hour long. Therefore, you will probably find that you will get the most from this text if your own study periods are relatively short.

Here in brief are your guides for using this text.

1 *Complete all the express frames in turn.*
2 *If you have any difficulty with an express frame, skip it and complete the frames of the sequence which directly follows.*
3 *Complete all the short review sequences.*
4 *Repeat a section if you have difficulty with a review sequence.*
5 *Keep your study periods brief.*

JAMES A. GOWEN

CONTENTS

TWELVE
OMITTED PARTS   243

THIRTEEN
MIXED AND ILLOGICAL
CONSTRUCTIONS   258

ONE

BASIC SENTENCE PARTS AND MAJOR PARTS OF SPEECH

SUBJECT AND PREDICATE

Almost all the low, dense fog disappeared within two hours after sunrise.

1A Draw a single line beneath the words of the subject in the following sentence, a double line beneath the words of the predicate.

Almost all the low, dense fog disappeared within two hours after sunrise.

□ The sentence is the basic unit of expression.

Wood burns.

This sentence expresses something about _____ .

Wood

□ The subject of a sentence names what the sentence is about.

Wood burns.

Wood is the _____ of this sentence.

subject

□ *Gold melts.*

The subject of this sentence is _____.

□ The predicate of a sentence asserts something about the subject.

Wood burns.

Burns is the predicate of this sentence because it asserts something about the subject _____.

Gold   □   *Gold melts.*

Melts is the _____ of this sentence.

□   *Men work.*

The subject of this sentence is _____. The predicate is _____.

□ All sentences have two parts: the naming part, which is called the _____, and the asserting part, which is called the _____.

□ Sentences usually have subjects and predicates made up of more than one word.

Mature men work diligently.

In this sentence *Mature men* is the _____, *work diligently* is the _____.

□   *The most popular girl came to the party.*

In this sentence, _____ is the subject, _____ is the predicate.

□   *Several tall, husky troopers arrived in a squad car.*

The subject of this sentence is _____.
The predicate is _____.

Left margin answers:

Gold

Wood

predicate

Men
work

subject
predicate

subject
predicate

The most popular girl came to the party

Several tall, husky troopers
arrived in a squad car

2

1B *Here are several problems.*

The subject of this sentence is _____.

The predicate is _____.

several problems
Here are

☐ In English sentences the subject generally comes before the predicate.

The rain came down.

In this sentence *The rain*, the _____, comes before *came down*, the _____.

subject
predicate

☐ The subject, however, may come after the predicate.

The rain came down.
Down came the rain.

The subject of both these sentences is _____.
The predicate is _____.

The rain
came down
(*down came*)

☐ *Down came the rain.*

In this sentence the _____ comes before the _____.

predicate
subject

☐ We often use *here* and *there* to introduce the predicate of a sentence. Neither of these words can be the subject.

Here comes Charlie.
Charlie comes here.

Although *Here* introduces the predicate in the first sentence, the subject of both of these sentences is the name _____.

Charlie

□ Sentences in which the predicate is introduced by *here* or *there* are often reversible.

> *Here are three tacks.*
> *Three tacks are here.*

Reverse the order of the subject and predicate of this sentence:

> *Here is your lost book.*

Your lost book is here. _____

□ *There* introducing the predicate of a sentence is sometimes an empty word that we can drop if we reverse the subject and predicate.

> *There are two cars in the garage.*

Rewrite this sentence, placing the subject before the predicate and dropping *There.*

Two cars are in the garage. _____

□ Reverse the order of the subject and predicate in this sentence, dropping *There.*

> *There is a car in the drive.*

A car is in the drive. _____

□ In sentences expressing a question, the predicate may be introduced by *when, where, how,* or *why.* If so, the subject may follow the predicate.

> *How are you?*

you　　The subject is not *How* or *are* but _____.

□ If *when, where, how,* or *why* introduces the predicate, it is part of the predicate.

> *Where is Herman?*

Herman　　The subject is not *Where* but _____. The pred-
Where is　　icate is _____.

☐ *How was George?*

The subject of this sentence is _____. The predicate is _____.

☐ No matter where it appears in a sentence, the _____ is always the part that names what the sentence is about. The _____ is always the part that asserts something about the subject.

REVIEW

Draw a single line beneath the words of the subjects of the following sentences, a double line beneath the words of the predicates.

☐ *Horses run.*

☐ *The four men are ready.*

☐ *Thousands of screaming teenagers greeted the young singer.*

☐ *Here stood the opposing forces.*

☐ *Three pretty little girls carried baskets of white carnations in the wedding procession.*

☐ *Where were you?*

1C *He gave us four old chairs and a table.*

chairs, table

List the nouns in this sentence: _____.

He, us

List the pronouns: _____.

□ The subject of a sentence names what the sentence is about, and the most important word in the subject is usually a name word called a noun.

The men left early.

men

The most important word in the subject of this sentence is the noun _____.

□ *The books are for sale.*

noun

The most important word in the subject of this sentence is the _____ *books.*

□ The term *noun* refers to any word that names a person (*Bob*), place (*Chicago*), object (*baseball*), quality (*beauty*), etc.

Ralph admires goodness.

Ralph

goodness

The two nouns in this sentence are _____ and _____.

□ Since it may not always be easy to distinguish nouns from other words, we should know that nouns change form in ways in which other words do not. For instance, nouns have a form ending in *'s*: *Bob's, Chicago's, baseball's, beauty's*. Thus we can say that *desk* [can, cannot] _____ be used as a noun but that *among* _____.

can

cannot

□

brought	Ed
Denver	with
to	furniture

6

Using the test described in the last frame, we know that only the following words from this group can be used as nouns: _____.

Denver, Ed, furniture

☐ *He gave us a bundle of used wood.*

The nouns in this sentence are _____.

bundle, wood

☐ *The team will **play** in the stadium.*

The nouns in this sentence are _____.

team, stadium

☐ Another **kind of** name word is the pronoun. One of the most important characteristics of pronouns is that they function as noun substitutes. Thus we say that pronouns stand for nouns.

John drove. He was extremely cautious.

The pronoun *He* in the second sentence stands for the noun _____ in the first.

John

☐ *The men left early, but they were delayed on the way.*

The pronoun _____ stands for the noun _____.

they   men

☐ Notice that, unlike nouns, pronouns do not have a form ending in *'s*. Thus, while we say *men's work,* we do not say *they's work.* Rather, we use another form entirely: _____ *work.*

their

☐ you   day
    them   we
    house   bridge

Testing each of these words by adding *'s* to them, we can see that _____, _____, and _____ are nouns and that _____, _____, and _____ are pronouns.

house   day   bridge
you   them
we

7

In the following sentences label the nouns N and the pronouns PRON.

N
Helen

PRON
she

N
performance

□ *Helen came early, but she left before the performance began.*

PRON
We

N
snow,

PRON
they

N
summers.

□ *We miss the snow, but they miss the hot summers.*

N
snow

PRON
they

PRON
she

N
camp

□ *The snow was quite deep, but they waited while she cleaned up the camp.*

VERBS

1D *The riding academy is down the street.*

is

The verb in this sentence is _____.

□ The predicate of every sentence contains at least one verb, a word that expresses either action or condition.

John drove.

drove

The predicate of this sentence is the verb _____, a word that expresses action.

8

action
predicate

condition

worked   was

drive

drank

bring, ask, give

V   V
sleeps   becomes
V
is

□ A verb is any word that expresses _____ or condition. The _____ of every sentence contains at
least one verb.

□   *Tom is here.*

The verb in this sentence is *is*. The eight forms of the verb
be (*am, are, is, was, were, be, being, been*) do not express
an action but rather a _____ of the subject.

□   *He worked late.*

     He was tired.

The verbs in these sentences are *worked* and *was*. The verb
_____ expresses action; the verb _____
expresses condition.

□ One important characteristic of verbs is that each has a
form to indicate past time. *Went* is such a form of *go, drove*
is such a form of _____.

□ The form of the verb *drink* which indicates past time is
_____.

□   *bring*   *ask*
     however   *within*
     newspaper   *give*

By asking which of the words in this list have a form to
indicate past time, we can see that the only ones which can
be used as verbs are _____.

□   *John usually sleeps well, but he becomes restless if there*
     is noise in the house.

Label the verbs in this sentence with a V. Remember that
verbs are those words which are used to express action or
condition and which have a form to indicate past time.

Label the verbs in the following sentences with a V.

V
leave

☐ *We leave tomorrow.*

V
delivers

☐ *The postman delivers our mail by truck.*

V
is

☐ *He is here now.*

V
runs
V
circles
V
contains

☐ *The belt runs through this loop here and circles the section of the motor which contains the carburetor.*

ADJECTIVES AND NOUN DETERMINERS

sudden, ripe
Those, the

1E *Those sudden showers drenched the ripe corn.*

The adjectives in this sentence are _____.
The noun determiners are _____.

☐ Nouns and pronouns often have descriptive words related to them.

Tall peaks border the valley.

peaks

In this sentence the descriptive word *Tall* is related to the noun _____.

☐ Descriptive words related to nouns or pronouns are called adjectives.

Tall peaks border the valley.

adjective

Tall, then, is an _____.

10

□   *Dry leaves fall.*

Dry

In this sentence the adjective is _____.

□ The term we use to express the relationship which an adjective has to its noun is *modify*.

   Black cars discolor rapidly.

In this sentence the adjective *Black* modifies the noun

cars

_____.

□   *I dislike large, noisy parties.*

large   noisy
parties

In this sentence the adjectives _____ and _____ modify the noun _____.

□ One important characteristic of adjectives is that they have forms to indicate more or most of the quality they express. For instance, *large* has the forms *larger* and *largest*. *Noisy*

noisiest

has the forms *noisier* and _____.

□ Many adjectives indicate more with an added *er*, most with an added *est*. Thus the adjective *bright* indicates more of the quality by the form _____, most by the form

brighter
brightest

_____.

□ Other adjectives indicate more or most by their use together with *more* or *most*. The adjective *beautiful*, for instance, indicates more of the quality when added to *more: more beautiful*. It indicates most when added to *most:* _____

most beautiful

_____.

□ Adjectives, then, have two identifying characteristics. One, they modify nouns; two, with few exceptions, they can indicate more or most of the quality they express.

   The small child played happily.

We know that *small* is an adjective because it modifies the

child
smallest

noun _____ and because it has the form *smaller* to indicate more and the form _____ to indicate most.

11

□   *John made an accurate count.*

We know that *accurate* is an adjective because it modifies

the noun _____ and because it can indicate more

by the form *more accurate* and most by the form _____

_____ .

count

most

accurate

□   *The restless audience greeted the young speaker with*
    enthusiastic cheers.

Label the adjectives in this sentence ADJ.

ADJ   ADJ
restless   young

ADJ
enthusiastic

□ A small but important group of words traditionally classed
as adjectives are more accurately classed as noun determiners. Of this group the most frequently used are the
articles, *a (an)* and *the*.

The apples are tasty.
Red apples are tasty.

These examples show how a noun determiner differs in
function from an adjective. *Red* describes the noun *apples.*
The [does, does not] _____ describe the same
noun.

does not

□ Unlike adjectives, which describe nouns, noun determiners
identify nouns. Besides the articles, *a (an)* and *the*, other
noun determiners are *my, our, your,* and *their,* which are
forms of pronouns, and *this, that, these,* and *those,* which
are often called demonstrative adjectives. Notice that, unlike adjectives, noun determiners [can, cannot] _____
indicate more or most.

cannot

□ Adjectives, then, describe nouns or pronouns and can indicate more or most. Noun determiners identify nouns and
cannot indicate more or most.

The new furniture has arrived.

Of the words related to the noun *furniture, The* is a(n)
_____ and *new* is a(n) _____ .

noun determiner

adjective

12

□ *He gave this large package to me.*

this
large

Of the words related to *package*, _____ is a noun determiner, _____ is an adjective.

In the following sentences, label the adjectives ADJ and the noun determiners N-D.

N-D	ADJ
An	easy

N-D	ADJ
the	hard

□ *An easy way often becomes the hard way.*

N-D	ADJ
Our	new

N-D	ADJ
that	long

□ *Our new car broke down on that long stretch of road between here and Syracuse.*

N-D	ADJ
those	large

N-D	ADJ
the	fresh

□ *Those large containers hold the fresh chemicals.*

ADVERBS

1F *With his extremely long legs he covered the distance very quickly.*

extremely
long   very   quickly
quickly   covered

This sentence contains three adverbs: _____ modifies _____; _____ modifies _____; _____ modifies _____.

□ Adjectives modify nouns or pronouns. Adverbs, the other large class of modifiers, modify verbs, adjectives, or other adverbs.

He ran rapidly.

verb

In this sentence the adverb *rapidly* modifies the _____ *ran.*

13

□ Characteristically adverbs end in *ly*. We can form adverbs from many adjectives by adding this ending. For instance, the adverb form of the adjective *proper* is *properly*. The adverb form of the adjective *beautiful* is _____.

beautifully

□ *True* is an adjective, *truly* is an _____.

adverb

□ An adverb modifies by expressing *how, when,* or *where.*

The stream flowed rapidly.

The adverb *rapidly* modifies the verb *flowed* because it expresses _____ the stream flowed.

how

□ Of course not all adverbs end in *ly.*

We arrived there late.

In this sentence the adverbs *there* and *late* modify the verb *arrived*. *There* expresses _____ and *late* expresses _____.

where
when

□ Even if it does not end in *ly*, any modifier that expresses _____, _____, or _____ is an adverb.

how   when   where

□ Since adverbs express *how, when,* or *where*, we have a simple substitution test to determine which words in a sentence function as adverbs. If we can replace a word with *thus* (*so*), *then,* or *there*, we know it is an adverb. For instance, in the sentence *He went outside*, we can replace the adverb *outside* with the word _____.

there

□   *He plays happily outside sometimes.*

Using the substitution test described in the last frame, we can determine that the adverbs in this sentence, all modifying the verb *plays*, are _____, _____, and _____.

happily [thus]
outside [there]
sometimes [then]

□ Adverbs modify adjectives as well as verbs.

It was little.
It was quite little.

quite
little

In the second sentence the adverb _____, for which *so* can be substituted, modifies the adjective _____.

□ Adverbs can modify other adverbs as well as verbs and adjectives.

He retired early.
He retired very early.

early
then

In this sentence the adverb *very*, for which *so* can be substituted, modifies another adverb, _____, for which _____ can be substituted.

□ Adverbs that modify adjectives and other adverbs normally come directly before the words they modify.

Much later he told me his very odd story.

odd
adjective

In this sentence the adverb *very* modifies _____, an _____.

□   *He told me much later his very odd story.*

later   adverb

In the same sentence, with its words slightly rearranged, the adverb *much* modifies _____, an _____.

□   *He told me his very odd story much later.*

told

Notice that in the last three example sentences the adverb *later*, together with the adverb modifying it, has appeared in three different positions, yet the meaning of the three sentences is the same. *Later*, which modifies _____, a verb, can appear in any of several positions without altering the meaning of the sentence.

verbs

□ Although adverbs modifying adjectives or other adverbs normally appear directly before the words they modify, adverbs modifying ＿＿＿＿＿＿＿ may appear in several positions within the sentence.

□   *Rarely he / gives a party / .*

can

The adverb *Rarely* [can, cannot] ＿＿＿＿＿＿＿ be moved to any of the positions marked by the slanted line.

□ Show with a slanted line where the adverb *slowly* can appear in this sentence.

*/The car/ drove/
around the corner/.*

The car drove around the corner.

Label all the adverbs in these sentences ADV.

ADV   **ADV**
very   *accurately*

□   *The store owner reported his income very accurately.*

ADV   **ADV**
adequately   *badly*

□   *One adequately large gasket can keep your hose from leaking badly.*

ADV   **ADV**
Lately   *strangely*

□   *Lately he has behaved strangely.*

16

In the following sentences, label the nouns N, the pronouns PRON, the verbs V, the adjectives ADJ, the noun determiners N-D, and the adverbs ADV.

N-D ADJ   N
The simple plan
ADV   V   N
soon changed matters.

☐ *The simple plan soon changed matters.*

N-D   N
Those men
V   ADV
came late.

☐ *Those men came late.*

PRON   V   PRON
He gave her
N-D   N
a   rose.

☐ *He gave her a rose.*

N-D   ADJ
A   large
N   V
house stood
ADV   ADV
there once.

☐ *A large house stood there once.*

17

TWO
BASIC SENTENCE PATTERNS

SUBJECT—VERB AND SUBJECT—VERB—DIRECT OBJECT PATTERNS

2A Label the following sentences according to the basic patterns they follow: *subject-verb* (S-V) or *subject-verb-direct object* (S-V-DO).

(a) **S-V-DO**

(b) **S-V**

(a) *John makes radios.*

(b) *John works rapidly.*

---

subject

predicate

□ In the last section we learned that all sentences have two basic parts: the naming part, called the _____, and the asserting part, called the _____.

□ *Boys play.*

Boys

play

In this two-word sentence, the noun _____ is the subject, and the verb _____ is the predicate.

□ Notice that such sentences as *Boys play* can be expanded by adding modifiers.

> *Active boys play outside.*

In this sentence the adjective _____ is added to the noun *boys*; the adverb _____ is added to the verb *play*.

Active
outside

□ *All active boys play outside often.*

The addition of modifiers does not change the basic pattern of subject plus verb, abbreviated S-V.

> *The horse ran away.*

This sentence, then, has the basic pattern _____.

S-V

□ Although every predicate contains at least one verb, some verbs, even with modifiers, cannot complete the predicate.

> *Paul swam . . . .*
> *Paul made . . . .*

In the first example the predicate is [complete, incomplete] _____; in the second it is _____.

complete   incomplete

□ Since a noun-verb group such as *Paul made* is incomplete, it cannot be a sentence of the S-V pattern.

> *Paul made cabinets.*

In this sentence the noun _____ completes the predicate.

cabinets

□ Words which complete the predicate belong to a group of sentence parts called predicate complements, or simply complements.

> *Paul made cabinets.*

In this sentence *cabinets* is a predicate complement, or simply a _____.

complement

19

□ As we will see, there are several kinds of complements. The complement which receives the effect of an action verb is called the direct object.

Paul made cabinets.

direct object
made

Cabinets, then, is a complement called a _____ because it receives the effect of the action verb _____.

□ *He gave a party.*

party

The direct object of the verb *gave* is _____.

□ Sentences with a direct object have the basic pattern *subject-verb-direct object*, abbreviated S-V-DO.

The shortstop threw the ball.

ball

This sentence follows the S-V-DO pattern. The direct object is the noun _____.

□ *The minister spoke well.*
The minister gave a fine sermon.

second

Only the [first, second] _____ sentence has an S-V-DO pattern.

□ *The minister spoke well.*

S-V

This sentence has an _____ pattern.

□ *The relay team performed extremely well today.*
The relay team ran an excellent race today.

S-V
S-V-DO

The first sentence has the pattern _____. The second sentence has the pattern _____.

REVIEW

Label the following sentences according to their basic patterns, using the abbreviations S-V or S-V-DO.

S-V-DO

□ *Bob drove the car all the way to Chicago.*

20

S-V	□ *The car ran well all the way to Chicago.*
S-V-DO	□ *A man with a beard held the tape.*

INDIRECT OBJECT AND OBJECTIVE COMPLEMENT PATTERNS

2B Label the following sentences according to the basic patterns they follow: *subject-verb-indirect object-direct object* (S-V-IO-DO) or *subject-verb-direct object-objective complement* (S-V-DO-OC).

(a) S-V-DO-OC

(b) S-V-IO-DO

(a) *They elected me chairman.*

(b) *They gave me the chairmanship.*

□ A sentence which has a direct object may have one additional complement as part of its basic structure.

> *The shortstop threw the ball.*
> *The shortstop threw John the ball.*

threw

ball

The second sentence has an additional complement, the noun *John*, between the verb _____ and the direct object _____.

□ A complement which appears between the verb and the direct object is called an indirect object because it receives the indirect effect of an action verb.

> *Helen made her friends a cake.*

cake

friends

In this sentence the direct object is the noun _____.
The indirect object is the noun _____.

□ *He handed Cathy the newspaper.*

Cathy

The indirect object in this sentence is _____.

verb

direct object

□ The indirect object always appears between the _____ and the _____.

21

□ An indirect object characteristically expresses *to* or *for whom.* Thus the sentence *Helen made her friends a cake* can be expressed in another way: *Helen made a cake*

for _____ *her friends.*

□   *The paymaster issued us the checks.*

Using the *to*-or-*for* device shows us that this sentence can be expressed in the following way: *The paymaster issued*

the checks to us _____.

□ The sentence pattern S-V-DO, then, can be expanded to include an indirect object. Using IO to stand for indirect object, this pattern can be abbreviated _____.

S-V-IO-DO

□   *Nelson wrote the Major a letter.*

does   This sentence [does, does not] _____ have an S-V-IO-DO pattern.

□   *He called me a taxi.*
    He called me a liar.

Using the *to*-or-*for* device, we see that only the [first, second] _____ sentence fits the S-V-IO-DO pattern.

first

□   *He called me a taxi.*
    He called me a liar.

Notice the difference between these two sentences. In the first, which has the S-V-IO-DO pattern, the indirect object *me* and the direct object *taxi* refer to a different person and thing. In the second sentence *me* and *liar* refer to [the same, different] _____ person(s).

the same

□ If a sentence has two complements which refer to the same person or thing, the first is the direct object and the second is the objective complement.

    He called me a liar.

me   The direct object in this sentence is _____; the
liar   objective complement is _____.

22

	☐ *We elected Harry president.*
direct object objective complement	In this sentence *Harry* is the _____; *president* is the _____.
after	☐ Unlike indirect objects, objective complements always come [before, after] _____ the direct object.
	☐ Thus the sentence pattern S-V-DO can be expanded to include an objective complement. Using OC to stand for objective complement, this pattern can be abbreviated
S-V-DO-OC	_____.
	☐ *Helen gave me a nickel.* *Helen considered me a friend.*
S-V-IO-DO S-V-DO-OC	The first sentence has the pattern _____. The second has the pattern _____.
	☐ *The judges awarded Marilyn Ross a prize.* *The judges voted Marilyn Ross the winner.*
S-V-IO-DO S-V-DO-OC	The first sentence has the pattern _____. The second sentence has the pattern _____.
	☐ Unlike direct or indirect objects, which are normally nouns or pronouns, an objective complement is occasionally an adjective. *Elliot considered the neighborhood a slum.* *Elliot considered the neighborhood dirty.*
noun adjective	Both of these sentences have an objective complement. In the first it is a(n) [noun, adjective] _____, *slum.* In the second it is a(n) _____, *dirty.*

□ When the objective complement is an adjective, it modifies the direct object.

Rita left the apartment spotless.

In this sentence the [direct object, objective complement] _____ *spotless* modifies the _____ _____ *apartment.*

| objective complement |
| direct object |

□ *The careless cook baked the cookies black.*
   The family found the kitchen a mess.

Both sentences have an S-V-DO-OC pattern. The [first, second] _____ sentence has an adjective as the objective complement; the _____ sentence has a noun.

| first |
| second |

□ *We thought her foolish.*
   We gave her a dime.

These sentences have different patterns. The first has the pattern _____. The second has the pattern _____.

| S-V-DO-OC |
| S-V-IO-DO |

REVIEW

Using the appropriate abbreviations, identify the following sentences according to the patterns they follow.

S-V-IO-DO	□ *I gave him my book.*
S-V-DO-OC	□ *Mr. Hawkins thought Bob foolish.*
S-V-DO-OC	□ *The reporters called the candidate a pirate.*

2C Identify the following sentences according to their basic patterns. S-V-SC is the abbreviation for patterns having subjective complements.

(a) S-V-SC

(b) S-V-DO

(a) *Earl became the president.*

(b) *Earl saw the president.*

□ Complements following condition verbs are different from those following action verbs.

> *Rosie bought a doll.*
> *Rosie is a doll.*

Doll in the first sentence follows the action verb *bought* and is its direct object. *Doll* in the second sentence follows the condition verb *is* but is not its direct object; rather, it identifies the subject, the noun _____.

Rosie

□ Complements following condition verbs identify the subject rather than receive the effect of an action.

> *Mr. Adkins is a tennis star.*
> *Mr. Adkins trains the tennis star.*

The noun *star* receives the effect of an action verb in the [first, second] _____ sentence, but it identifies the subject in the _____ sentence.

second

first

□ Condition verbs, unlike action verbs, can link complements to the subject.

> *The car was a wreck.*

The condition verb *was* links the complement _____ to the subject _____.

wreck

car

□ A condition verb that links the complement to the subject is called a linking verb.

> *Jim is chairman.*

Because *is* joins its complement *chairman* to the subject *Jim,* it is a _____ verb in this sentence.

linking

□ Since the complement of a linking verb refers to the same person or thing as the subject, we call it the subjective complement.

> *Jim is chairman.*

In this sentence *chairman* is the _____.

subjective complement

□ The subjective complement of linking verbs has other names you may have heard—predicate nominative, for instance, or predicate noun. For convenience here we will use only the one name, subjective _____.

complement

□ A subjective complement is always joined to the subject by a linking verb.

> *Pierre is a French name.*

In this sentence the verb _____ is a linking verb.

is

□   *Pierre is a French name.*

The condition verb *is* is a _____ verb because it joins the _____ complement *name* to the subject *Pierre.*

linking
subjective

□ English contains many words besides the forms of *be* which serve as linking verbs.

> *She is a friend.*
> *She seemed a friend.*

In the second example the condition verb *seemed* functions as a _____ verb, and the noun *friend* is the _____.

linking
subjective complement

26

subject	□ Later in this book we shall deal with the important groups of condition verbs which function as linking verbs. It is important now only to remember that the subjective complement, which a linking verb joins to the subject, refers to the same person or thing as the _____.
	□ Adjectives as well as nouns and pronouns may be subjective complements.
	The car is blue.
is *car*	In this sentence the linking verb _____ joins the adjective *blue* to the subject, the noun _____.
	□ Adjectives that are complements of linking verbs always modify the subject of the sentence.
	The skies were overcast.
overcast subject	The adjective _____ modifies the noun *skies*, the _____ of this sentence.
	□ *The skies were overcast.*
subjective complement	The adjective *overcast* is the _____ in this sentence.
subjective complement	□ Using SC to stand for subjective complement, the sentence pattern having a linking verb and a _____ can be abbreviated S-V-SC.
	□ *The chairman seemed happy.* *The chairman cast the deciding vote.*
first	Only one of these sentences has an S-V-SC pattern, the [first, second] _____.
	□ *I am editor of the school paper.* *I chose Reed to help me.*
first	Only the [first, second] _____ sentence has the S-V-SC pattern.

Identify the subjective complements in the following sentences.

editor

☐ *I am editor of the paper.*

competent

☐ *This secretary is competent.*

they

☐ *It was they who followed us here.*

REVIEW: SENTENCE PATTERNS

Using the appropriate abbreviations, identify the basic sentence patterns of each of the following sentences.

S-V-DO-OC

☐ *He considered her careless.*

S-V

☐ *The paper came late.*

S-V-SC

☐ *This check is good.*

S-V-DO

☐ *Ernest Hemingway flew light planes.*

S-V-DO-OC

☐ *This city's voters elected John Rogers their city commissioner.*

S-V-SC

☐ *I am he.*

S-V-IO-DO

☐ *Her parents gave her a watch.*

28

THREE
PHRASES

VERB PHRASES

3A *Should he be leaving now?*

The verb phrase in this sentence is composed of the auxiliary verb(s) _____ and the main verb(s) _____ .

Should ... be leaving

☐ We often use groups of words called phrases which function as single words. For instance, the verb phrase consists of two or more words that together function as a verb.

> *He drives.*
> *He is driving.*

In the second sentence the verb phrase _____ has the same function as the verb _____ in the first sentence.

is driving
drives

□ A verb phrase consists of the main verb with one or more auxiliary verbs preceding it.

He is driving.

In this sentence the verb phrase consists of the main verb _____ and the auxiliary verb _____.

driving   is

□ In English the main verb is always the last verb in a verb phrase.

He has been driving.

In this sentence the main verb is _____.

driving

□   *He has been driving.*

In this sentence *has been driving* is a verb _____ consisting of the _____ verb *driving* and two _____ verbs, *has* and *been.*

phrase
main
auxiliary

□ We use the various forms of *be, have,* and *do* as main verbs, but we also use them as auxiliary verbs in verb phrases.

Bob has a pen.
Bob has written the editorial.

In the [first, second] _____ sentence *has* is the main verb. In the _____ it is an auxiliary verb.

first
second

□   *She did go quickly.*
    She did the dishes.

Did is a main verb only in the [first, second] _____ sentence.

second

□ Some auxiliary verbs, called modal auxiliaries, have only one form: *can, could, may, might, must, shall, should, will, would.* Since these verbs are incomplete by themselves, we normally do not use them as main verbs. These verbs are always _____ verbs.

auxiliary

30

☐ *The students will have finished by noon.*

This sentence has two auxiliary verbs, _____ and

_____ .

will
have

☐ *They might have been working since dawn.*

This sentence has [two, three] _____ auxiliary
verbs preceding the main verb _____ .

three
working

☐ One or more words often appear between the auxiliary and
main verbs of a verb phrase.

> *Peter can come.*
> *Peter can always come.*

In the second sentence the adverb _____ separates the two verbs of the verb phrase _____ .

always
can come

☐ Sometimes we join the adverb *not* to auxiliary verbs.

> *Peter cannot come.*

In this sentence the adverb *not* is joined to the _____

_____ can.

auxiliary
verb

☐ Combined forms like *cannot* are often contracted, or
shortened.

> *Peter can't come.*

The contraction *can't* consists of the auxiliary varb _____
and the adverb _____ .

can
not

☐ *Peter can't come.*

Even though it contains a contraction, the verb phrase in
this sentence consists only of the two verbs _____
and _____ .

can
come

31

□ We often form contractions of auxiliary verbs and certain personal pronouns—*I, you, he, she, it, we,* and *they.*

> *I will do it.*
> *I'll do it.*

In the second sentence _____ is a contraction of the personal pronoun _____ and the auxiliary verb _____.

I'll

I

will

□ *They would play if you asked them.*

> *They'd play if you asked them.*

In the second sentence *They'd* is a contraction of the personal _____ *They* and the _____ *would.*

pronoun

auxiliary verb

□ Sentences expressing a question often begin with an auxiliary verb which is separated from the main verb.

> *Will the bank return my canceled checks?*
> *The bank will return them soon.*

Although the verb phrase is separated by *the bank* in the first sentence, the predicate of both sentences contains the verb phrase _____.

will return

□ *Did the House of Representatives pass the bill?*

The predicate of this sentence contains the verb phrase _____.

Did . . . pass

32

Identify the verb phrases in the following sentences.

Will . . . be going

☐ *Will Mel be going with us?*

should have been working

☐ *He should have been working four days.*

(woul)d forget

☐ *I'd forget it as soon as possible.*

Can . . . expect

☐ *Can the constituents in this district actually expect the incumbent to keep his promises?*

did . . . finish

☐ *Where did she finish?*

VERBALS AND VERBAL PHRASES

3B *Flying was once a daring sport, difficult to learn.*

to learn   flying
daring

The above sentence contains three verbals: the infinitive _____, the gerund _____, and the participle _____.

verbs

☐ Verbs have forms which we use as nouns or modifiers. These are called verbals because they are forms of _____ even though they serve as nouns or modifiers.

infinitives

☐ One verbal is the infinitive, a form of the verb introduced by *to. To sleep, to fly,* and *to write* are examples of verbals called _____.

☐ *He went to the library to study.*

to study

The infinitive in this sentence is _____.

33

□ Infinitives should not be confused with prepositional phrases that begin with *to*. Remember that infinitives consist of the introductory word *to* followed by a _____ rather than a noun.

verb

□ We often use infinitives as noun substitutes.

To swim is good exercise.

The infinitive _____ is the subject of this sentence. Here it is used as a _____ substitute.

To swim
noun

□ *Robert asked to go.*

In this sentence the infinitive *to go*, used as a noun, is the direct _____ of the verb *asked*.

object

□ Infinitives also serve as modifiers—as substitutes for adjectives or adverbs.

John's desire to play was great.

In this sentence the infinitive _____ is used as an adjective substitute modifying the noun _____.

to play
desire

□ *John played to win.*

In this sentence the infinitive _____ is used as an adverb substitute modifying the verb _____.

to win
played

□ The infinitive is a verbal that may serve as a noun substitute; it may also serve as a modifier—either as an _____ or as an _____ substitute.

adjective
adverb

□ Another verbal is the form of the verb ending in *ing*. When used as a noun substitute, this verbal is called a *gerund*.

To swim is good exercise.
Swimming is good exercise.

In the second sentence the gerund _____ is identical in meaning and use to the infinitive _____ in the first sentence. Both are noun substitutes.

Swimming
To swim

34

□ When used as a noun substitute, the verb form that ends in *ing* is a verbal called a _____.

□ Two verbals we use as noun substitutes are the _____ and the _____.

□ The *ing* form of a verb is also used as an adjective substitute. In this use it is a verbal called a participle.

> *Hunting requires patience.*
> *The hunting party waited until dawn.*

The participle _____ in the second sentence is identical in form to the gerund _____ in the first sentence.

□ *Hunting requires patience.*
> *The hunting party waited until dawn.*

Hunting is a _____ in the first sentence because it serves as a noun substitute. The same word is a _____ in the second sentence because it serves as an adjective substitute modifying the noun _____.

□ The participle ending in *ing,* identical to the gerund ending, is one of the two basic forms of verbs used as adjective substitutes. This form is called the present participle. *Going* is the present participle of *go; stealing* is the _____ participle of _____.

□ Besides the present participle, verbs have one other basic participial form, the one used as the main verb with the auxiliary *have.* This form is called the past participle.

> *They have completed the work.*
> *The completed work is on the table.*

Completed is the main verb following *have* in the first sentence. In the second it is a _____ participle modifying the noun _____.

35

□ *The swimming coach called for a delayed workout.*

In this sentence _____ is a present participle modifying _____; _____ is a past participle modifying _____.

swimming
coach   delayed
workout

□ The three kinds of verbals, then, are the _____, the _____, and the _____.

infinitive
gerund   participle

□ *To run is hard work.*
Running is hard work.
The man running is the coach.

Each of these three sentences contains a verbal. The verbal *To run* in the first is a(n) _____; the verbal *Running* in the second is a(n) _____; and the verbal *running* in the third is a(n) _____.

infinitive
gerund
participle

3C *By swimming the distance slowly, we eventually reached the far shore.*

The verbal phrase in this sentence is the object of the preposition _____. It consists of the gerund, _____, the direct object of the gerund, _____, and the adverb, _____.

By   swimming
(the) distance
slowly

□ We distinguish verbals from nouns, adjectives, and adverbs because they retain some of the characteristics of verbs. For instance, verbals are often modified by adverbs, forming phrases which function as units.

To write is our aim.
To write easily is our aim.

The second sentence has an infinitive phrase consisting of the infinitive *to write* modified by the adverb _____.

easily

36

□ *Working hastily often causes errors.*

The subject of this sentence is a gerund phrase consisting of the _____ *Working* modified by the _____ *hastily.*

gerund adverb

□ All three kinds of verbals—infinitives, participles, and gerunds—may take direct objects if they are based on action verbs.

To return the letter was easy.

The noun _____ is the direct object of the infinitive _____ in this sentence because it receives the action of the verbal.

letter
To return

□ *Giving lessons was his way of earning money.*

This sentence has two gerunds. The gerund _____ has a direct object, _____; the gerund _____ _____ also has a direct object, _____.

Giving
lessons
earning money

□ A verbal phrase with a direct object may also have an indirect object.

Helen agreed to lend me her coat.

The direct object of the infinitive *to lend* is _____; the indirect object is _____.

coat
me

□ If a verbal is based on a linking verb, it may have a noun, pronoun, or adjective as a subjective complement.

Being accurate requires concentration.

The adjective *accurate* is the subjective complement of the [participle, gerund] _____ *being.*

gerund

□ *It is not easy to become president.*

The noun _____ is the subjective complement of the infinitive _____.

president
to become

□ Remember that verbals with their complements and modifiers function together as substitutes for nouns or adjectives.

> *The job was easy.*
> *Fastening the bolts securely was easy.*

In the second sentence the gerund phrase, composed of the gerund *fastening* with its object *bolts* and adverb-modifier *securely*, has the same function as the noun _____ in the first sentence.

job

□ *He hoped to read the novel soon.*

Here the direct object of the verb *hoped* is an infinitive phrase composed of the infinitive, _____, its direct object, _____, and the adverb, _____.

to read
novel   soon

□ *The ship bringing medicine reached port.*

This sentence has a participial phrase composed of the participle _____ and its direct object, _____.

bringing   medicine

□ *The ship bringing medicine reached port.*

The participial phrase *bringing medicine* modifies as a single unit the noun _____.

ship

□ *Finding a suitable job is difficult.*

The gerund phrase in this sentence is _____. It acts as the [subject, direct object] _____ of the sentence.

Finding a suitable job
subject

□ *The team hoped to upset their cross-town rival.*

The infinitive phrase in this sentence is _____ _____. It is the [subject, direct object] _____ _____ of the verb *hoped*.

to upset their cross-town rival
direct object

38

□   *The regents expected a report covering the incidents.*

The verbal phrase in this sentence is _____

_____, a participial phrase modifying the noun

_____.

covering the incidents

report

REVIEW

Identify each of the verbals and verbal phrases in the following sentences. Identify also their kind and their function.

□   *The men carrying the money were robbed.*

carrying the money
participial phrase
modifier of *men*

verbal (phrase): _____
kind: _____
function: _____

□   *To be a journalist was his main ambition.*

To be a journalist
infinitive phrase
subject

verbal (phrase): _____
kind: _____
function: _____

□   *The doctor tried giving the patient a new diet.*

giving the patient a new diet
gerund phrase
direct object

verbal (phrase): _____
kind: _____
function: _____

□   *He asked to be included in the study group.*

to be included in the study group
infinitive phrase
direct object

verbal (phrase): _____
kind: _____
function: _____

□   *The laughing children toured the museum noisily.*

laughing
participle
modifier of *children*

verbal (phrase): _____
kind: _____
function: _____

3D *Carson traveled alone for long periods.*

The prepositional phrase in this sentence consists of the preposition _____, its object _____, and the adjective _____.

for periods
long

□ Certain words which we call prepositions express the relationship of a noun or pronoun with some other word in the sentence.

The airports near Chicago are busy.

The word that expresses the relationship between the noun *Chicago* and the subject *airports* is the preposition_____.

near

□ A word that expresses the relationship between a noun or pronoun and some other word in a sentence is a _____.

preposition

□ The noun or pronoun which the preposition relates to another word is called the object of the preposition.

The airports near Chicago are busy.

In this sentence *Chicago* is the _____ of the preposition _____.

object
near

□ A preposition, then, expresses the relationship between its _____ to some other word in a sentence.

object

□ A preposition and its object form what we call a prepositional phrase.

The airports near Chicago are busy.

In this sentence *near Chicago* is a _____.

prepositional phrase

	☐ If the object of a preposition has modifiers, then they are part of the prepositional phrase.
	The airports near large cities are busy.
near large cities	Here the prepositional phrase is _____.
	☐ The prepositional phrase *near large cities* consists of the preposition *near*, its object _____, and the adjective modifying the object, _____.
cities	
large	

of bass	**3E** *A school of bass swam swiftly beneath the surface.*
school	In this sentence the prepositional phrase _____
beneath the surface	modifies _____, and the prepositional phrase
swam	_____ modifies _____.

	☐ Prepositional phrases normally modify the words to which they are related. In other words, prepositional phrases function like the one-word modifiers, adjectives and
adverbs	_____.
	☐ For instance, a prepositional phrase may modify a noun or pronoun and thus function as an adjective.
	The golden cross stood on the hill.
	The cross of gold stood on the hill.
	The prepositional phrase *of gold* in the second sentence
adjective	functions as an _____. It modifies the noun *cross* just as the adjective *golden* modifies this same noun in the first sentence.
	☐ Prepositional phrases, unlike adjectives, usually follow the nouns they modify.
	The car at the end of the line is the newest.
	The prepositional phrase *at the end* modifies the noun
car of the line	_____; the prepositional phrase _____ _____ modifies the noun *end*.

☐ Like an adjective, a prepositional phrase can also serve as a subjective complement following a linking verb.

> *The cloth is silky.*
> *The cloth is like silk.*

The prepositional phrase *like silk* in the second sentence has the same function as the subjective complement _____ in the first sentence.

silky

☐　*Our bus was on time.*

In this sentence the linking verb _____ joins the prepositional phrase _____ to *bus*, the subject of the sentence.

was
on time

☐ Like adverbs, prepositional phrases can express *how, when,* or *where.*　Prepositional phrases, therefore, can function as _____ as well as adjectives.

adverbs

☐　*Our bus came on time.*

The prepositional phrase *on time* modifies the verb _____.

came

☐　*Our bus came on time.*

In modifying the verb *came,* the prepositional phrase *on time* expresses _____ the bus came.

when

☐　*He swam to the far shore with difficulty.*

In the foregoing sentence the prepositional phrase _____ _____ expresses *where,* and the prepositional phrase _____ expresses *how.* Both modify the verb _____.

to the far shore
with difficulty
swam

☐ Prepositional phrases, unlike adverbs, sometimes also express *why.*

> *Mr. Kelley travels on business.*

In this sentence the prepositional phrase _____ expresses *why.*

on business

□ *During August I went by plane to Hawaii for a rest.*

Of the four prepositional phrases in this sentence, *During August* expresses _____, *by plane* expresses _____, *to Hawaii* expresses _____, and *for a rest* expresses _____.

when
how   where
why

□ Prepositional phrases functioning as adverbs generally modify verbs. And like adverbs that modify verbs, these phrases can appear apart from the verb in other positions in a sentence.

After the party we went home.
We went home after the party.

after the party
went

In both sentences the prepositional phrase _____ _____ modifies the verb _____ even though it does not appear next to the verb in either.

□ *I disliked him from the beginning.*

/I disliked him from the beginning.

Mark with a slanted line the other position in this sentence which the prepositional phrase can occupy.

REVIEW

Identify each prepositional phrase in the following sentences and the word each modifies.

of the seven hurdles
modifies *last*
  with difficulty
  modifies *cleared*

□ *Bob cleared the last of the seven hurdles with difficulty.*

with the Hoe modifies *Man*
of the consequences modifies *picture*
  of human depravity modifies *consequences*

□ The Man with the Hoe *is a frightening picture of the consequences of human depravity.*

Complete the following frames.

☐ *He did not arrive here until yesterday.*

did ... arrive

The verb phrase in this sentence is _____.

☐ *The man on the corner watched us as we tried to park in a narrow space.*

on the corner

in a narrow space

man

to park

The prepositional phrases here are _____ and _____. The first modifies the noun _____, the second modifies the infinitive _____.

☐ *The apples with white markings will be sold at a discount.*

with white markings

at a discount

adjective

adverb

The prepositional phrases in this sentence are _____ _____ and _____. The first functions as an _____; the second functions as an _____.

☐ *His ambition was to win the high jump title.*

infinitive

to win the high jump title

The verbal phrase in this sentence, an _____ phrase, is _____.

☐ *By coming early, we escaped the traffic jamming the freeway on-ramps.*

gerund

coming early

participial

jamming the freeway on-ramps

This sentence contains two verbal phrases, the _____ phrase _____ and the _____ phrase _____.

□   *To get ahead was his reason for working that hard.*

This sentence contains the infinitive phrase _____
_____, which functions as the _____.
It also contains the gerund phrase _____,
which functions as the object of the _____ for.

To get ahead   subject
working that hard
preposition

FOUR

COMPOUND AND COMPLEX PATTERNS

COMPOUND SENTENCE ELEMENTS AND COMPOUND SENTENCES

4A *We packed four suitcases and an overnight bag.*

The _____ of this sentence is compound. It consists basically of two nouns, _____ and _____, joined by the coordinating conjunction _____.

direct object
suitcases
bag
and

☐ We often have two or more parts in a particular sentence element. For instance, a sentence may have two or more nouns as its subject.

Peter and Karen saw the play.

The subject of this sentence has two parts, the nouns _____ and _____.

Peter   Karen

46

□ Sentence elements having two or more parts are called compound.

Peter and Karen saw the play.

compound

This sentence has a _____ subject.

□ A sentence may also contain a compound verb.

The family worked and saved for years.

worked   saved

The compound verb in this sentence is composed of the verbs _____ and _____.

□ We join the parts of compound elements with words like *and.* This word expresses the relationship of the parts of a

compound

_____ element which have equal rank.

□ *And* belongs to a group of words called coordinating conjunctions. *Conjunction* means ''that which joins'' and *coordinate* means ''of equal rank.'' Any word that joins elements of equal rank, then, is a _____.

coordinating
conjunction

□ The most common coordinating conjunctions are *and, or,* and *but.*

Books and newspapers can be found in the library or the study.

coordinating
conjunctions

This sentence contains two _____, *and* and *or.*

□   *You should send a gift or a card.*

or

In this sentence the coordinating conjunction _____ joins the two nouns of the direct object, _____

gift

card

and _____.

□ Compound elements joined by coordinating conjunctions may have more than two parts.

Balls, bats, and gloves littered the dugout.

The compound subject of this sentence is a series of [two, three] _____ nouns.

three

□ *We can go by train, plane, car, or bus.*

The object of the preposition _____ is a compound series of four nouns.

by

□ *He passes, runs, and kicks well.*

This sentence has a compound series of [nouns, verbs] _____ .

verbs

4B *He did not know whether to go or to stay.*

The compound direct object is joined by the correlative form _____ .

whether ... or

□ We often use pairs of words as conjunctions joining compound elements in a sentence. Such pairs as *both... and, either ... or,* and *neither ... nor* are forms of conjunctions which we call correlatives.

You should send both a gift and a card.

In this sentence the nouns _____ and _____ and joined by the correlative _____ .

gift   card
both ... and

□ *The day was neither warm nor sunny.*

In this sentence the _____ *neither ... nor* joins two adjectives, _____ and _____ .

correlative
warm   sunny

48

□ Another common correlative form is *not only . . . but also.*

> *The settlers discovered not only corn but also tobacco growing in the new land.*

In this sentence the correlative *not only . . . but also* joins the two nouns of the compound _____, *corn* and *tobacco.*

direct object

□ *Whether . . . or* is another correlative.

> *All cars, whether new or old, should have their brakes checked regularly.*

The correlative _____ joins the two adjectives *new* and *old,* which modify _____.

whether . . . or
cars

□ Coordinating conjunctions and correlatives join phrases as well as single words.

> *Jim went to a football game and to a track meet on the same day.*

Here the prepositional phrases _____ and _____ are joined by the coordinating conjunction *and.*

to a football game
to a track meet

□ *Either breaking new trails of thought or broadening old ones, scientists are constantly active.*

The correlative _____ joins two participial phrases, _____ and _____.

Either . . . or
breaking new trails of thought
broadening old ones

□ *Insulted, Alfred didn't know whether to reply in kind or to walk indignantly away.*

The correlative _____ joins two _____ phrases, *to reply in kind* and *to walk indignantly away.*

whether . . . or
infinitive

49

4C *He arrived late, but he had a good excuse.*

The coordinating conjunction *but* joins two independent
_____ to form this _____ sentence.

□ A sentence may contain more than one subject-predicate group.

Helen helped, but Mary refused.

This sentence contains two subject-predicate groups,
Helen helped and _____.

Mary refused

□ Each subject-predicate group in a sentence is called a clause.

Helen helped, but Mary refused.

This sentence contains two separate subject-predicate
groups. In other words, it contains two _____.

clauses

□ Clauses that can stand by themselves if taken out of a sentence are called independent clauses.

Helen helped, but Mary refused.

Since *Helen helped* and *Mary refused* can stand by themselves, they are _____ clauses.

independent

□ Sentences composed of two or more independent clauses are called compound sentences.

Dr. Lee teaches calculus; and his wife teaches history.

This compound sentence is composed of two _____
_____.

independent
clauses

□ Independent clauses in compound sentences are normally joined by coordinating conjunctions.

Dr. Lee teaches calculus, and his wife teaches history.

The independent clauses in this _____ sentence
are joined by the coordinating conjunction _____.

compound
and

50

□ The common coordinating conjunctions used to join independent clauses are *and, but, or, nor, for,* and *yet.* Any one of these may join two or more independent clauses in a _____ sentence.

compound

□ *The trees have lost their leaves, and the sky is ashen gray.*

The independent clauses in this compound sentence are joined by the _____ conjunction *and.*

coordinating

□ *The boat trembled alarmingly, but few of the passengers became panicky.*

The independent clauses in this compound sentence are joined by the coordinating conjunction _____.

but

□ We often use correlatives such as *either . . . or, neither . . . nor,* and *whether . . . or* to join independent clauses in a compound sentence.

   Either you go or I stay.

The independent clauses in this sentence are joined by the correlative _____.

Either . . . or

□ *Neither will the crank turn nor will the motor start.*

The independent clauses in this sentence are joined by the _____ *Neither . . . nor.*

correlative

□ An independent clause must be able to stand alone. Don't mistake a compound sentence element for an independent clause in a compound sentence.

   The water rose and then receded.

The coordinating conjunction *and* [does, does not] _____ join independent clauses in this sentence.

does
not

□ *The plane rose rapidly through the fog and pointed its nose west.*

The tree fell finally, and the lumberjacks stripped the branches from its trunk.

second

first

The [first, second] _____ sentence contains two independent clauses; the _____ sentence contains a compound predicate only.

□ *The tree fell finally, and the lumberjacks stripped the branches from its trunk.*

compound

independent clauses

This is a _____ sentence because it is composed of two _____ .

□ *Her dress was green, and her gloves were white.*
She wore a green dress and white gloves.

first

Only the [first, second] _____ sentence here is a compound sentence.

REVIEW

Complete the frames following the three example sentences below.

(a) *Either that chair is blue or I am color-blind.*
(b) *We can go forward or stand our ground.*
(c) *In spring the trees grow new foliage rapidly and the grass turns green almost overnight.*

a   c

□ Of the three sentences above, two are compound: sentences _____ and _____ .

predicate

□ The compound element of sentence *b* is the [subject, predicate, direct object] _____ .

□ Each of the sentences above uses a coordinating conjunction or a correlative:

Either ... or
or
and

Sentence *a* uses _____

Sentence *b* uses _____

Sentence *c* uses _____

SUBORDINATE CLAUSES; SUBORDINATING CONJUNCTIONS; COMPLEX SENTENCES

complex
main (independent)
subordinate
if

4D *I can finish the work if I have time.*

This is a _____ sentence, composed of the _____ clause *I can finish the work* and the _____ clause *if I have time.* The subordinating conjunction in the sentence is _____.

□ Many sentences have clauses that cannot stand alone.

Bob went home because he was ill.

can
cannot

Of the two clauses in this sentence, *Bob went home* [can, cannot] _____ stand alone, and *because he was ill* [can, cannot] _____.

□ Clauses that cannot stand alone are called subordinate clauses because they depend for their meaning upon the independent clause to which they are related.

Bob went home because he was ill.

subordinate

The clause *because he was ill* is a _____ clause.

□ The independent clause upon which subordinate clauses depend is called the main clause.

Bob went home because he was ill.

main

This sentence is composed of one _____ clause and one subordinate clause.

□ Remember that a clause is any group of words having a subject and verb. Even subordinate clauses, therefore, have a _____ and a _____.

subject   verb

□ *He waited until she left.*

He waited
until she left

The main clause in this sentence is _____.
The subordinate clause is _____.

□ *He waited until she left.*

she
left

The subject of the subordinate clause is _____.
The verb is _____.

□ Sentences having one or more main clauses and one or more subordinate clauses are called complex sentences.

I will go if Mr. Kerr asks me.

complex
I will go
if Mr. Kerr asks me

This _____ sentence is composed of the main clause _____ and the subordinate clause _____.

□ A subordinate clause is normally introduced by a word showing the relationship of that clause to the main clause.

I will go if Mr. Kerr asks me.

if

The word which expresses the relationship of the subordinate clause to the main clause is _____.

□ *If, because, although,* and *unless* are examples of words called subordinating conjunctions.

I will go if Mr. Kerr asks me.

subordinating
conjunction
subordinate
main

If is a _____ because it shows the relationship between the _____ clause *if Mr. Kerr asks me* and the _____ clause *I will go.*

☐   *I will not see her unless she returns.*

The subordinating conjunction in the above sentence is
_____. It shows the _____ between
the subordinate clause *unless she returns* and the main
clause *I will not see her.*

☐ We use certain words such as *when, where, how,* and *why*
both as adverbs and as subordinating conjunctions.

> *When will Tom write his paper?*
> *Tom will write his paper when he has time.*

In the first sentence *When* is used as a(n) _____.
This same word is used in the second sentence as a(n)
_____.

☐   *Tom will write his paper when he has time.*

When is a subordinating conjunction in this sentence because it shows the relationship between the subordinate

clause _____ and   the   main
clause _____.

☐ Words such as *since, until, before,* and *after* are used both
as prepositions and as subordinating conjunctions.

> *Hitler retained power until the end.*
> *Hitler retained power until he died.*

Until is used as a _____ in the first sentence and as a _____ in the second.

☐   *Hitler retained power until he died.*

We   know   that   *until*   is   a   _____   in   this
sentence because it shows the relationship between the

_____ clause *until he died* and the _____
clause *Hitler retained power.*

Underline the subordinate clauses in the following complex sentences and label the subordinating conjunctions S-C.

S-C
unless you are
willing to practice

☐ *You can't learn to write unless you are willing to practice.*

S-C
because their
differences were
too great

☐ *The managers were unable to reach an agreement because their differences were too great.*

S-C
until they have
lost their leaves

☐ *The trees should not be pruned until they have lost their leaves.*

S-C
before the alumni
made their bequest

☐ *This library had fewer than a thousand books before the the alumni made their bequest.*

RELATIVE PRONOUNS AND ADJECTIVES

4E *Mr. Peters asked me who came.*

who

is

who came

In this sentence the relative pronoun is _____.
It [is, is not] _____ the subject of the subordinate clause _____.

□ Some pronouns are also used to show the relationship between a subordinate clause and the main clause in a sentence.

I told my father who would go.

In this sentence the pronoun *who* shows the relationship between the subordinate clause _____ and the main clause _____ .

who would go
I told my father

□ Pronouns that express the relationship between a subordinate clause and the main clause are called relative pronouns.

I told my father who would go.

In this sentence *who* is a _____ .

relative pronoun

□ The relative pronouns are *that, which, what,* and the forms of *who* (*who* and *whom*). Relative pronouns are like subordinating conjunctions. They show the relationship of a _____ clause to the _____ clause of a sentence.

subordinate   main

□ *The teacher asked us who had finished.*

In this sentence the relative pronoun _____ shows the relationship of the subordinate clause, _____ , to the main clause, _____ _____ .

who
who had finished
The teacher asked us

□ Although relative pronouns are like subordinating conjunctions, we speak of them separately because they serve two purposes: a relative pronoun may be the subject or an object of the subordinate clause as well as the word that shows the relationship of the _____ clause to the _____ clause.

subordinate
main

□ *He asked me who had eaten.*

In this sentence the relative pronoun *who* is the [subject, direct object] _____ of the subordinate clause *who had eaten.*

subject

57

□ If the relative pronoun is not the subject of the subordinate clause, it is sometimes omitted.

Sadie is the girl he left behind.

he left behind

The writer of this sentence omitted the relative pronoun *whom* from the subordinate clause _____.

□ *This is the book which I requested.*

Lindbergh was an unknown flier who gained fame overnight.

first

subject

The relative pronoun may be omitted only from the [first, second] _____ sentence because it is not the _____ of the subordinate clause.

subject

□ A relative pronoun may be omitted if it is not the _____ of the subordinate clause.

□ Cross out any unnecessary relative pronouns.

This is the problem that gave me the most trouble.
This is the problem which I found most difficult.

which

4F *The man whose name I mentioned is his uncle.*

whose
whose name I
mentioned

The relative adjective _____ introduces the subordinate clause _____.

□ *Whose, which,* and *what* are used as relative adjectives. These words are distinguishable from relative pronouns when they modify a noun or pronoun in the subordinate clause.

The teacher whose book I used is Mr. Finley.

In this sentence the relative adjective *whose* joins the subordinate clause *whose book I used* to the main clause. It is also an adjective modifying the noun it precedes,

book

_____.

58

□ *Hank indicated which place I should take.*

In this sentence the relative adjective *which* joins the subordinate clause *which place I should take* to the main clause, and it modifies the noun _____.

place

□ *He asked me what dog was mine.*

relative adjective

In this sentence *what* is a _____ modifying *dog*. At the same time it joins the subordinate clause

what dog was mine

_____ to the main clause *He asked me.*

□ The relative adjectives *which* and *what* each have a form ending in *ever.*

Give me whatever money you can spare.

In this sentence *whatever* is a relative adjective modifying

money

the noun _____.

□ *This indicator shows whichever tank is out of gas.*

The subordinate clause in this sentence is related to the

relative adjective

main clause by the _____ *whichever.*

REVIEW

Underline the subordinate clauses in the following sentences. Label the relative pronouns R-PRON and the relative adjectives R-ADJ.

R-ADJ
what road I can take

□ *Don't try to tell me what road I can take.*

R-PRON *who have retired*	☐ *Four history professors who have retired collaborated in the preparation of this history series.*
R-PRON *that I wanted to go*	☐ *The reason that I wanted to go was silly.*
R-ADJ *whose car to use*	*I simply wanted to know whose car to use.*
R-PRON *which had become* *too small*	*A new wing was added to the hospital which had become too small.*

NOUN, ADJECTIVE, AND ADVERB CLAUSES

that he had been unfair direct object	**4G** *The manager feared that he had been unfair.* This sentence has a noun clause, _____. It serves as the _____ in the sentence.
adjective	☐ Subordinate clauses, unlike independent clauses, are groups of words that function as one word. That is, a subordinate clause may function as a noun or as one of the two kinds of one-word modifiers, an _____ or adverb.

□ Subordinate clauses serving as nouns are called noun clauses.

> *Mr. Elliot believed the story.*
> *Mr. Elliot believed that I had received the book.*

that I had received the book

In the second of these sentences the noun clause _____ _____ has the same function as the noun *story* has in the first sentence.

□ Relative pronouns introducing noun clauses often have the suffix *ever*.

> *Whoever can come is welcome.*

noun clause
relative pronoun

The subject of this sentence is the _____ *Whoever can come;* it is introduced by the _____ *Whoever.*

□ The examples in the last two frames show that a noun clause can serve as the subject or the direct object in a sentence. Noun clauses can serve any function that a noun can.

> *Our representative is whomever we elect.*

noun
subjective

In this sentence the _____ clause *whomever we elect* is the _____ complement of the linking verb *is*.

□ *You may give a card to whoever needs one.*

whoever needs one
to

In this sentence the noun clause _____ is the object of the preposition _____.

clause
noun

□ A noun clause is any subordinate _____ that functions as a _____.

4H *Tom is a man whom you can trust.*

The adjective clause in this sentence is _____
_____. It modifies the noun _____.

whom you can trust   man

□ Subordinate clauses also serve as modifiers. Those subordinate clauses that modify nouns or pronouns are called adjective clauses.

The man whose car I used returned last night.

In this sentence the subordinate clause *whose car I used* is an _____ clause modifying the noun *man.*

adjective

□   *Ralph took the box that I built.*

The adjective clause in this sentence is _____;
it modifies the noun _____.

*that I built
box*

□ Adjective clauses, like prepositional phrases, normally follow the nouns they modify.

Al brought a friend whom he had met in France.

In this sentence the adjective clause _____
_____ follows the noun it modifies, _____.

*whom he had met in France
friend*

□   *The girl is a member of my sister's sorority.*

If we wished to add the adjective clause *whom I dated last night* to the sentence, we would place it directly after the word _____.

girl

4I *The driver who picked me up left me where I could catch the bus.*

The adverb clause in this sentence is _____.

where I could catch the bus

62

clause	□ Subordinate clauses can function as adverbs. Any clause expressing *how, when,* or *where* we call an adverb _____.
	□ An adverb clause may express *how, when,* or *where* in the same way that an adverb does.
	I threw the ball there. *I threw the ball where he could catch it.*
where he could catch it	The adverb clause in the second sentence that serves the same purpose as the adverb *there* in the first sentence is _____.
	□ *I threw the ball where he could catch it.*
threw *where*	The adverb clause modifying the verb _____ expresses [*how, when, where*] _____.
	□ *Pete came after I did.*
after I did *when*	The verb *came* is modified by the adverb clause _____ _____ expressing [*how, when, where*] _____.
	□ An adverb clause expressing *how* may modify an adjective as well as a verb.
	He is taller than I am.
taller	The adverb clause *than I am,* expressing *how,* modifies the adjective _____.
	□ An adverb clause may also modify an adverb.
	He runs faster than I can.
adverb adverb	The _____ clause *than I can* modifies the _____ *faster.*
	□ An adverb clause expressing *how, when,* or *where* normally modifies a particular word in the main clause of a sentence—a verb, _____, or _____.
adjective adverb	

□ An adverb clause, however, may express *why* as well as *how, when,* or *where.*

> *Mildred hurried because she was late.*

In this sentence the adverb clause *because she was late* expresses _____.

why

□ Such subordinating conjunctions as *because* and *since* introduce adverb clauses expressing *why.*

> *Mildred hurried because she was late.*

The adverb clause in this sentence is introduced by the subordinating conjunction _____.

because

Since the hill was steep

Since

□ *Since the hill was steep, we parked at the bottom.*

In this sentence the adverb clause _____ expresses *why.* The subordinating conjunction _____ joins it to the main clause.

□ In addition to the ideas of *how, when, where,* and *why,* adverb clauses express other ideas such as those of condition and concession.

> *I will come if I finish my work.*

The adverb clause *if I finish my work* expresses a [condition, concession] _____ of the speaker's coming.

condition

□ Two subordinating conjunctions used to introduce adverb clauses of condition are *if* and *unless.*

> *Rita will be unhappy unless she changes her attitude.*

The adverb clause expressing a condition in this sentence is _____.

unless she changes her attitude

64

□ Adverb clauses expressing concession are introduced by such subordinating conjunctions as *although* (*though*) and *while* (when used to mean *although*).

Though this car is good, that one is better.

The adverb clause expressing the concession that the car first mentioned has merits is introduced by the subordinating conjunction _____.

Though

□ Generally speaking, all adverb clauses of concession can be introduced by *although*, but they may be introduced by *while, whereas*, or *though*.

Whereas New York's population is growing, California's is growing even faster.

We recognize *Whereas New York's population is growing* as an adverb clause of concession because it can be introduced by *although* in place of _____.

Whereas

□ An adverb clause, then, expresses *how, when, where,* or *why*. It may also express a condition or a concession.

While Mabel is willing to wait if you are delayed, I am not.

The adverb clause *While Mabel is willing to wait* expresses the idea of _____; the adverb clause *if you are delayed* expresses the idea of _____.

concession
condition

Underline the adverb clauses in the following sentences.

although he knew the answer

☐ *He asked me why, although he knew the answer.*

If you wish

☐ *If you wish, you can give whoever comes a copy.*

unless he was drafted

☐ *The man whom I voted for had refused to run unless he was drafted.*

when you have time

☐ *Please come when you have time.*

because it no longer served a useful function

☐ *The typing pool was abolished because it no longer served a useful function.*

REVIEW: CLAUSES

Complete the following frames.

☐ *Whoever comes should open the windows that face the lake.*

Whoever comes

subject

This sentence contains a noun clause, _____, which serves as the _____ of the sentence.

☐ *Whoever comes should open the windows that face the lake.*

that face the lake

windows

There is also an adjective clause, _____, which modifies the noun _____.

66

that I promised you
if you'll help me

That he might come
which you did not
foresee
when you invited him

☐ *I'll give you the five dollars that I promised you if you'll help me.*

This sentence has an adjective clause, _____ _____, and an adverb clause, _____.

☐ *That he might come is a problem which you did not foresee when you invited him.*

This sentence has a noun clause, _____ _____, an adjective clause, _____, and an adverb clause, _____.

FIVE

TENSE

THE SIMPLE TENSES

worked
past *will work*
future *is*
present

5A *She worked yesterday and will work tomorrow; but today is her day off.*

The first verb in this sentence, _____, is in the _____ tense. The second verb, _____, is in the _____ tense. The third verb, _____, is in the _____ tense.

tense

☐ Verbs indicate time in relation to the action or condition they express. This quality of verbs is called tense.

He speaks forcefully.
He spoke forcefully.

The verb *speaks* in the first sentence indicates present time; it is in the present tense. The verb *spoke* in the second sentence indicates past time; it is in the past _____.

68

□ Verbs change form for certain tenses. The past tense of many verbs is formed by adding *d* or *ed* to the present-tense form. Complete this sentence with the past-tense form of the verb *sail:*

sailed

> We _____ to Honolulu last summer.

□ Auxiliary verbs joined to main verbs also indicate tense.

> *Two meetings convene today.*
> *Two meetings will convene tomorrow.*

will

The addition of the auxiliary verb _____ to the verb *convene* in the second sentence forms the future tense.

□ The three tenses just considered are sometimes called the simple tenses. These are the present, _____,

past
future

and _____ tenses.

□ *When the group meets today, those who arrived yesterday will propose a change in the location for next year.*

meets
arrived
will propose

This sentence has a verb in the present tense, _____, one in the past tense, _____, and one in the future tense, _____.

5B *Henry leaves tomorrow.*
Water boils at 100 degrees centigrade.
President Roosevelt's speech asks for social reform.

present
all

The _____ tense of the verb is correctly used in [the first, the first and second, all] _____ example(s).

69

□ The present tense of a verb indicates present time. It can also be used to indicate future time if it is clear from the sentence that the action expressed will take place in the future.

The executives leave now.
The executives leave tomorrow.

present
future

In the second sentence the verb is in the _____ tense but it indicates a _____ action.

□ *We will meet again Saturday.*

Omitting the auxiliary *will* from this sentence would change the verb to the present tense. The sentence [would, would not] _____ have the same meaning.

would

□ We also use the present tense to indicate a general rule such as a habit or a law of nature.

I always sleep late.
Those who sleep late are not necessarily lazy.

present

Since both of these sentences state a general rule, both verbs are in the _____ tense.

□ *The rains in Tahiti are often torrential.*

rule

The present tense is used here because the sentence expresses a general _____.

□ A writer may use the present tense to make past events seem more vivid. Used in this way, it is called the historical present.

Caesar's delays win him a month in which to prepare his defenses.

historical

Although the events expressed here happened in the past, the writer uses the _____ present.

70

□ *President Wilson argued valiantly for the League of Nations.*

argues
~~argued~~

Cross out the verb in this sentence and write above it the historical present form.

□ The historical present is no longer popular for narrative writing, but it is common in discussions of ideas contained in writing and speeches.

Hemingway romanticizes bullfighting in his book Death in the Afternoon.

This sentence does not indicate that Hemingway is writing now; rather, it simply expresses an idea about his book, using the _____ present.

historical

□ Complete this sentence with the form of the verb *reject* which indicates the historical present.

Walter Mather, in a column which appeared last week, _____ the language of the State Senate's recent mortage law.

rejects

---

went
belittled
hit

5C The past-tense form of *go* is _____. The past-tense form of *belittle* is _____. The past-tense form of *hit* is _____.

The past tense of a verb indicates completion in a past time.

The sailors searched for the lighthouse.

We know from the form of the verb that sailors completed their search at some time in the _____.

past

□ The past tense of most verbs in English is formed by adding *d* or *ed* to the present form. The past tense of *look* is _____; the past tense of *arrange* is _____.

looked   arranged

□ A number of English verbs, called irregular verbs, do not follow this pattern.

We _____ to class eariler yesterday.

The form of the verb *come* that completes this sentence is _____.

came

□ Although irregular verbs are comparatively few, they are among the most commonly used. Anyone who speaks English would not complete the first sentence below with *gived* or the second with *drived* but would use the correct forms automatically.

gave
drove

Last week I _____ him ten dollars.
The Smiths _____ to Michigan two months ago.

□ Certain irregular verbs such as *shut, cut, put,* and *hit* have a past-tense form identical to the present-tense form.

They shut the door now.
Yesterday they _____ the door.

shut

Complete the second sentence with the appropriate form of *shut.*

□ Verbs that have a past-tense form identical to the present-tense form cannot by themselves indicate tense. We can know the tense of these verbs only from context—that is, from their relationship to other words or sentences.

The Smiths put their car in storage last week.

We know that *put* is in the past tense because of the two words indicating past time, _____.

last week

future both	**5D** *I will be there.* *I am going to be there.* The verbs in both these sentences are in the _____ tense. In [the first, the second, both] _____ sentence(s) the verb form is correct.
will leave	☐ The future tense indicates future time only. Normally the future tense is introduced by the auxiliary verb *will*. *This station will leave the air at midnight.* The verb phrase _____ in this sentence is in the future tense.
will	☐ Until recently many authorities insisted that the auxiliary verb *shall* is the correct indicator of the future tense in sentences having *I* or *we* as the subject. The British still maintain this distinction between *shall* and *will,* but most writers in the United States now ignore it. It is accurate to say, then, that the normal indicator of the future tense in all uses is the auxiliary verb _____.
future	☐ We sometimes use *shall* to express strong intention or obligation. *I shall remain here.* *You shall go tomorrow.* In such uses, the auxiliary verb has additional meaning. Both *shall* and *will,* however, are basically indicators of the _____ tense.

73

□ Another common indicator of the future tense is the auxiliary verb phrase *going to* preceded by a present-tense
form of *be* (*am*, *are*, or *is*).

> *I will begin tomorrow.*
> *I am going to begin tomorrow.*

The auxiliary verb phrase in the second sentence which
takes the place of *will* in the first sentence is _____

_____ .

am going to

□   *Ralph will take his typewriter with him.*

An auxiliary verb phrase which can be substituted for *will*
in this sentence is *is* _____ .

going to

□ The auxiliaries *will* or *shall* and the auxiliary phrase *going
to* preceded by *am*, *are*, or *is* indicate the _____
tense.

future

REVIEW

Complete the following sentences with the appropriate
form of the verb indicated.

□ The present tense of go.

> *I* _____ *tomorrow.*

go

□ The historical present of *write.*

> *He* _____ *about Java.*

writes

□ The form of *radiate* indicating a general rule.

> *Heat* _____ *a kind of light.*

radiates

□ The past tense of *put.*

> *The President* _____ *the Ambassador in office.*

put

74

will (shall, or *am going to) be*	□ The future tense of be. I _____ here.

PRINCIPAL PARTS OF VERBS

present participle *watch* past participle *show*	**5E** *Watching* is the _____ of the verb _____. *Shown* is the _____ of the verb _____.

going	□ All verbs have a form ending in *ing*. This is called the present participle. Thus the present participle of the verb *go* is _____.
present participle *think*	□ *Thinking* is the _____ of the verb _____.
ing	□ The present participle of all English verbs ends in _____.
remembered	□ Verbs have another participial form, the past participle. This is the form of the verb which we use with the auxiliary *have.* Thus the past participle of *remember* is [*have*] _____.
have	□ While most verbs, like *remember,* have a past participle ending in *d* or *ed*, many do not. However, the past participle of any verb can be identified easily because it is the form we use with the auxiliary verb _____.
asked *risen*	□ The past participle of *ask* is _____; the past participle of *rise* is _____.
regular irregular	□ Verbs whose past participles are identical to their past-tense forms and end in *d* or *ed* are called regular. Those whose past participles are formed in some other way are called irregular. Thus *ask* is a(n) _____ verb; *rise* is a(n) _____ verb.

have □ Whether a verb is regular or irregular, the past participle is the form always used with the auxiliary verb _____.

---

help   helped   helped
go   went   gone
put   put   put

5F   List the principal parts of these three verbs:

help _____   _____   _____

go _____   _____   _____

put _____   _____   _____

□ All English verbs have three forms which may not vary regularly. These are called the principal parts.

Present	Past	Past Participle
look	looked	looked

*reach   reached
reached*

Since *look* is a regular verb, two of its principal parts are identical. The principal parts of *reach,* another regular verb, are _____, _____, and _____.

□ Distinguishing a verb's principal parts is more meaningful in regard to irregular verbs because most of these verbs have different forms in each part.

Present	Past	Past Participle
see	saw	seen

draw   drew   drawn

Another example is the irregular verb *draw.* Its principal parts are _____, _____, and _____.

□ Unlike those of regular verbs, the past participles of irregular verbs are seldom identical to the past-tense form.

I have [go] home.

past participle

We would use *gone,* the _____ of the irregular verb *go,* to complete this sentence.

□ A few irregular verbs, such as *shut, put, cut,* and *hit* have identical forms in all three principal parts. The past participle of *hit*—the form used with the auxiliary *have*—is

hit   cut

_____; the past participle of *cut* is _____.

76

List the principal parts of the following verbs.

think thought
thought

☐ think _____ _____ _____

let let let

☐ let _____ _____ _____

go went gone

☐ go _____ _____ _____

repeat repeated
repeated

☐ repeat _____ _____ _____

THE PERFECT TENSES

5G Each of the following sentences contains a verb in a different tense.

future perfect
present perfect
past perfect

She will have come. _____ tense

She has left. _____ tense

She had forgotten. _____ tense

☐ As its name indicates, the past participle of a verb shows that the action or condition is past.

This furniture has been made to last.

We know that the action of making is past because *made*,

past

the _____ participle of *make*, is used.

☐ Because it shows that an action or condition is past, the past participle of a verb can be joined to a present-tense form of *have* (*have* or *has*) to indicate that a past action or condition is continuing in the present.

The wind blew for three days.
The wind has blown for three days.

The fact that the past action of the wind's blowing con-tinues during the present can be expressed only by the

second

[first, second] _____ sentence.

77

□ *The wind has blown for three days.*

This sentence can show that the past action continues during the present because its verb is composed of the past participle _____ preceded by a present-tense form of *have*, _____.

blown
has

□ Joining the past participle of a verb to *have* (*has*), the present tense of the auxiliary verb, forms what is called the present perfect tense.

The wind has blown for three days.

The verb in this sentence is in the _____ tense.

present perfect

□ The present perfect tense is one of three perfect tenses; the other two are the past perfect and future perfect. English, then, has six tenses in all: the simple tenses—present, past, and future—and the perfect tenses—present perfect, past perfect, and future _____.

perfect

□ One of the advantages of having the three perfect tenses in addition to the simple tenses is that they allow us to express a prior action or condition continuing in a present, past, or future time.

I have walked all day.

We say that the verb *have walked* is in the present perfect tense because it can indicate that the prior action of walking continues during the _____ time.

present

☐ To indicate that a prior action or condition continues during the present, we use the present perfect tense. This is the form of the verb composed of a _____ -tense form of *have* plus the _____ of the main verb.

☐ We always use the present perfect tense to indicate that a prior action or condition continues during the present. We also use it to indicate that a completed past action or condition is in some way related to the present.

Mr. Brown has traveled extensively in Europe in preparation for his speech tonight.

Although Mr. Brown is not traveling in Europe during the present, the relationship between the past action of traveling and the present time is indicated by the use of the _____ tense.

☐ The present perfect tense always indicates a past action or condition which may either be continuing during the present time or is in some way _____ to the present.

☐ *We drove all night.*

If we wished to show that the driving continues during the present—or is in some way related to it—we would replace the past-tense form *drove* with the present perfect form of the same verb:

We _____ all night.

☐ By use of the past perfect tense we can indicate that a past action or condition continued prior to a definite past time. This tense is formed by joining the past participle of a verb to *had*, the past-tense form of *have*.

By yesterday noon it had rained for two days.

Because the past participle *rained* is joined to *had*, we know that the action of raining continued prior to a _____ time, yesterday noon.

79

□ *Had* plus the past participle of a verb is the past perfect tense of that verb.

> *Paul had worked on the design for two weeks.*

past perfect

The verb *had worked* is in the _____ tense.

□ Comparing the present perfect and past perfect tenses shows the difference in the way each expresses a past action or condition.

> *We have driven all day today.*
> *We had driven all day yesterday.*

The present perfect tense in the first sentence indicates that the past action of driving continues up to the present time. The past perfect tense in the second sentence indicates that the same past action continued up to a definite

past

_____ time.

□ We always use the past perfect tense to express a past action continuing during a past time. We can also use it to express a past action which was not continuous but was completed by a past time and related to it.

> *By the time Smith retired he had received two Pulitzer Prizes.*

Receiving the Pulitzer Prizes occurred before the retirement. In this sentence, then, the past actions expressed in the past perfect tense did not continue in the past time

related

but were _____ to it.

□ The future perfect tense is like the present perfect and past perfect tenses in that it also expresses a past action or condition. As you would expect, however, the future perfect tense indicates that the past action or condition

future

continues during, or is related to, a time in the _____.

□ The future perfect tense is composed of the past participle of a verb joined to a future form of *have* (*will have or shall have*).

We will have traveled through five countries.

will have traveled
future perfect

The verb in this sentence, _____, is in the _____ tense.

□ *By Thursday the plane will have flown for seven days.*

related future

The future perfect tense indicates that the action of flying continues during, or is _____ to, a _____ time, Thursday.

□ All three perfect tenses —present perfect, past perfect, and future perfect—express a prior action or condition that continues during, or is related to, a present, _____, or _____ time.

past
future

past

□ We form the perfect tenses by joining the _____ participle of the verb to a present, past, or future form of the auxiliary verb _____.

have

REVIEW

Each of the sentences below has a verb in one of the simple tenses. Change each to its perfect-tense form.

will have gone

□ *I will go tomorrow.*

had left

□ *I left yesterday.*

has cut

□ *This material cuts easily.*

set
sat

5H   Choose the correct forms in the following sentence.

They [*sat, set*] _____ *their books down before*
they [*sat, set*] _____ *down.*

□ The verbs *sit* and *set* can be confusing because they look somewhat alike. But they have different meanings. *Sit* refers to the act of being seated.

The children sit quietly.

Since the verb in this sentence refers to the act of being seated, the verb *sit* [is, is not] _____ correct.

is

□ *Set* refers to the act of placing or adjusting something.

She set the plant on the table.

Since the verb in this sentence refers to the act of placing something, a plant, the verb _____ is correct.

set

□   *He* [*sat, set*] *his watch.*

Since the sentence refers to the act of adjusting something, a watch, the correct verb is _____ .

set

□ The verb *sit* has two forms, *sit* and *sat*. The verb *set* has only the one form.

Today they sit down.
Yesterday they [*sat, set*] *down.*

The correct form to complete the second sentence is _____ .

sat

□ Remember that the past-tense form of *sit* is *sat*, not *set*.

Last night we [*sat, set*] *in the auditorium until eleven.*

The correct form for this sentence is _____ .

sat

82

□ The verb *sit* (*sat*), then, refers to the act of being seated. The verb *set* refers to the act of placing or adjusting something. Complete these sentences.

set

set

sat

The mechanic [*sat, set*] _____ *his gauge.*

The mechanic [*sat, set*] _____ *his gauge on the bench.*

The mechanic [*sat, set*] _____ *on the floor.*

□ Complete these sentences.

sat

set

The crowd finally [*sat, set*] _____ *down after giving the speaker a five-minute ovation. The girls* [*sat, set*] _____ *their purses on the floor.*

5I Choose the correct forms for the following sentence.

laid

lay

He [*lay, laid*] _____ *his watch on the night-table before he* [*lay, laid*] _____ *down for a nap.*

□ The verbs *lie* and *lay* are often confused because they look somewhat alike. Their meanings, however, are different. *Lie* refers to the act of reclining.

The children lie down for a nap at twelve.

Since the verb in this sentence refers to the act of reclining,

is

lie [*is, is not*] _____ the correct verb.

□ The verb *lay* refers to the act of placing something.

She will [*lie, lay*] *the wreath on the tomb.*

Since this sentence refers to the act of placing something,

lay

the correct verb is _____.

□ *Lie*, meaning to recline, has three forms: *lie, lay, lain*. It does not have a form *laid*. Complete these sentences.

lay

lain

Yesterday he [*lay, laid*] _____ *down early.*

He has [*lain, laid*] _____ *down early before.*

□ Complete these sentences. Remember that the forms of *lie* are *lie, lay, lain.*

lie

lay

The girls [*lie, lay*] _____ down now.

The girls [*lay, laid*] _____ down yesterday.

□ *Lay*, meaning to place something, has only two forms, *lay* and *laid.* Complete these sentences.

lay

laid

He will [*lie, lay*] _____ down the paper.

He has [*lain, laid*] _____ down the paper.

□ One source of confusion between *lie* and *lay* is that the past-tense form of *lie* (*lay, lain*) is identical to the present-tense form of *lay* (*laid*). Remember, then, that *lay* means to recline only in the past tense. It means to place something only in the present tense. Complete these sentences.

lay

lay

Yesterday Charlie [*lay, laid*] _____ down.

Now they [*lie, lay*] _____ their work down.

□ Complete these sentences with the appropriate form of *lie* (*lay, lain*) or *lay* (*laid*).

lay

lie

Please _____ the books on the counter.

Please _____ down now.

□ Complete these sentences.

lie

lay

Remember that the baby is to [*lie, lay*] _____ down at two.

Remember to [*lie, lay*] _____ the panel on the floor.

□ Complete these sentences.

laid

lain

The electricians [*lay, laid*] _____ the conduit along the ditch.

The adults very seldom have [*lain, laid*] _____ down before midnight.

Complete the following sentences.

lying
sat

□ *Before* [laying, lying] _____ *down, he* [sat, set] _____ *for awhile on the edge of his bunk.*

lay

□ *The tourist from Germany* [lay, laid] _____ *in the sand all day.*

sat

□ *They have* [sat, set] _____ *on the porch for a long time now.*

laid
set
sat

□ *Bob finally* [lay, laid] _____ *down his work. He* [sat, set] _____ *his watch before he* [sat, set] _____ *down.*

CONSISTENCY OF TENSE

comes
~~*came*~~

kills
~~*killed*~~

5J Replace any incorrect words in the following sentences.

After Beowulf slays the monster Grendel, he believes that the countryside is safe. However, on the night following, Grendel's mother came to the warriors' hall seeking revenge and killed one of Hrothgar's great chieftains.

□ Problems in tense arise if we ignore the logical relationship between the verb of a subordinate clause and that of the main clause.

He leaves the paper when he goes to work.

goes
present

Since the two actions expressed are connected in the present time, both the verb *leaves* of the main clause and the verb _____ of the subordinate clause are in the _____ tense.

□   *He left the paper when he [go] to work.*

past

Since the verb *left* is now in the _____ tense, we must complete the sentence with the form of the bracketed verb in the same tense, _____.

went

□   *He left the paper when he went to work.*

is

Went, the past tense of the verb in the subordinate clause, [is, is not] _____ logical because the two actions are connected in a past time.

□ Replace the incorrect verb in this sentence with its correct form.

ran

~~runs~~

When I asked him to stop, he runs away.

□ If we choose the present tense in telling a story or discussing ideas, we should use the present tense consistently.

Othello's extreme jealousy leads him to kill Desdemona. His realization of Iago's trickery came too late.

comes

Since *leads* is in the present tense, consistency requires that we change *came* to its present-tense form, _____.

□   *The writer lists a number of grave dangers in growing inflation. His article, however, contained few suggestions for its remedy.*

contained   contains

To make the tense of this sentence sequence correct, we must replace the verb _____ with _____.

□ Whether we choose the present or past tense, we should be consistent. Cross out and replace the incorrect verbs in this sentence sequence.

watched

~~watches~~

decided

~~decides~~

During the talk the crowd became restless. Mr. Zimmer watches the audience uneasily and decides to end the talk immediately. His presence of mind saved the situation from becoming dangerous.

86

□ Cross out and replace the incorrect verbs in this sentence sequence.

speaks

~~spoke~~

drops

~~dropped~~

> Jordan Baker, one of Fitzgerald's most memorable characters, appears at the party along with the others. Nick spoke to her, and then she dropped from his sight in the crowd of moving figures.

5K Complete this sentence.

rises

> The father told his child that the sun always [*rises, rose*] _____ in the East.

□ Recall that the present tense is always used in expressing a general rule. Complete this sentence.

boils

> We knew that water [*boils, boiled*] _____ at a higher temperature there.

□ When expressing a general rule, we are not concerned with time; therefore, we use the _____ tense, no matter what the tense of the related verbs in the sentence is.

present

□ Complete this sentence.

is

gives

> Madame Curie discovered that radium [*is, was*] _____ an element that [*gives, gave*] _____ off particles of energy.

□ Make sure that the following sentences do or do not deal with a general rule before completing them.

divide

divided

> The instructor explained that single-cell animals [*divide, divided*] _____ to reproduce themselves. The students watched through their microscopes while a group of tiny single-cell animals [*divide, divided*] _____ .

□ Complete these sentences.

It was well known in the eighteenth century that the ocean [covers, covered] _____ *three-quarters of the earth's surface.*

covers

He discovered early that students generally [want, wanted] _____ *to learn.*

want

5L Complete each of the following sentences with the correct infinitive of the verb *receive*.

to receive

The salesman hopes _____
the order before next Monday.

On Monday the salesman said he was very pleased _____ *the order the previous Saturday.*

to have received

□ Since infinitives and participles are verbals, they share certain qualities of tense with verbs. Verbals, however, have only two tense forms, the present and the perfect.

to look
to have looked

The first verbal is a present infinitive; the second is a perfect _____.

infinitive

□ The present infinitive of the verb *give* is _____; the perfect infinitive is _____.

to give
to have given

□ We use the present form of an infinitive if the action it expresses occurs at the same time as that expressed by a related verb.

The senators will be pleased to hear from their constituents.

The hearing and the pleasure [will, will not] _____ occur at the same time. The present infinitive is therefore the [correct, incorrect] _____ choice.

will

correct

88

	□ *Senators are pleased to hear from their constituents.*
present	Since the hearing and the pleasure occur at the same time, the _____ infinitive *to hear* is the correct choice for this sentence.
	□ This principle is useful for choosing infinitives related to verbs in all tenses.
	The senators were pleased [to hear, to have heard] from their constituents.
present to hear	Even though the related verb *were* is in the past tense, we use the _____ infinitive [*to hear, to have heard*] _____ to complete the sentence because the hearing and the pleasure occurred at the same time in the past.
	□ Complete these sentences with the correct form of the infinitive *to learn*.
to learn	*I have been hoping _____ more from him.*
to learn	*I had been hoping _____ more from him.*
present infinitive do not	□ If the action expressed by the infinitive occurs at the same time as that expressed by the related verb, we use the _____. We [do, do not] _____ match the tense of the infinitive with that of the related verb.
	□ If the action of the infinitive precedes the action of the related verb, we use the perfect infinitive.
	The team is happy to have won yesterday's game.
preceded	The perfect infinitive is correct in this sentence because the victory [preceded, followed] _____ the team's being happy.

□ Complete this sentence.

On his return to San Francisco, the conductor said that the members of the orchestra were pleased [to play, to have played] _____ *before such large audiences in Japan.*

to have played

□ We often use infinitives related to verbs expressing future possibility—*plan, intend, expect, hope,* and the like. Such verbs require a present infinitive. Complete this sentence.

I expect [to travel, to have traveled] _____ *before I retire.*

to travel

□ If we remember that the perfect infinitive expresses a completed action, while the present infinitive does not, we will have little trouble choosing the correct infinitive form.

Rudolf Hess hoped to find asylum in England.

Since the finding [was, was not] _____ completed at the time of the hoping, the present infinitive is the [correct, incorrect] _____ choice.

was not

correct

□ *The store owner plans [to sell, to have sold] the entire stock before Christmas.*

The infinitive required to complete this sentence is _____, the _____ infinitive.

to sell
present

□ Complete this sentence.

The workers intend [to strike, to have struck] _____ *before June 15.*

to strike

90

5M Choose the correct participle of the verb *leave* to complete the following sentences.

_____ yesterday, Roger arrived in Akron this morning.

_____ the room, George stumbled on the edge of the rug.

□ The participle, like the infinitive, has a present and a perfect form.

> *working*
> *having worked*

The first is an example of a _____ participle; the second is an example of a _____ participle.

□ The present participle of *go* is _____; the perfect participle is _____.

□ If the action expressed by the participle occurs at the same time as the action expressed by the related verb, we use the present participle.

> *Flying across the Alps, we saw the Matterhorn.*

Although the related verb *saw* is in the past tense, the _____ participle *Flying* is the correct choice because flying and seeing occurred at the same time.

□ Complete this sentence.

> [*Turning, Having turned*] _____
> right, Ralph felt his rear wheel strike the curb.

□ We use the perfect participle if the action expressed by the participle is prior to the action expressed by the related verb.

Having arrived late last night, he overslept this morning.

is

The perfect participle, *Having arrived,* [is, is not] _____

did

the correct choice because the arrival [did, did not] _____ occur before the oversleeping.

□ Choose the correct participle to complete these sentences.

Working

[*Working, Having worked*] _____ *rapidly, Bill accomplished more than the others.*

Having finished

[*Finishing, Having finished*] _____ *his assignment last week, Bill can begin another now.*

□ We use the perfect participle only if the action it expresses

before

occurs [before, during] _____ the action of the

present

related verb. In all other cases we use the _____ participle.

REVIEW

Complete the following sentences.

to arrive

□ *The Smiths plan* [*to arrive, to have arrived*] _____ *in Paris before the summer heat.*

exists

□ *The lecturer explained why he doubted that life* [*exists, existed*] _____ *on Mars at the present time.*

goes

□ *In a copyrighted article, Paul Dillon expresses his belief that a two-party system is not only desirable but necessary. He* [*goes, went*] _____ *on to show how a single-party system can lead to dictatorship.*

Having left

□ [*Leaving, Having left*] _____ *early, Bob missed all the fun.*

92

to sell

☐ *The firm intended [to sell, to have sold]* _____
all the obsolete models by Christmas.

93

SIX
VOICE

ACTIVE AND PASSIVE FORMS

The canary was fed by William.

6A Rewrite this sentence, changing the verb to the passive voice.

William fed the canary.

_____

□ Verbs have a quality called voice. This term refers to the two forms of verbs in all tenses which allow us to show whether the subject acts or receives the action.

I see the audience.
I am seen by the audience.

first

second

In the [first, second] _____ sentence the subject *I* acts. In the _____ sentence the subject *I* receives the action of the verb.

□ If the subject of a sentence acts, the verb is in the active voice.

The winner bowled a perfect game.

active

winner

The verb *bowled* is in the _____ voice because it expresses an action of the subject, _____.

94

□ If the subject receives the action, the verb is in the passive voice.

A perfect game was bowled by the winner.

In this sentence the subject *game* receives the action; the verb phrase *was bowled* is in the passive _____.

voice

□ We form the passive voice with the appropriate form of *be* plus the past participle of an action verb.

The meeting was canceled.

The passive voice of the verb in this sentence is formed with the auxiliary verb *was* plus the _____ participle *canceled*.

past

□   *The hunter was killed by a stray bullet.*
     A stray bullet killed the hunter.

The verb in the first sentence is in the _____ voice; the verb in the second is in the _____ voice.

passive
active

□ Rewrite this sentence, changing the verb to the passive voice.

The Hudsons bought a new stereo console.

_____

A new stereo console was bought by the Hudsons.

□ Rewrite this sentence, changing the verb to the active voice.

An important game was won by Syracuse.

_____

Syracuse won an important game.

second
active

6B *Bob was given a new assignment by Dr. Kenworth.*
Dr. Kenworth gave Bob a new assignment.

The [first, second] ＿＿＿＿＿＿＿ sentence is more direct and concise because its verb is in the ＿＿＿＿＿＿＿ voice.

---

object
by

□ *The carpenter added four rooms.*
Four rooms were added by the carpenter.

These sentences show that changing the verb from the active to the passive voice obliges us to express the real actor, *carpenter*, as the ＿＿＿＿＿＿＿ of the preposition ＿＿＿＿＿＿＿ .

□ Making the real actor the object of the preposition *by* places the actor in a secondary position grammatically. This may weaken the expressive power of a sentence.

The rich are often envied by the poor.
The poor often envy the rich.

second
active

The [first, second] ＿＿＿＿＿＿＿ sentence is more direct and concise because the verb is in the ＿＿＿＿＿＿＿ voice.

□ We should be careful not to use a passive verb unless it is necessary.

A corsage was brought to Helen by her date.

This sentence is obviously weak because it uses a passive verb unnecessarily. Rewrite it, changing the verb to the active voice.

date brought her a
corsage

Helen's ＿＿＿＿＿＿＿＿＿＿＿＿＿＿＿＿＿ .

Sanchez smashed a long double to deep center field.	□ *A long double to deep center field was smashed by Sanchez.*
	Robinson fielded the ball and threw quickly to third.
	Rewrite the weaker sentence of these two so that it is as direct and concise as the other.
	_____
The second	**6C** *The wheel was devised long before recorded history. Mexico was conquered by Cortez.*
	[The first, The second, Both] _____ sentence(s) could have an active verb.
passive	□ Although we should avoid using the passive voice, it is occasionally useful and necessary. Obviously if we do not know who or what acts, we must use the _____ voice.
	□ *Five valuable furs were stolen from the home of Helen Gardiner.*
	If the thief is unknown, we can give this sentence a verb in the active voice only by using a vague subject such as *someone.*
	Someone stole five valuable furs from the home of Helen Gardiner.
	It is obvious from these examples that the passive voice is better than the active voice if the real actor [is, is not]
is not	_____ known.

□　*Someone or something broke our picture window during our absence.*

Since the real actor, the person or thing that broke the window, is unknown, this sentence would be better if its verb were in the passive voice and the vague subject, *Someone or something,* omitted.

was broken

Our picture window _____ *during our absence.*

□　*Someone must have given Bob incorrect instructions.*

Mr. Hopkins gave Bob incorrect instructions.

Bob must have been given incorrect instructions.

One of these sentences would be better with its verb in the passive voice. Rewrite it.

_____

□ The passive voice is also useful if the real actor is unimportant.

Automobiles, flash floods, a tornado, an exploding boiler, and a misplaced stepladder injured five hundred persons over the holiday weekend.

The writer's use of the active voice in this sentence obliged him to list all the possible causes of injury. If he listed them realizing they were unimportant to his story but wishing to use the active voice, he burdened his reader and himself unnecessarily. This sentence would be far more concise with the verb in the passive voice and with the real actors unexpressed.

were injured

□　*Five hundred people* _____ *over the holiday weekend.*

active

passive

passive

□ Since the _____ voice is generally more direct and concise than the _____ voice, we should not employ the _____ without good reason.

98

unimportant will not	☐ We choose the passive voice if the real actor is unknown or _____. In both cases the real actor [will, will not] _____ be expressed.

Rewrite any sentence below which can be improved by a change in voice. Mark good sentences C.

☐ *China was once called Cathay.*

C

_____

Mr. Jones mixed the
paint carefully and
applied it to the
undercoated panels.

☐ *The paint was mixed carefully by Mr. Jones and applied by him to the undercoated panels.*

_____

_____

The Giants' two start-
ing tackles were
injured during yes-
terday's scrimmage.

☐ *Someone or something injured the Giants' two starting tackles during yesterday's scrimmage.*

_____

_____

AVOIDING SHIFTS IN VOICE

Althought it was
foggy, we saw the
Statue of Liberty as
we entered New York
Harbor.

6D *Although it was foggy, the Statue of Liberty was seen as we entered New York Harbor.*

Rewrite this sentence to correct the shift in voice.

_____

_____

□ If we carelessly shift from the active to the passive voice, our sentences tend to be awkward and ambiguous.

A crash was heard as Roger entered the room.

This sentence has a shift in voice, leaving ambiguous the question of who did the hearing. The verb *was heard* is in _____ voice, and the verb *entered* is in the _____ voice.

passive
active

□   *A crash was heard as Roger entered the room.*

Correcting the shift in voice makes it clear that Roger did the hearing and the entering: *Roger* _____ *as he entered the room.*

heard a crash

□   *Smith stayed at his desk until the assignment was written.*

Correcting the shift in voice makes it clear that Smith did the staying and the writing: *Smith stayed at his desk* _____ .

until he had written the assignment

□ We should also avoid shifting voice in related sentences.

I have two tennis rackets, one heavier than the other.
The heavy racket is used for practice games.

To improve this sentence sequence, we should rewrite the [first, second] _____ one, changing the verb to _____ voice.

second
active

□ Correct the shift illustrated in the last frame by rewriting the second sentence.

_____

I use the heavy racket for practice games.

□   *First, Mr. Miller mixed the powder with an equal part of solvent. When it had hardened slightly, a heavy coat was applied to the raw lumber.*

We can improve this sentence sequence by correcting the shift in voice. Rewrite the weak sentence.

_____
_____

When it had hardened slightly, he applied a heavy coat to the raw lumber.

Rewrite the following sentences when necessary to correct a shift in voice. Mark correct sentences C.

Dave fired hastily at the elk just as soon as he saw it.

☐ *Dave fired hastily at the elk just as soon as it was seen.*

_____

_____

☐ *Government defense contracts exert an immense economic influence.*

_____

_____

C

☐ *The scissors were found because my mother suggested that I look under my bed.*

I found the scissors because my mother suggested that I look under my bed.

_____

_____

☐ *Professor Chaney has written four books. Also, seven talks have been given by him during the last year.*

Also, he has given seven talks during the last year.

_____

_____

☐ *The plane was missed because I overslept.*

I missed the plane because I overslept.

_____

_____

SEVEN
MOOD

INDICATIVE AND IMPERATIVE MOODS

indicative imperative	**7A** *She is leaving.* *Leave!* The first sentence illustrates the _____ mood; the second sentence, the _____ mood.

□ Certain verb forms can indicate the manner, or way, in which we view an action or condition. This characteristic of verbs is called mood.

> *You will go.*
> *Go!*

different

The mood, or manner of viewing the same action, is [identical, different] _____ in these two sentences.

□ *You will go.*
   Go!

mood

Because the verbs in these two sentences indicate a different manner of viewing the same action, we say that the verb of each is in a different _____.

102

☐ English has three moods: the indicative, the imperative, and the subjunctive. The indicative is the mood of verbs stating a fact.

The car started easily.

Since *started* is used to state a fact, it is in the indicative

mood   _____ .

☐   *Roses are not always red, nor are violets always blue.*

Are, the verb used twice in this statement of fact, is in the

indicative   _____ mood.

☐ We recognize a verb as being in the indicative mood if it

statement   fact   is used in a _____ of _____ .

☐ Verbs used in commands are in the imperative mood.

You are ready.
Be ready.

The verb *are* is in the indicative mood. The verb *Be* is in

imperative   the _____ mood.

☐ The form of the verb that indicates the imperative mood is the root form. *Be* is the root form of that verb. All other English verbs have a root form identical to the present-tense form without the *s.*

Apply yourself.

imperative   *Apply,* the root form of that verb, indicates the _____ mood.

□ Since the root form of all verbs except *be* is identical to the present-tense form without the *s*, it is not always distinguishable except in use. The root form of the verb used to indicate the imperative mood does not require the implied subject *you*.

[You] *leave!*

imperative

Here we recognize *leave* as the root form indicating the _____ mood because it does not require the subject *you*.

□ [*You*] *should wait.*
[*You*] *get ready!*

second
imperative

We can tell that the verb of the [first, second] _____ sentence is in the _____ mood because it does not require the subject *you*.

□ The imperative mood is basically the mood of command, but we use it also for making requests and giving instructions.

Please return the book.
Turn left at the next corner.

you

Although neither of these sentences is a command, we say that both verbs are in the imperative mood because both lack the subject _____.

□ *You should go by way of Chicago.*
Go by way of Chicago.

indicative
imperative

Although the instructions given in these two sentences are identical, the verb phrase of the first sentence is in the _____ mood, while the verb of the second is in the _____ mood.

□ *Please return the book.*

you

We know that the verb *return* of this request is in the imperative mood because it lacks the subject _____.

indicative	□ The mood of statement is the _____ mood. The mood of command, used also to make requests and give instructions, is the _____ mood.
imperative	

7B Complete this sentence.

see	*It is better that Mrs. Green* [*see, sees*] _____ *the teacher herself.*

□ *You are here.*
Be here.

By comparing these sentences, we can see that the form of the verb indicating the imperative mood is _____ .

Be

□ *Be* is the root form of that verb. The root form of all other verbs in English is the present-tense form without the *s* ending. Thus the root form of *thought* is *think*; the root form of *gone* is _____ .

go

□ *Be here.*
I ask that you be here.

Notice that the use of the root form *be* has a certain mild imperative force in the *that* clause of the second sentence. We would use the same form in this sentence:

be

I insist that Bob _____ *given another chance.*

□ We often join *that* clauses to predicates which express advice, preference, or necessity. In such clauses, use of a verb's root form has a mild imperative force. Thus we say *She is dismissed* but *He requested that she* _____ *dismissed.*

be

□ The following sentences illustrate the difference in meaning signified by different verb forms following predicates that express advice, preference, or necessity.

I insist that the work is complete.
I insist that the work be complete.

In the first sentence the use of the present-tense form *is* indicates that the *that* clause expresses a statement of fact.

root

In the second sentence the use of the _____ form *be* indicates that the *that* clause expresses a mild command.

□ The root form is necessary in *that* clauses following verbs of advice, preference, and necessity if a mild command is intended.

I move that the meeting [be, is] adjourned.

be

Since the verb of parlimentary motion is a verb of advice, the correct form of the verb in the *that* clause is _____.

□ Complete these sentences.

answer
be

I prefer that Thurlow [answer, answers] _____.
I demand that the bill [be, is] _____ paid now.

□ *It is better* may be similar in meaning to *I suggest* or *I prefer*. If so, *that* clauses following *It is better* require the verb's root form. Complete these sentences.

stay
stay

I prefer that she [stay, stays] _____.
It is better that she [stay, stays] _____.

□ Similarly, *It is necessary* may have the same meaning as *I demand* or *I insist*.

repeat

It is necessary that John [repeat, repeats] _____ the courses.

106

□ Keep in mind that verbs of advice, preference, and necessity may be followed by more than one *that* clause. Complete this sentence.

be be

> *The manager suggested that all employees [be, are]* _____ *on time and that they [be, are]* _____ · *careful in answering customers' complaints.*

□ Complete this sentence, making sure you have a reason for each choice.

return

pay

> *I insist that Mr. Edwards [return, returns]* _____ *the books now and that he [pay, pays]* _____ *the fines that are due on them.*

REVIEW

Complete the following sentences with the appropriate form of *be*.

am

□ *I* _____ *here now.*

be

□ *I insist that you* _____ *here tomorrow.*

be

□ *Please* _____ *here tomorrow.*

be

be

□ *I suggest that we all* _____ *ready and that we* _____ *open to any possibility that arises.*

SUBJUNCTIVE MOOD

7C *We would call more often if she was nearer.*

was

were

To correct this sentence, we would replace _____ with _____.

□ We often find it necessary to indicate that an action or condition is contrary to fact. Such expressions require the subjunctive rather than the indicative mood.

If I am there tomorrow, I can help.
If I were there tomorrow, I could help.

Both of these sentences are introduced by clauses expressing the possibility of the speaker's presence at a particular place. If the speaker does not in fact expect to be present, he will use the [first, second] _____ sentence.

second

□ Verb forms indicating that the conditions expressed are contrary to fact are in the subjunctive mood.

If I am there tomorrow, I can help.
If I were there tomorrow, I could help.

The verb *am* in the first sentence is in the indicative mood. The verb *were* in the second sentence is in the _____ mood.

subjunctive

□ Clauses introduced by *if* which express conditions contrary to fact require a verb in the subjunctive mood.

If Bob were thrifty, he would save more.

The subjunctive form of the verb *be* in the *if* clause of this sentence is _____.

were

□   *If he were ready, he could go.*

The verb form *were* in this sentence's *if* clause indicates that the subject *he* is not ready. In other words, the form of the verb indicates the _____ mood.

subjunctive

□ Notice that the verb *were* used as a subjunctive form does not indicate past time.

We would stop if the light were red now.

In this sentence the verb *were*, normally past tense, refers to a [past, present] _____ condition contrary to fact.

present

□ The subjunctive *were* is identical to one of the past-tense forms of *be*. However, the other past-tense form, *was*, is normally not used to indicate the subjunctive mood in formal writing. Complete this sentence with the verb form indicating the subjunctive mood.

If he [was, were] _____ *here, we would go.*

were

□ All English verbs except *be* have only one past-tense form, which we use to express present and future conditions contrary to fact.

If space scientists flew to the moon tomorrow, they could not survive.

The *if* clause in this sentence concerns a future action. To show that the condition expressed is not possible, the speaker used the _____-tense form of the verb *fly*.

past

□ To indicate that a present or future condition is contrary to fact, we use the past-tense form of the verb. The mood of such verbs is _____.

subjunctive

□ *If prosperity brought peace, economists would have clearer goals.*

The correct form of the verb *bring* [is, is not] _____ used in this sentence.

is

7D Complete this sentence with the appropriate subjunctive form of *be*.

If he _____ *here, he would have left on time.*

□ In expressing past rather than present or future conditions contrary to fact, we use the past perfect tense of the verb. Compare these sentences:

Because she married him, she is happy.
If she had married him, she would be happy.

The second sentence uses the subjunctive mood to express a past condition contrary to fact; the subjunctive mood is indicated by the past _____ tense of the verb *marry—had married.*

□ Indicators of the subjunctive mood in *if* clauses dealing with present or future conditions are *were* and the _____ tense of other verbs. The indicator of the subjunctive mood in *if* clauses dealing with past conditions is the _____ _____ tense of the verb.

□ *If the President had vetoed the bill, Congress would have passed it anyway.*
If the President vetoed the bill, Congress would pass it anyway.

In both of these sentences the verb of the *if* clause is in the subjunctive mood. The [first, second] _____ sentence expresses a present or future condition contrary to fact with the _____ tense form of the verb. The _____ sentence expresses a past condition contrary to fact with the _____ tense form.

110

□ Complete these sentences with the appropriate form of the verb *swim*.

swam

had swum

They would freeze if they _____ today.
They would have frozen if they _____
yesterday.

□ Complete these sentences.

had come

They would have gone if I [came, had come] _____
with them.

came

They would go if I [came, had come] _____
with them.

7E *If the car had been in good repair, we would have gone.*

The introductory clause in this sentence can be written another way without changing the meaning of the sentence.

Had the car been in
good repair

_____, *we would have gone.*

□ We can express the idea contained in some *if* clauses having a verb in the subjunctive mood without using the *if*.

If I were to go now, I would be early.
Were I to go now, I would be early.

The subordinate clauses in both these sentences have the same meaning. In the first sentence the clause is introduced by _____. In the second sentence it is introduced by _____, the form of the verb indicating the _____ mood.

If
Were
subjunctive

111

□ *Were* and *had* used subjunctively can introduce clauses without *if*.

> *Were I to go, I would meet you.*
> *Had I gone, I would have met you.*

Both subordinate clauses in these sentences can be introduced by *if*:

I were

I had

> If _____ to go . . . .
> If _____ gone . . . .

□ *If the cake fell, we would have no dessert.*

We cannot replace *If the cake fell* with *fell the cake*. We can, however, replace the *if* clause in this sentence with one introduced by the verb rather than *if*.

> *If the cake were to fall, we would have no dessert.*

Were the cake to fall

> _____, we would have no dessert.

□ *If the telephone had been connected, we would have called.*

Rewrite the subordinate clause in this sentence, omitting the introductory *if*.

Had the telephone been connected

> _____, we would have called.

---

were

7F Complete this sentence.

> *He drives as though he [was, were] _____ on the Indianapolis Speedway.*

112

□ A clause introduced by *as if* or *as though*, like those introduced by *if*, may also express a condition contrary to fact.

> *Atomic weapons cannot be treated as though they were firecrackers.*

We know from the verb *were* that the condition expressed in the clause introduced by *as though* [is, is not] _____ contrary to fact.

is

□ *Atomic weapons cannot be treated as though they were firecrackers.*

Since it indicates that the condition expressed is contrary to fact, the verb *were* is in the _____ mood.

subjunctive

□ *He looked as if he had seen a ghost.*

The verb _____ in this sentence is in the subjunctive mood.

had seen

□ Complete these sentences with the subjunctive form of the bracketed verbs:

> *He spends money as though it [grows, grew] _____ on trees.*

grew

> *It felt as if the sky [fell, had fallen] _____ on us.*

had fallen

□ Complete these sentences.

> *She acts as if she [was, were] _____ God.*

were

> *Though still young, he behaved as though he [was, were] _____ ninety.*

were

Complete the following sentences with the form of *be* which indicates the subjunctive mood.

Were

□ _____ the company to go out of business now, *500 people would be out of work.*

had been

□ *The coach explained that if the team _____ in better shape it would not have lost so badly.*

were

□ *The gaudy Pacific sunsets can make the buildings of Honolulu look as though they _____ on fire.*

USE OF INDICATIVE AND SUBJUNCTIVE MOODS

is
were

7G *John behaves as though he [is, were] crazy.*

If the chances are good that John really is crazy, the appropriate verb form is _____. If we know that John is not really crazy, then the correct form is _____.

subjunctive
does not

□ The advantage of having a subjunctive mood is that we can express clearly whether or not we consider a condition contrary to fact, or at best improbable.

He would ask her if he were wise.

The writer here indicates by his use of the _____ mood in the *if* clause that he [does, does not] _____ consider the subject *he* wise.

114

□ In contrast, we use the indicative mood in *if* clauses to suggest that the conditions expressed may be factual.

If he is wise, he will ask her.

indicative

The verb in the *if* clause of this sentence is in the _____ mood. In this way the writer indicates that the subject *he* may or may not be wise.

□ *If I were elected President, I would insist on tax reform.*
If I am elected President, I will insist on tax reform.

subjunctive
indicative

The verb of the *if* clause in the first sentence is in the _____ mood. The verb of the *if* clause in the second sentence is in the _____ mood.

□ *If I were elected President, I would insist on tax reform.*
If I am elected President, I will insist on tax reform.

first

The speaker of the [first, second] _____ sentence thinks his election is impossible, or at best improbable.

□ *If I am fired from this job, I can easily get another.*

indicative

Because he uses the _____ mood in the *if* clause, we know that this speaker thinks his being fired is possible.

□ *If I became a teacher ....*

poor

Without knowing what the remainder of this sentence is, we can tell that the speaker believes his chances of becoming a teacher are [good, poor] _____.

□ *If I became a teacher ....*

subjunctive

The verb form in this *if* clause indicates the _____ mood.

115

were subjunctive	□ *He acts as though he [is, were] ill.* Assuming that the writer of this sentence thinks that the subject *He* is not really ill, he will use _____, the verb in the _____ mood.
is indicative	□ *He acts as though he [is, were] ill.* If the writer thinks it likely that the subject *He* really is ill, he will use _____, the form of the verb in the _____ mood.
is indicative	□ *He spends money as though he [is, were] a millionaire.* If the writer wishes to indicate that the subject *He* may be a millionaire, he will complete the sentence with _____, the _____ form of the bracketed verb.
were subjunctive	□ *He spends money as though he [is, were] a millionaire.* If the speaker wishes to express doubt that the subject *He* is a millionaire, he will complete the sentence with _____, the _____ form.
were subjunctive	**7H** *Ralph behaves as though he [is, were] the most important man on earth.* *Ralph wishes he [is, were] the most important man on earth.* Both of the above sentences should be completed with _____, the verb in the _____ mood.
were	□ Logic often demands the subjunctive mood because the conditions expressed are clearly contrary to fact. Complete this sentence with the logical verb. *John speaks as though New York [is, were] _____ a mile from Cleveland.*

□   *John speaks as though New York were a mile from Cleveland.*

Because New York and Cleveland are a good deal more than a mile apart, the clause introduced by *as though* logically requires *were*, the verb indicating the _____ mood.

subjunctive

□ *Wish* is an unusual verb: because it always expresses a condition contrary to fact, it is normally followed by a verb in the subjunctive mood.

I am taller than he.
I wish that I were taller than he.

The verb *were* following the verb _____ in the second sentence indicates the subjunctive mood.

wish

□   *Helen wishes that her vacation [was, were] longer.*

Since it follows the verb *wish*, the correct verb form to complete this sentence is _____, the form of *be* indicating the _____ mood.

were
subjunctive

□ Complete this sentence.

Hank wishes he [was, were] _____ finished now.

were

Complete the following frames.

☐ *Senator Rogers speaks as though the relations between labor and management [have, had] never been better.*

If the writer of this sentence agrees with the Senator's views, he will complete this sentence with _____, the form of the verb indicating the _____ mood. If he disagrees, he will complete it with _____, the form of the verb indicating the _____ mood.

have
indicative
had
subjunctive

☐ Complete the following sentences with the logical form of the verb *drive.*

drove

Mr. Hendricks wishes that his son _____ more carefully.

With all the breakdowns we had between San Francisco and Los Angeles, I felt as though I _____ all the way from New York.

had driven

AVOIDING SHIFTS IN MOOD

71 *Outline your paper first. Then you should follow your outline as closely as possible.*

The problem with this sentence sequence is that the writer has shifted from the _____ to the _____ mood.

imperative   indicative

□ Shifting carelessly from one mood to another—for instance, from the imperative to the indicative mood—makes our writing awkward and confusing.

Wash the floor first. Then you should spread an even coat of wax on it.

The writer of the above sentences has shifted from the

_____ mood in the first to the _____ mood in the second sentence.

□ We can correct this shifting construction in either of two ways. We can place the verbs of both sentences in the indicative mood:

You should wash the floor first. Then you should spread and even coat of wax on it.

Or we can place the verbs of both sentences in the imperative mood:

*Wash the floor first.
Then spread an even
coat of wax on it.*

_____

_____

*You should turn the
switch down; and
then for added
safety you should
unplug the set.*

□   *Turn the switch down; and then for added safety you should unplug the set.*

Rewrite this sentence, using the indicative mood.

_____

_____

*Turn the switch down;
and then for added
safety unplug the set.*

□ Now rewrite the sentence, using the imperative mood.

_____

_____

7J   Replace the incorrect verbs in the following sentence.

*send
~~sends~~
notify
~~notifies~~*

Last week Mrs. Abram suggested that Dr. Elliott sends her a new bill and that he notifies her of her appointment date.

□ Recall that verbs expressing advice, preference, or necessity are often followed by a clause introduced by *that*. In such clauses we use the root form of the verb, which is *be* and the present-tense form without the *s* of all other verbs.

I ask that she be dismissed.

Since the verb *ask* expresses a preference, the verb in the clause, the root form *be*, [is, is not] _____ appropriate.

is

□ Two or more *that* clauses often follow verbs of advice, preference, or necessity.

I move that a committee _____ appointed and that it _____ given full power.

Both *that* clauses follow the verb of parliamentary motion, a verb expressing advice. The verb required in both clauses is _____, the root form.

be

□ When more than one *that* clause follows a verb of advice, preference, or necessity, be sure to use the root form of the verb in all of the clauses. Complete this sentence.

It is necessary that she [goes, go] _____ later and that Mrs. Harper [helps, help] _____ her now.

go
help

□ *The President requests that Congress work on the tax bill during this session and that its effort is unremitting.*

Correct the illogical shift in construction by substituting the correct form of the incorrect verb.

... that its effort
be
~~is~~ unremitting

□ *It is preferable that he goes to college now and enlist in the service later.*

Correct this shifting construction by substituting the correct form of the verb for the incorrect one.

go
... that he ~~goes~~
to college now ...

7K Replace the incorrect word in the following sentence with the correct form.

If he were twenty pounds heavier and if his arm was healed, he would have received an offer to play professional football.

were
~~was~~

☐ Shifting carelessly from the indicative to the subjunctive mood creates awkward and confusing sentences.

If I were wealthier than I am, and if I get a new job, I would be happy.

The writer here shifts carelessly from the _____ mood in the first *if* clause to the _____ mood in the second.

subjunctive
indicative

☐ *If I were wealthier than I am, and if I get a new job, I would be happy.*

Since both *if* clauses in this sentence express conditions contrary to fact, both require verbs in the _____ mood.

subjunctive

☐ *If I were wealthier than I am, and if I get a new job, I would be happy.*

Correct the shifting construction of this sentence by crossing out the incorrect verb and substituting its correct form.

got
. . . and if I ~~get~~ a new job . . .

☐ Correct the shift in this sentence.

Ralph would be promoted if he had more training in microwave theory and if he gets along better with his fellow workers.

got
. . . if he ~~gets~~ along better . . .

☐ Correct the shift in this sentence.

The garden would be prettier if you took out those hedges and replace them with small flowering shrubs.

replaced
. . . and ~~replace~~ them . . .

121

Correct any shifting construction you find in the following sentences. Mark correct sentences C.

C

□ *I insist that this child be treated with more patience and that he receive more remedial training.*

Then ~~you should~~ . . .

□ *Before assembling the control, check all parts against the parts list provided. Then you should group the unassembled parts according to the positions they will occupy.*

were
. . . if he ~~was~~ free . . .

□ *If I had more time and if he was free, we could have entered our sloop in Sunday's regatta.*

. . . diplomatic corps
hire
~~hires~~ more . . .

□ *He asks that the government take a more active interest in African problems and that the diplomatic corps hires more technicians familiar with the political situation there.*

C

□ *We would go if there were time and if the car were in good shape.*

122

EIGHT

SUBJECT-VERB AGREEMENT

VERB AGREEMENT WITH REGULAR AND IRREGULAR NOUNS

8A *He does his work.*
  They do theirs.

In the first sentence the verb *does* is the [singular, plural] _____ form to agree with the subject _____.
In the second sentence *do* is the _____ form to agree with the subject _____.

singular *He*
plural
  They

□ The most important relationship in any sentence is that between the subject and the verb. This relationship requires that the verb agree with its subject. For instance, we say *I am here* but not *We am here;* the present-tense form of *be* which agrees with *we* is _____.

are

□ The subject, then, determines what form of the verb we use. In other words, the verb must agree with the _____.

subject

123

singular plural	☐ The subject of a sentence may be either singular or plural. If it refers to a single person or thing, it is _____; if it refers to more than one person or thing, it is _____.
	☐ *Newspapers affect public opinion.*
Newspapers more than one	The subject of this sentence is the noun _____; we call it plural because it refers to [one, more than one] _____ thing.
	☐ *He arrives early tomorrow.*
He singular	The subject of this sentence is the pronoun _____; we call it _____ because it refers to a single person.
	☐ A singular subject requires the singular form of a verb.
	Water [*freeze, freezes*].
singular	Since the subject of this sentence is singular, we must complete the sentence with *freezes*, the _____ form of the bracketed verb.
contains *does*	☐ Singular verbs in the present tense end in *s* or *es*. The singular form of *contain* is _____; the singular form of *do* is _____.
go receive	☐ Plural subjects require the plural form of the verb, the present-tense form without the *s*. The plural form of *goes* is _____; the plural form of *receives* is _____.
plural	☐ Verbs have different forms for singular and plural subjects only in the present and present perfect tenses. Recall that the present perfect tense is formed by adding one of the present-tense forms of *have* (*has* or *have*) to the past participle. With singular subjects we use *has* before the past participle. With _____ subjects we use *have* before the past participle.

□　*Hank has finished.*

　The Smiths have finished.

These examples show that subject-verb agreement in the present perfect tense involves only the auxiliary *have*. A singular subject requires [*has, have*] _____. A plural subject requires _____.

□ Complete these present perfect tense verbs.

　He _____ gone. They _____ gone.

has
have

has　have

8B　Choose the correct verb for each of the following sentences.

　The data [*is, are*] _____ *complete.*

　The alumni [*is, are*] _____ *here.*

　The theses [*is, are*] _____ *ready.*

are
are
are

□ Unlike all other verbs, which have only two present-tense forms, *be* has three present-tense forms: *am* (used only with the subject *I*), *is*, and *are*.

　One is gone; three are left.

Is agrees with [singular, plural] _____ subjects, *are* with _____ subjects.

singular
plural

□ In addition, *be* is the only verb that has singular and plural past-tense forms.

　One was gone; three were left.

The past-tense form of *be* which agrees with singular subjects is _____; the form that agrees with plural subjects is _____.

was
were

□ Except for *be*, all verbs in English have singular and plural forms only in two tenses, the _____ tense and the _____ perfect tense.

present
present

125

past

□ *Be* is the only verb that has a singular and a plural form in the _____ tense, *was* and *were*.

□ We who speak English regularly do not need a list of rules for subject-verb agreement. We choose the correct form of a verb for a subject with little difficulty; for most of us the choice is automatic. Complete these sentences with either *fill* or *fills*.

fills

fill

    This machine _____ the bottles.

    These tubes _____ the machine.

□ However, we can choose the correct form of the verb only if we know whether the subject is singular or plural. We know, for instance, that *machine* is _____ and that *tubes* is _____.

singular

plural

□ The majority of nouns in English have a plural form ending in *s* or *es*, but some do not. The plural of *car* is _____. But the plural of *child* is _____.

cars

children

□ Most of the irregular plural forms of nouns are so familiar to us that we use them without being aware that they are irregular. We unconsciously recognize *men* as the plural of _____ and *women* as the plural of _____.

man   woman

□ We don't say *two foots* but rather *two* _____. Similarly, we don't say *two tooths* but rather *two* _____.

feet

teeth

□ Certain plural forms borrowed from Latin and Greek present difficulties because we use them less often. We may have to be careful in identifying *crises* as the plural of *crisis* and *analyses* as the plural of _____.

analysis

126

	☐ A noun ending in *sis* would have an almost unpronounceable plural form if it were made by the addition of yet another *s* sound. Try to pronounce *thesis* with *es* added to it. It can be done; but because the sound is unpleasant and difficult to make clearly, we form the plural of nouns ending in *sis* by changing the *i* before the final *s* to *e*. Thus the
theses	plural of *thesis* is _____.
	☐ *Hypothesis* and *basis* are two other nouns of this kind. Complete the plural formations of the incomplete words in these sentences.
hypotheses *bases*	The hypothes[is, es] _____ are given. The bas[is, es] _____ are clearly presented.
alumnus	☐ The Latin and Greek plural forms of certain nouns borrowed from these languages remain a part of English. For instance, we find *foci*, the Latin plural form of *focus*, used by a few writers. We also find *alumni* used regularly as the plural of _____.
criteria	☐ Also popular is the plural form *phenomena* for the noun *phenomenon*. The noun *criterion* has a similarly formed plural. These three criteri[a, ons] _____ are valuable aids.
memorandum	☐ In Latin, nouns ending in *um* have a plural formed by exchanging that ending for *a*. Consequently, we often find *curricula* as the plural form of *curriculum* and *memoranda* as the plural form of _____.

127

□ Fortunately, these irregular forms are passing from the language. The forms *curriculums* and *memorandums* are now accepted. We must be aware, however, that these nouns have two plural forms in common use. *Medium* is another noun which follows this pattern.

Two influential _____ *are radio and television.*

A sentence such as this may be completed with one of

media
mediums

two plural forms of the noun *medium:* _____ or

_____ .

□ The noun *data* is the plural of the less familiar singular noun *datum*. Until recently *data* served as both a singular and plural noun, but the use of *datum* by scientists to refer to a single fact has brought the singular form into general use. Now *datum* refers to a single fact, *data* to a number of related facts. Complete these sentences.

was
were

That datum [*was, were*] _____ *important.*
That data [*was, were*] _____ *important.*

□ Our use of the relatively few nouns with irregular forms should follow current practice. If in doubt about the form of a noun, we should consult the dictionary.

No response required.

□ Complete this frame only if you have a dictionary ready at hand. Look up each word.

The noun *index* has two plural forms in general use,

indexes   indices
species (identical to
singular form)

_____ and _____ . The noun *species*

has only one plural form, _____ .

□ Complete the following sentences.

were

□ *He discovered that his major hypotheses [was, were]* _____ *not supported by other findings.*

return

□ *The alumni [returns, return]* _____ *every year during Home-coming Week.*

are

□ *The South American political crises [is, are]* _____ *the concern of North Americans.*

was

□ *The datum [was, were]* _____ *crucial.*

were

□ *His criteria [was, were]* _____ *carefully stated.*

VERB AGREEMENT WITH SINGULAR NOUNS HAVING PLURAL FORMS

8C Complete these sentences.

is

Mumps [is, are] _____ *among a number of mild contagious diseases.*

are

Statistics [is, are] _____ *sometimes misleading.*

□ Some nouns ending in *s* or *es* are plural in form but singular in meaning. If a plural form refers to a number of things considered as a unit, it requires a singular verb.

A thousand dollars is too much to pay.

Although plural in form, *dollars* takes the [singular, plural]

singular

_____ verb *is* because the amount of dollars is considered a single unit.

129

□ Some nouns referring to numbers of things are singular or plural depending on their meaning.

> *Over three thousand orders have been mailed.*
> *Over three thousand dollars has been stolen.*

In the first sentence here, *orders* is [singular, plural] _____ because it refers to a number of separate things. In the second sentence *dollars* is _____ because it refers to a number of things considered as a unit.

plural
singular

□ Complete these sentences only after you have determined whether the subject of each has a singular or a plural meaning.

> *In this heat, fifteen minutes [seem, seems]* _____ *like a long time.*
> *During today's hot weather, fifteen persons [has, have]* _____ *been hospitalized.*

seems

have

□ Complete these sentences.

> *Thirty thousand dollars [was, were]* _____ *set aside as a sinking fund.*
> *Thirty thousand engineers [is, are]* _____ *employed by aerospace firms.*

was

are

□ Nouns ending in *s* or *es* may be either singular or plural, depending on meaning. *News*, for instance, is a descendant of a plural word meaning novelties, but it is now considered singular.

> *The news [was, were]* _____ *frightening.*

was

□ *The United States* is also normally singular.

> *Like other nations, the United States [suffer, suffers]* _____ *from technological unemployment.*

suffers

130

□ English has several singular nouns ending in *ics—physics*, *mathematics*, and *economics*, for example. Normally, nouns ending in *ics* require a singular verb:

is

> *Civics* [*is, are*] _____ *the study of political responsibility.*

□ *Civics, physics,* and similar words always refer to a subject of study, a single thing, and are therefore [singular, plural]

singular

> _____ .

□ Certain commonly used nouns ending in *ics*, such as *athletics, statistics,* and *politics*, may have a singular or a plural meaning.

> *Athletics was the subject of the debate.*
> *Athletics are pursued with zeal in many great universities.*

singular

plural

In the first sentence *Athletics* refers to sports considered as a whole and requires a [singular, plural] _____ verb. In the second sentence *Athletics* refers to a number of sports and requires a _____ verb.

□ Complete these sentences only after determining whether *Statistics* refers to a single thing or to more than one thing.

is

> *Statistics* [*is, are*] _____ *taught during the fall semester.*

were

> *Statistics* [*was, were*] _____ *gathered carefully.*

□ Complete these sentences.

are

> *His politics* [*is, are*] _____ *a product of careful study.*

is

> *Politics* [*is, are*] _____ *seldom considered an ennobling profession.*

□ Several singular nouns with plural forms cause difficulty because they are often given plural verbs even though they refer to only one thing. For instance, since we say *Smallpox is contagious*, we should also say *Measles* _____ *contagious*.

is

□ Although they end in *s*, *measles* and *mumps* refer to [one, more than one] _____ thing and are therefore [singular, plural] _____.

one
singular

□ Unlike *measles and mumps*, nouns like *scissors*, *pants*, *trousers*, and *tweezers* refer to two-part objects and normally take plural verbs.

are   The pants [*is, are*] _____ *mine*.
are   The scissors [*is, are*] _____ *dull*.

□ Complete these sentences.

has   *Mumps* [*has, have*] _____ *broken out among the school children*.

have   *The tweezers* [*has, have*] _____ *rusted*.

8D Complete the following sentence.

is

Hawthorne's Twice Told Tales [*is, are*] _____ *a fascinating group of stories*.

□ The titles of books, plays, poems, and the like are sometimes plural in form.

Dickens' Pickwick Papers *is a delightful book.*

Although plural in form, *Pickwick Papers* is the title of a single book and thus requires the [singular, plural]

singular   _____ verb *is*.

□ Cross out the incorrect verb in this sentence and substitute the correct form:

Shakespeare's Merry Wives of Windsor *are definitely on the program of the summer festival.*

is
~~are~~

□ Complete this sentence.

Hedgley's "The Three Faces of China" [*paint, paints*] _____ *a dreary picture of the Chinese commune system.*

paints

REVIEW

□ Complete the following sentences.

need

□ *These pinking shears* [*needs, need*] _____ *sharpening.*

is

□ *"Capitol Reports"* [*is, are*] _____ *a summary of political events in Washington.*

was

□ *Basic economics* [*was, were*] _____ *the subject of Professor Williams' talk.*

is

□ *Three dollars* [*is, are*] _____ *too much to pay for that.*

were

□ *The statistics* [*was, were*] _____ *provided by over seventy fieldworkers.*

133

8E *Some* [*is, are*] *left.*

If *Some* refers to a number of matches, the correct verb is _____. If it refers to an amount of pie, the correct verb is _____.

are

is

☐ Pronouns as subjects of sentences present few problems of subject-verb agreement. We automatically choose the correct verb form in sentences like these:

hope

has

> *They* [*hopes, hope*] _____ *for the best.*
> *He* [*has, have*] _____ *gone.*

☐ Certain words traditionally classed as pronouns, however, are singular or plural depending on the way we use them. The pronoun *all* is an example. Complete these sentences.

Are

Is

> [*Is, Are*] _____ *all of the guests here?*
> [*Is, Are*] _____ *all of the pie gone?*

☐ If the pronouns *any, all, some, more,* and *most* refer to a number of things, they are plural.

> *Some of the ships* [*has, have*] *left.*

plural

have

Some, the subject of this sentence, refers to a number of ships and is therefore [*singular, plural*] _____. The correct form of the verb is _____.

☐ If *any, all some, more,* or *most* refers to a quantity, it is singular.

> *Some of the milk* [*has, have*] *soured.*

quantity

has

Some, the subject of this sentence, refers to a _____ of milk and is therefore singular. The correct form of the verb is _____.

134

□ *More than enough* [*was, were*] *on hand.*

was

were

If *More* refers to a quantity of cheese, the correct form of the verb is _____ . If *More* refers to a number of bottles, the correct form is _____ .

□ Complete these sentences.

have

has

All of the men [*has, have*] _____ *arrived.*
All of the sand [*has, have*] _____ *washed away.*

8F *None of the children* [*is, are*] *here.*

The generally acceptable form of the verb to complete this sentence is _____ .

are

□ Until recently, strict teachers of English insisted that the pronoun *none* is always singular. Therefore, they considered the verb *are* in such sentences as *None are left* to be [*correct, incorrect*] _____ .

incorrect

□ Since *none* is equivalent to *not one* or *not any*, this pronoun logically requires a [*singular, plural*] _____ verb.

singular

□ However, usage affects strictly grammatical logic. Now it is generally accepted that *none* follows the pattern of *any*, *all*, *some*, *more*, and *most*. That is, in reference to a quantity it is singular; in reference to a number of things it is plural.

are

is

Of the cars, none [*is, are*] _____ *left.*
Of the pie, none [*is, are*] _____ *left.*

□ Although some English texts still insist on the strictly logical use of *none*, we find that even in better books and magazines *none* has a [*singular, plural*] _____ verb if it refers to a quantity and a _____ verb if it refers to a number.

singular

plural

□ *None* [*has, have*] *come.*

If *None* refers to students, the verb generally accepted as correct is _____. If it refers to cement, the correct verb is _____.

have
has

8G Complete these sentences.

was

> *Only one of the many problems* [*was, were*] _____ *considered.*

was

> *Each of the four trees* [*was, were*] _____ *treated with insecticide.*

was

> *Neither of the two members* [*was, were*] _____

□ Pronouns such as *one* and *each* are always singular. If the verb follows the pronoun directly, we have no difficulty choosing the correct form.

is

> *One* [*is, are*] _____ *left.*

has

> *Each* [*has, have*] _____ *a book.*

□ *Each* and *one* are often modified by prepositional phrases which separate them from their related verbs.

> *One of the children is left.*

The subject of this sentence is not children but rather the pronoun _____.

One

□ *One of the children is left.*

of

Children is the object of the preposition _____.
The verb *is* does not agree with *children* but with the pronoun _____.

One

136

□ *Each of the three men by the stairs has a book.*

The subject of this sentence is neither *stairs*, the object of the preposition _____, nor *men*, the object of the preposition _____.

□ *Each of the three men by the stairs has a book.*

The verb *has* agrees with the subject of the sentence, the singular pronoun _____.

□ *One of the stamps in their collections [is, are] extremely rare.*

The correct form of the verb is _____ because it must agree with the subject _____.

□ *Either* and *neither* are two other singular pronouns often separated from their verbs by modifying prepositional phrases.

Either [comes, come] today.
Either of the parents [comes, come] today.

The subject of each of these sentences is _____.
The correct verb form in both cases is therefore _____.

□ Complete this sentence.

Neither of the two women teaching history [is, are] _____ over thirty.

Complete the following sentences.

has	☐ *Neither of the two men who promised to help us move the bricks* [*has, have*] _____ *showed up.*
was	☐ *Only one of the qualified men* [*was, were*] _____ *available to the residents of Fallbrook as consultant on forming a new government.*
were	☐ *None of the committee members* [*was, were*] _____ *available for comment.*
has	☐ *Either of the two prizes on the lists* [*has, have*] _____ *been offered as a substitute.*

VERB AGREEMENT WITH STRUCTURALLY COMPLEX SUBJECTS

are	**8H** Complete these sentences.
was	*The golf clubs on the shelf in the front closet* [*is, are*] _____ *mine.* *A collection consisting of four paintings by Klee and two by Cézanne* [*was, were*] _____ *donated to the museum.*

☐ A noun may be separated from its related verb by phrases and clauses.

The treasurer of several campus organizations graduates today.

The verb *graduates* is separated from its subject, the noun

treasurer of several campus organizations	_____, by the prepositional phrase _____ _____.

138

□ *The treasurer of several campus organizations graduates today.*

The verb *graduates* agrees with the singular subject
treasurer, not the plural noun *organizations*, which is the
object of the preposition _____ .

of

□ If one or more plural nouns appear between a singular
subject and its verb, we might choose erroneously the
plural form of the verb. We can avoid error by identifying the subject before choosing the verb.

*Each of the ten switches on the four panels [turns, turn]
on a separate light.*

Each

turns

The subject of this sentence is the pronoun _____ .
The correct form of the verb is _____ .

□ Another common mistake is to choose the singular form of
a verb when one or more singular nouns separate it from a
plural subject.

*The members of the group within the club [expect,
expects] to form a committee.*

expect

members

The correct form of the verb is _____ because it
must agree with the subject _____ .

□ The best way to assure that the verb agrees with its subject is to tie them together mentally, ignoring all intervening words.

*Almost every one of the people standing in the aisles
remains until the performance is over.*

one

. . . remains

The subject and verb of this sentence are _____
. . . _____ .

□ *The team of research engineers and physicists assigned
to the studies [report, reports] today.*

Join the subject of this sentence mentally with each of the
verb forms. The form that agrees with the subject, the noun
_____ , is _____ .

team   reports

139

□ Remember also that the subject might not be the first element in a sentence.

Of their five children only one of the older girls [is, are] courteous.

is

one

The correct form of the verb is _____ because it agrees with the subject _____ .

□ Complete these sentences.

In all these years just one of our fraternity members [has, have] _____ played varsity football.

has

Before the flight the test engineers in charge of research and development [is, are] _____ responsible for the fueling operation.

are

---

81 Complete these sentences.

is

There [is, are] _____ only one of several solutions given in the book.

are

Here [is, are] _____ the only three tickets I could get.

□ We often introduce a form of *be* with *there*. When identifying the subject of sentences having this pattern, remember that *there* is never the subject.

There are three lamps in the room.
Three lamps are in the room.

lamps

The pattern of these sentences is different, but both have the same subject, the plural noun _____ .

□   *There are three lamps in the room.*

after

When *there* introduces a form of *be*, the subject of the sentence comes [before, after] _____ the verb.

140

□ *There was one problem remaining to be solved.*

The singular verb _____ introduced by *There* agrees with the singular subject _____ .

was
problem

□ *There [has, have] been in all only one satisfying method.*

Since the subject of this sentence is _____ , a singular noun, the correct form of the verb is _____ .

method
has

□ Similarly, we sometimes introduce a form of *be* with the adverb *here*. Like *there, here* cannot be the subject of a sentence.

   Here are the tickets.

The subject of this sentence is not *Here* but the plural noun _____ .

tickets

□ *Here [is, are] the men who will move the piano.*

Since the verb must agree with the subject _____ , the correct form is _____ .

men
are

□ Complete these sentences.

   There [is, are] _____ *the first tennis racquet I ever owned.*
   Here [was, were] _____ *the two people he admired the most.*

is

were

8J Complete these sentences.

   Mr. Wilson, accompanied by his son, [arrives, arrive] _____ *tomorrow.*
   Mr. Wilson and his son [arrives, arrive] _____ *tomorrow.*

arrives
arrive

□ Some subjects are compound; that is, they have two or more parts joined by a conjunction such as *and* or *or*.

Salt and pepper are the most common seasonings.

The compound subject of this sentence consists of two singular nouns, _____ and _____ .

Salt   pepper

□ Even though each element joined by *and* in a compound subject is singular, the whole subject is plural because it refers to more than one thing.

Hiking and swimming [is, are] favorite pastimes.

and

are

Since the two gerunds of the compound subject in this sentence are joined by _____ , the correct form of the verb is _____ .

□ A compound subject joined by *and* may, of course, have more than two singular elements.

Baseball, basketball, and football [is, are] popular spectator sports.

Even though each of the three nouns of the compound subject in the sentence is singular, the correct form of the verb is _____ .

are

□ We do not consider a noun joined to the subject by *together with*, *accompanied by*, or *in addition to* part of a compound subject. These phrases serve as prepositions rather than conjunctions.

Ralph, together with his father, helps plan our trips.

together with

Father is not part of a compound subject. Rather, it is joined to *Ralph* by a phrase serving as a preposition, _____
_____ .

□ *Ralph and his father help plan our trips.*
Ralph, together with his father, helps plan our trips.

Notice the difference between the subject of these two sentences. Because the subject of the first has two elements joined by *and*, it is compound and requires *help*, the [singular, plural] _____ form of the verb. The subject of the second is not compound; it requires *helps*, the _____ form of the verb.

plural

singular

□ *A nail in addition to a hammer* [*is, are*] *required.*

nail

is

The subject of this sentence is the noun _____; the form of the verb that agrees with it is _____.

□ *A check accompanied by a receipt* [*was, were*] *in this envelope.*
A check and a receipt [*was, were*] *in this envelope.*

second

first

The subject of the [first, second] _____ sentence is compound; the subject of the _____ sentence is not.

□ Complete these sentences with the correct form of the verb.

was

were

A check accompanied by a receipt [*was, were*] _____ *in this envelope.*
A check and a receipt [*was, were*] _____ *in this envelope.*

□ Complete these sentences.

is

are

A table in addition to a chair [*is, are*] _____ *needed.*
A table and a chair [*is, are*] _____ *needed.*

8K Complete these sentences.

Cream cheese and chives [*is, are*] _____ *a good sandwich spread.*

Each finger and thumb [*has, have*] _____ *been injured at one time.*

□ In some instances the elements of a compound subject joined by *and* refer to only one person or thing. Such compound subjects require the singular form of the verb.

The president and general secretary [*opens, open*] *the meeting.*

If the two nouns of the compound subject, *president* and *secretary*, refer to only one person who has two titles, the correct form of the bracketed verb is _____.

□ *My friend and helper* [*was, were*] *with me.*

If both nouns of the compound subject in this sentence refer to the same person, the correct form of the bracketed verb is _____. If each refers to a different person, the correct form is _____.

□ Some elements of a compound subject joined by *and* may refer to two or more things so closely related that the subject is singular in meaning.

Cottage cheese and salad dressing is a popular snack.

Although compound, the subject of this sentence refers to a single dish. The [singular, plural] _____ verb *is* is the correct choice.

□ Complete this sentence.

The corporation's profit and loss [*is, are*] _____ *the subject of this report.*

144

□ Determine which of these compound subjects is singular and which is plural before completing these sentences.

Salad and dessert [is, are] _____ included in the dinner.

Bread and butter [is, are] _____ served at English teas.

□ If *each* or *every* modifies singular elements of a compound subject joined by *and*, we think of each part separately, and the singular form of the verb is correct.

Each nickel and each dime falls into place automatically.

Since the singular nouns *nickel* and *dime* are modified by *each*, the [singular, plural] _____ verb form *falls* is correct.

□ *Each* or *every* may appear only once in modifying the elements of a compound subject.

Every sailboat and motorboat moored here [sells, sell] for less than $1,000.

Since _____ modifies the two nouns of this compound subject, the correct form of the bracketed verb is _____.

□   *Each parent and teacher is individually responsible for the child's education.*

The singular verb *is* agrees with this compound subject because its elements are modified by _____.

□ Complete these sentences.

A saw and a chisel [is, are] _____ efficient only when sharp.

Each saw and chisel [is, are] _____ efficient only when sharp.

□ Complete these sentences.

is

Every actor and musician [*is, are*] _____ *on the payroll.*

is

Each dog and cat [*is, are*] _____ *to receive some kind of prize.*

8L Complete these sentences.

Either the mayor or the committee members [*is, are*]

are

_____ *responsible.*

Either the committee members or the mayor [*is, are*]

is

_____ *responsible.*

□ Compound subject joined by the conjunction *or* are like those joined by *and* modified by *each* or *every:* the elements are separate, and the verb must agree with each element separately rather than with the whole subject.

Plastic or glass is suitable for milk containers.

Since the compound subject of this sentence is composed

or

of two singular nouns joined by the conjunction _____, the singular verb *is* is correct.

□   *Miss Porter or Mrs. Peters* [*takes, take*] *the notes at our meetings.*

Since the singular elements of this compound subject are

or

joined by _____, the correct form of the verb is

takes

_____, the singular form.

□ Complete these sentences.

is

Every Saturday and Sunday [*is, are*] _____ *a holiday.*

is

Saturday or Sunday [*is, are*] _____ *a holiday.*

146

□ Like *and, or* may join more than two elements in a compound subject. If the elements are singular, the verb must be singular, no matter how many elements the subject contains.

fits

> A table, a chair, or a bookcase [*fits, fit*] _____ into this space.

□ However, if all the elements joined by *or* in a compound subject are plural, the verb must be plural.

> *Days, weeks, or even months* [*passes, pass*] *as rapidly as a minute.*

plural

pass

Since all the elements of this compound sentence are [*singular, plural*] _____, the correct form of the verb is _____.

□ Complete these sentences.

are

> *Plastic bottles, cups, or glasses* [*is, are*] _____ *included in the basket.*

is

> *An icepick, a knife, or a nail* [*is, are*] _____ *useful in marking leather.*

□ A compound subject may have both a singular and a plural element joined by *or*. In such cases the verb should agree with the element nearer it.

> *Five small roses or a single gardenia* [*makes, make*] *an attractive corsage.*

makes

Since the singular noun *gardenia* is nearer the verb, the correct form is _____.

□ *A single gardenia or five small roses* [*makes, make*] *an attractive corsage.*

roses

make

Since the plural noun _____ is nearer the verb, the correct form is _____.

□ We often use the conjunction *or* in the correlative form *either . . . or.* The addition of *either* to *or* in a compound subject does not change the principles of agreement.

> *Either he or she* [*was, were*] *there all day.*
> *He or she* [*was, were*] *there all day.*

was   The correct verb for both sentences is _____.

□ Complete this sentence.

are
> *Either apples or pears* [*is, are*] _____ *served for dessert.*

□ Another correlative form used in compound subjects is *neither . . . nor.* When choosing a verb to agree with a compound subject having this correlative, follow the same principles that apply to subjects having *or* or *either . . . or.*

> *Neither Mr. Blake nor Mr. Shaw* [*was, were*] *here.*
> *Either Mr. Blake or Mr. Shaw* [*was, were*] *here.*

Since the separate elements of both subjects of these sentences are singular, the correct form of the verb for both

was singular   is _____, the [singular, plural] _____ form.

□ These principles of subject-verb agreement apply to compound subjects whose elements are joined by *or, either . . . or*, and *neither . . . nor*: if the separate elements of the

singular   compound subject are singular, the verb must be _____

_____; if the separate elements are plural, the verb must

plural   be _____.

□   *In the beginning of the play neither characters nor incidents* [*is, are*] *convincing.*

Because the separate elements of this compound subject

plural   are [singular, plural] _____, the correct verb is

are   _____.

□ *Neither the trees nor the solitary cloud* [*seems, seem*] *real.*

The compound subject in this sentence is composed of a singular and a plural noun. Since the noun closer to the verb is [singular, plural] _____, the correct verb is _____.

singular
seems

□ Complete this sentence.

Neither the foreman nor the other jury members [*was, were*] _____ *ready to reach a decision.*

were

□ Complete these sentences.

have

Either the owner or his two assistants [*has, have*] _____ *been here.*

is

Either the apples or the watermelon [*is, are*] _____ *enough for the picnic lunch.*

REVIEW

Complete the following sentences.

is

□ *Every rooftop and tree* [*is, are*] _____ *covered with snow.*

review

□ *Either the manager or his assistants* [*reviews, review*] _____ *the plant's personnel needs regularly.*

has

□ *One of the twenty boats in the offshore fishing fleets* [*has, have*] _____ *a radar-equipped bridge.*

stands

□ *Robert Ellsworth, in addition to the four other accused perjurers,* [*stands, stand*] _____ *trial today.*

is

□ *Fish and chips* [*is, are*] _____ *a popular inexpensive dinner in England.*

VERB AGREEMENT IN SUBORDINATE CLAUSES

8M *One of the four tools that [was, were] broken can be mended.*

If this sentence means that only one of four broken tools can be mended, the correct verb is _____ . If it means that only one of the four is broken and can be mended, the correct verb is _____ .

were

was

☐ A verb in a subordinate clause must agree with its subject, not with the subject of the main clause.

Mr. John knows who I am.

In the clause *who I am*, the verb *am* agrees with the subject of the clause, the pronoun _____ , not with the subject of the main clause, *Mr. John.*

I

☐ *I heard that you were on vacation.*

In the noun clause introduced by *that*, the verb _____ agrees with its subject, the pronoun _____ .

were

you

☐ As the sentences in the last two frames illustrate, *who, which,* and *that* are often not the subjects of the clauses they introduce but simply relative pronouns. That is, they may serve merely to introduce the clause. This sentence is similar:

The courses which he takes are rather difficult.

The subject of the adjective clause *which he takes* is not the relative pronoun *which* but the pronoun _____ .

he

☐ In some clauses *who, which,* or *that* is the subject of the clause.

The men who were late are waiting.

The subject of the clause *who were late* is _____ , the relative pronoun.

who

150

□ *The men who were late are waiting.*

The verb *were* does not agree with *men*, the subject of the sentence, but rather with _____, the relative pronoun which serves also as the subject of the subordinate clause.

who

□ If one of the relative pronouns *who, which,* or *that* is the subject of the clause it introduces, the verb of the clause must agree with the relative pronoun.

The car that was on sale went for very little.

that

Here the verb *was* agrees with the relative pronoun _____.

□ Problems of subject-verb agreement arise because *who, which,* or *that* used as the subject of a clause may be singular or plural, depending on the word it stands for.

The bell which rings at noon is out of order.

Which, the subject of the subordinate clause in this sentence, stands for the noun *bell*. Since the noun it stands for is singular, *which* is also _____.

singular

□ *The bells which ring at noon are out of order.*

bells
plural

In this sentence, *which* stands for the noun _____ and is therefore [singular, plural] _____.

□ *The members who are present will leave shortly.*
This is the clerk who saw the robbery.

plural
members
singular
clerk

In the first sentence *who* is [singular, plural] _____ because it stands for the noun _____. The same word in the second sentence is _____ because it stands for the noun _____.

151

□ When choosing a verb to agree with *who, which,* or *that,* we must determine whether the relative pronoun is singular or plural.

Independent farms that [*produces, produce*] *dairy products are decreasing in number.*

Since *that* in the above sentence is [singular, plural] _____, the correct verb is _____.

plural *produce*

□ If only one noun or pronoun precedes *who, which,* or *that,* we have no difficulty determining whether the relative pronoun is singular or plural.

The executive who [*needs, need*] *four secretaries is overworked or lazy.*

In this sentence *who* can refer only to the noun _____. The correct form of the verb is therefore _____.

executive

needs

□ More than one noun or pronoun may precede *who, which,* or *that* in a sentence.

The workers in the factory who [*was, were*] *unhappy formed a union.*

Who obviously cannot refer to *factory;* it must refer to _____. The correct form of the verb is _____.

workers   were

□ Some problems of this kind are more difficult to solve.

Three pictures of the collection which [*is, are*] *worth $100,000 are on display.*

In this sentence *which* may refer to either *pictures* or *collection.* If it refers to *pictures,* the correct form of the verb is _____; if it refers to *collection,* the correct form is _____.

are

is

□ Notice how the verb form in an adjective clause may affect the meaning of the entire sentence.

Three pictures of the collection which are worth $100,000 are on display.

Since *are* is used here to agree with *which*, the clause refers to the worth of the [pictures, collection] _____ .

pictures

□ *Three pictures of the collection which [is, are] worth $100,000 are one display.*

If the clause introduced by *which* refers to the worth of the whole collection to which the pictures belong, the correct verb is _____ .

is

□ *One of the professors who [speaks, speak] today is sitting on the platform.*

If we wish to say that only one professor is scheduled to speak, we use the verb _____ . If we wish to say that the professor is only one of several who are scheduled to speak, we use the verb _____ .

speaks

speak

□ *Several sections of the road that were in poor repair have collapsed.*

The form of the verb which agrees with *that* indicates that [all, part] _____ of the road was in poor repair.

part

□ *Frank, one of the fraternity brothers who date Mary, stopped by.*

Of the fraternity brothers, Frank [is, is not] _____ the only one who dates Mary.

is not

□ *Frank, one of the fraternity brothers who date Mary, stopped by.*

If we wish to show that Frank is the only fraternity brother dating Mary, we substitute the verb _____ for the verb _____ .

dates

date

Complete the following frames.

☐ *One of the models which [has, have] a three-speed transmission sells for under $4,000.*

If only the one model has a three-speed transmission, the correct verb is _____. If all the models have three-speed transmissions, the correct verb is _____.

has

have

☐ *One of the books that [deals, deal] with Egyptian culture is missing.*

If only the one book deals with Egyptian culture, the correct verb is _____. If all the books mentioned do, the correct verb is _____.

deals

deal

☐ *The keys of the typewriter which [has, have] been damaged will not strike properly.*

If only the keys are damaged, the correct verb is _____.
If the whole typewriter is damaged, the correct verb is _____.

have

has

154

NINE
PRONOUNS

AGREEMENT IN PERSON

9A Identify the following words according to person.

(a) second	(e) third
(b) third	(f) first
(c) first	(g) third
(d) third	(h) third

(a) you _____ (e) boat _____

(b) she _____ (f) I _____

(c) we _____ (g) it _____

(d) each _____ (h) he _____

□ Pronouns are name words like nouns; but unlike nouns, pronouns refer to someone or something that they do not specifically name.

I dislike liver.

Instead of using his own name, the speaker refers to himself with the pronoun _____.

I

□ *Do you know whether he likes liver?*

This sentence contains two pronouns: the pronoun referring to the person spoken to is _____; the pronoun referring to the person spoken about is _____.

you

he

155

□ One way we identify pronouns is by person. Those which refer to (or include) the person speaking are of the first person.

I told him we will be there.

I

we

The two first-person pronouns in this sentence are _____ and _____.

□ Pronouns of the second person refer to those who are spoken to. *You* is a pronoun of the _____ person.

second

□ The third person includes all pronouns that refer to someone or something spoken about.

He told me it was ready.

He   it

The two pronouns of the third person in this sentence are _____ and _____.

□ First-person pronouns refer to (or include) the person _____. Second-person pronouns refer to the person spoken _____. Third-person pronouns refer to the person or thing spoken _____.

speaking

to

about

□   *Someone gave us the book you forgot.*

Identify the three pronouns in this sentence according to person.

us

you

Someone

first person: _____

second person: _____

third person: _____

□ The third person includes most of the pronouns in our language. *He, she, it, they, some*, and *everything* are among the many pronouns of the _____ person; all of them refer to persons and things spoken _____.

third

about

third	□ It is not meaningful to identify nouns according to person because we use pronouns instead of nouns in referring to ourselves speaking or to the person we are speaking to. However, since nouns refer to persons or things spoken about, we can consider them as being of the _____ person.
I you *book*	□ All nouns and pronouns, then, are identifiable according to person. *You say that I borrowed the book?* This sentence contains one noun and two pronouns: _____ is of the first person, _____ is of the second person, and _____ is of the third person.
me ~~*you*~~	**9B** Cross out and replace any incorrect word in this sentence. *I really enjoy swimming because it makes you feel invigorated.*
I second	□ Identifying pronouns according to person helps us to avoid illogical shifts in our writing. *I prefer movies that make you laugh.* The writer of this sentence shifted illogically from the first-person pronoun _____ to the _____-person pronoun *you*.
first	□ *I prefer movies that make me laugh.* This sentence is logical because both the pronouns *I* and *me* are of the [first, second] _____ person.

☐ *From where we stood you could see Mt. Shasta.*

first
we

This writer begins his sentence with the _____-person pronoun _____. He then shifts illogically to the _____-person pronoun _____.

second   you

☐ *From where we stood you could see Mt. Shasta.*

you   we

To improve this sentence, we would replace the pronoun _____ with the pronoun _____.

☐ *I should buy a map because you could get lost without one.*

you   I

We can improve this sentence by replacing the pronoun _____ with the pronoun _____.

☐ Correct the error in this sentence.

us
~~you~~

We liked the extended tour because the guides let you take side trips.

9C   *The chemist worked late in the laboratory; he did not return home until after eleven o'clock.*

antecedent   *he*

Chemist is the _____ of the pronoun _____.

☐ A pronoun of the third person usually refers to a word which precedes it.

Carl came late, but he left early.

Carl

The pronoun *he* in this sentence refers to the noun _____.

☐ The word to which a pronoun refers is its antecedent.

Carl came late, but he left early.

antecedent

In this sentence *Carl* is the _____ of *he*.

☐ *A person can complete the test if he tries.*

antecedent
he

In this sentence *person* is the _____ of the pronoun _____.

158

Anyone *he*	☐ *Anyone who wishes can come provided he warns the office in advance.* In this sentence _____ is the antecedent of the pronoun _____.

he ~~they~~	**9D** Correct this sentence. *If anyone wishes a copy, they can have one.*

second third	☐ A pronoun must agree with its antecedent in person. *If anyone goes out in this weather, you should wear a hat.* The pronoun *you* does not agree with its antecedent *anyone* because *you* is the _____ person and *anyone* is of the _____ person.
he ~~you~~	☐ Normally we use the third-person pronoun *he* (*him*) to agree with *one, anyone, anybody,* or *person* because these are also of the third person. *If anyone goes out in this weather, you should wear a hat.* Correct this sentence by crossing out the incorrect pronoun and replacing it with the correct one.
he ~~you~~	☐ Correct the error in this sentence. *If a person is applying for a job, you should be well dressed.*
he ~~you~~	☐ Correct the error in this sentence. *When anyone disagrees with a speaker's point of view, you should let the speaker explain himself completely before attacking the point.*

Correct the following sentences where necessary. Mark correct sentences C.

we
~~you~~

☐ *As we entered the stadium you could hear what sounded like a million voices shouting.*

he
~~you~~
him
~~you~~

☐ *When a person is really anxious for an education, you should let nothing stop you from getting it.*

C

☐ *If anyone is interested, he should contact Mr. Blair.*

we
~~you~~

☐ *From where we stood you could see the coastline as far as the cape.*

AGREEMENT IN NUMBER AND GENDER

(a) plural
(b) singular
(c) singular or plural
(d) singular
(e) plural
(f) singular

9E Identify the following words according to number.

(a) we _____ (d) I _____
(b) he _____ (e) they _____
(c) you _____ (f) person _____

plural
more than one

☐ We identify pronouns according to number as well as person. That is, we identify the pronouns of the three persons as either singular or plural. *I* is a singular pronoun of the first person because it refers to only one person. *We* is a _____ pronoun of the first person because it refers to [one, more than one] _____ person.

160

singular plural	☐ The second-person pronoun *you* is unusual; it can refer to one person or to two or more persons. Therefore, *you* is either _____ or _____ in number, according to the way we use it.
singular plural	☐ The third-person pronouns *he, she,* and *it* are _____ in number. The third-person pronoun *they* is _____ in number.

it has ~~they have~~	**9F** Correct the error in this sentence. *Swimming across a river like this is difficult because they have such strong currents.*

singular	☐ A pronoun must agree with its antecedent in number as well as in person. *A man can succeed if he works hard.* In this sentence the pronoun *he* agrees with its antecedent *man* in number because both words are [singular, plural] _____.
plural *motor*	☐ *Running an electric motor too long will overheat them.* The pronoun *them* is incorrect because it is [singular, plural] _____, while its antecedent, _____, is singular.
it	☐ Complete this sentence with the pronoun which agrees in number with *motor.* *Running an electric motor too long will overheat* _____.
clothes they	☐ *Buy cotton clothes in a size larger than you need because it can shrink.* The pronoun *it* does not agree in number with its antecedent _____. We correct this sentence by substituting the pronoun _____ for *it.*

□ Cross out the incorrect pronoun and replace it with the correct one.

it
~~*they*~~

A person has to be careful when landing a trout because they can slip off the hook.

□ Correct this sentence.

it
~~*they*~~

Riding a strange horse can be dangerous if you do not know how they will behave.

---

its
~~*their*~~

9G Correct this sentence.

Every single record in his massive collection has their individual protective jacket.

□ Though the possessive forms such as *his*, *her*, *its*, and *their* are related to pronouns, we use them to identify nouns.

The players forgot their equipment.

equipment

In this sentence the possessive form *their* identifies the noun _____.

□ Although used to identify nouns, *his*, *her*, *its*, and *their* are forms of pronouns and have antecedents.

The players forgot their equipment.

players

In this sentence the possessive *their* has an antecedent, the noun _____.

□ The possessive forms of pronouns must agree with their antecedents. *His*, *her*, and *its* agree with [singular, plural]

singular   plural

_____ antecedents; *their* agrees with _____ antecedents.

□   *Clerks receive their paychecks every Friday.*

Clerks
is

Since the antecedent of their is the plural noun _____, their [is, is not] _____ the correct possessive form.

162

□ *An engineer can improve [his, their] job opportunities by further study.*

Since the antecedent *engineer* is singular, the correct form of the possessive is _____, the singular form.

his

□ Correct this sentence.

its
~~their~~

A car will not start easily if their battery is weak.

9H Correct this sentence.

his
~~their~~

Any employee in the two production departments may take their vacation this month.

□ We sometimes mistakenly use *they, them,* or *their* to agree with a singular antecedent if we are not sure whether the antecedent is masculine or feminine.

A student can expect to receive their degree in four years.

Since *student* is singular, the possessive their [does, does not] _____ agree with it.

does not

□ One way we can solve this problem is by using both the masculine and feminine singular forms. Complete this sentence.

her

A student can expect to receive his or _____ *degree in four years.*

□ Using *his* or *her* however, is cumbersome. A better way is to use a masculine singular pronoun or possessive (*he, him,* or *his*) to agree with an antecedent which is either masculine or feminine. Complete this sentence.

his

A student can expect to receive[his, her] _____ *degree in four years.*

□ *Each player may discard any card* _____ *wishes.*

Since a card player may be either masculine or feminine, we can complete this sentence with the pronoun _____.

he

□ Only if an antecedent is clearly feminine do we use a feminine singular pronoun or possessive.

A graduate seldom remembers [*his, her*] *teachers.*

If the graduate is from a coeducational college, we would complete the sentence with the possessive _____.

his

If the graduate is from a women's college, we would complete the sentence with _____.

her

□ The masculine singular forms *he*, *his*, and *him* agree with words such as *one*, *anyone*, and *person*. Complete this sentence.

If anyone has a question, [*he, she, they*] _____ *can ask it now.*

he

□ Complete this sentence.

A person can remember a lot when [*he, she, they*] _____ *concentrates.*

he

□ In the few instances in which *one, anyone, person*, and the like refer to one member of a strictly femine group, we use a feminine singular pronoun or possessive.

Anyone who wishes may hand in [*his, her, their*] *paper now.*

If a teacher made this announcement in a class limited to girls, he would complete the sentence with _____.

her

□　*Each member should pay [his, her] dues on the first of
every month.*

If *member* refers to a masculine or a feminine person, the
correct completion is _____. If *member* refers
to a person belonging to a women's club, the correct completion is _____.

9I Complete these sentences.

*Everyone who participated received a prize of some kind
for [his, their] _____ part in the performance.*
*Everyone enjoyed the show because [he, they] _____
found it amusing.*

□ Choosing pronouns to agree with *everybody* and *everyone*
requires special care because they may be both singular
and plural.　First of all, we know that they are singular
because we use them with the singular form of the verb.

Everyone [works, work] _____ to earn money.

□ Since we use a singular form of the verb with *everybody*
and *everyone*, we also use the singular pronoun *he* (*him*)
and the possessive *his* to agree with them.　Complete this
sentence.

*Everybody going on the trip should wax [his, their]
_____ skis.*

□ The only sentences requiring the feminine singular pronoun *she* (*her*) are those in which *everybody* or *everyone* refers to one of a group strictly feminine.

Everyone please take [his, her] nameplate when [he, she] leaves.

her

she

his

he

If we were to address this sentence only to a gathering of women, we would complete it with _____ and _____. If we were to address it to a gathering of men and women, we would complete it with _____ and _____.

□ Occasionally, using a singular pronoun or possessive to agree with *everybody* or *everyone* is confusing.

Everyone was so hungry that he could not wait for dinner.

he

This sentence would not be confusing if we substituted the pronoun *they* for the pronoun _____.

□ If *everyone* or *everybody* is the antecedent, choose a singular pronoun or possessive to agree with it unless the singular form is illogical.

Everyone enjoyed reading his small part on stage. They felt disappointed, however, that the audience was so small.

is

The pronoun *they* in the second sentence [is, is not] _____ used correctly.

□ Complete these sentences.

his

they

Everyone who can should make it [his, their] _____ job to replace the missing papers.
Everyone enjoyed the play so much that [he, they] _____ applauded for ten minutes.

166

Correct the following sentences where necessary. Mark correct sentences C.

they were
~~he was~~

□ *Everybody found the movie so sad that he was unable to hold back his tears.*

their
~~his~~

he
~~they~~

□ *Any person who wishes to become a journalist should make sure that they will be prepared to accept the challenge which a career in journalism offers.*

his
~~their~~

□ *Every student should hand in all their class cards before the end of registration week.*

C

□ *Anyone who expects me to help him had better be sure that he realizes how much work is involved.*

its
~~their~~

□ *Using a spinning reel is relatively easy because their rewind mechanism is simpler than that of other kinds.*

PROBLEMS OF AGREEMENT AND REFERENCE

9J Complete these sentences.

it

their

Either the car or the truck could pull a trailer if [it, they] _____ had a hitch. Unfortunately, both the car and the truck carry too little gas in [its, their] _____ tank(s) for the trip.

□ Choosing a pronoun or possessive to agree with a compound antecedent requires care. We must first of all indentify the antecedent.

Bob and Pete brought their rattlesnake to the party.

Bob [and] Pete

The antecedent of the possessive *their* is _____ and _____ .

□ Any antecedent whose elements are joined by *and* is plural and requires a plural pronoun or possessive. Complete this sentence.

Mrs. Smith told Bob and Pete to take the rattlesnake along with [him, them] _____ when [he, they] _____ left.

them

they

□ A compound antecedent joined by *or, either . . . or,* or *neither . . . nor* is singular if its elements are singular. Complete this sentence.

Neither the spaniel nor the pointer could be judged until [it, they] _____ demonstrated [its, their] _____ abilities in the hunting events.

it

its

□ If both elements of a compound antecedent joined by *or, either . . . or,* or *neither . . . nor* are plural, the pronoun or possessive must be plural to agree with it.

Neither the owners nor the team members were pleased with [his, their] _____ club's performance in the series.

their

□ Complete these sentences.

Mr. Elliott and John remembered to bring [his, their] _____ own money. However, neither Mr. Elliott nor John wanted to spend all [his, their] _____ savings on the trip.

their

his

□ Complete these sentences.

You can expect the detergent or the solvent to do [its, their] _____ work rapidly.
You can expect the detergent and the solvent to do [its, their] _____ work rapidly.

its

their

Mrs. Roberts handed
her coat to Helen.
or
Mrs. Roberts handed
Helen's coat to her.

9K *Mrs. Roberts handed Helen her coat.*

Rewrite this sentence to clarify the ambiguous reference.

_____

☐ Our use of a pronoun or possessive will be ambiguous unless it refers clearly to its antecedent.

> *Mr. Tichenor gave Jim his pencil.*

We cannot tell whose pencil Mr. Tichenor gave Jim because *his* can refer either to _____ or to _____ .

Mr. Tichenor
Jim

☐ Sentences which have two or more possible antecedents preceding a pronoun or possessive are confusing. It is best to rewrite such sentences so that the pronoun or possessive has only one possible antecedent preceding it. Complete the revision below.

> *Mr. Tichenor gave Jim his pencil.*
> *Mr. Tichenor* _____ *to Jim.*

gave his pencil

☐ *Mr. Tichenor gave his pencil to Jim.*

It is clear now that the pencil belongs to _____ .

Mr. Tichenor

☐ *The committee members submitted questions to the congressmen about their voting duties.*

This sentence is ambiguous. Because *their* can refer either to the _____ or to the _____ , we cannot tell whose voting duties the questions are about.

committee members
congressmen

□ *The committee members submitted questions to the congressmen about their voting duties.*

If the voting duties are the committee members', the sentence will be clear if *their* has only the one antecedent preceding it:

about their voting duties to the congressmen

    The committee members submitted questions _____

_____ .

□ *The oil will not lubricate the engine if its temperature is too high.*

This sentence is not clear because *its* has two possible

oil   engine

antecedents, _____ and _____ .

□ *The oil will not lubricate the engine if its temperature is too high.*

If *its* in this sentence refers to oil, we can rewrite the sentence this way:

the oil
the engine

    If the temperature of _____ *is too high, it will not lubricate* _____ .

□ *The oil will not lubricate the engine if its temperature is too high.*

If *its* refers to *engine*, we can rewrite the sentence this way:

the engine
the oil

    If the temperature of _____ *is too high,* _____ *will not lubricate it.*

9L *Although the car's windshield was cracked, it was safe to drive.*

Rewrite this sentence correctly.

its windshield was cracked, the car

    Although _____
was safe to drive.

170

□ Pronouns and possessives refer to nouns or pronouns, not modifiers or possessive forms of nouns.

> *Randy tried to hold the bull's tail, but it kicked him anyway.*

Since we expect *it* to refer to the noun *tail* rather than the possessive form *bull's* which modifies *tail*, this sentence seems to mean that the bull's _____ rather than the bull kicked Randy.

tail

□ *Randy tried to hold the bull's tail, but it kicked him anyway.*

Since the antecedent cannot be the possessive form of the noun, we can correct the reference problem in this sentence by changing *bull's* to *bull* and *it* to *its*:

> *Randy tried to hold its tail, but _____ kicked him anyway.*

the bull

□ *In Kerr's article "The Multiversity," he discusses the crisis facing American universities.*

Since *he* cannot refer to *Kerr's*, we should substitute *his* for *he* and *Kerr* for *Kerr's*, changing their positions in the sentence:

> *In _____ article "The Multiversity," _____ discusses the crisis facing American universities.*

his   Kerr

□ *Jim recharged the car's battery even though it had four flat tires.*

Rewrite this sentence to clarify the reference of *it*. Follow the pattern used in the last three frames.

> *Jim recharged _____ had four flat tires.*

its battery even
though the car

171

□ *Who, whose, whom, which,* and *that* introducing adjective clauses have antecedents.

> *This is the car that I bought.*

That introducing the adjective clause *that I bought* has a noun for its antecedent, _____.

car

□ *Who, whose, whom, which,* or *that* should have a noun antecedent, never a possessive form of a noun used to identify another noun.

> *Joe's wife, whom I played football with in college, is quite attractive.*

Since we expect *whom* to have a noun as its antecedent, this sentence seems to suggest that _____ rather than _____ played football in college.

Joe's wife
Joe

□ *Joe's wife, whom I played football with in college, is quite attractive.*

To correct the ambiguity in this sentence, we must re-arrange its parts so that *whom* has *Joe* rather than *Joe's* for its antecedent.

> *Joe, whom I played football with in college, has* _____ _____.

an attractive wife

□ *We met the Senator's children, who spoke so ably before the Congressional Committee yesterday.*

Rewrite this sentence to clarify the reference of *who.*

> *We met the children* _____ *spoke so ably before the Congressional committee yesterday.*

of the Senator who

□ *The truck's headlights which had been driven into the field lighted up the roadway.*

Clarify the reference of *which.*

> *The* _____ *which had been driven into the field lighted up the roadway.*

headlights of the
truck

172

9M *Actors have to work hard because it is a demanding profession.*

Rewrite this sentence correctly.

Actors have to work hard _____

because acting is a demanding profession

☐ Pronouns must have logical antecedents.

Because my father is an engineer, I decided to study it.

The antecedent of *it* in this sentence can be only *engineer*. However, a person does not study "engineer" but rather _____ .

engineering

☐ *Because my father is an engineer, I decided to study it.*

A pronoun lacking a logical antecedent must be replaced with the appropriate noun.

Because my father is an engineer, I decided to study _____ .

engineering

☐ *The Mexicans are happy even though it has a low average national income.*

Clarifying this sentence requires this substitution:

The Mexicans are happy even though _____ *has a low average national income.*

Mexico

☐ *Although doctors are often overworked, it is a rewarding profession.*

Correct the pronoun error in this sentence.

Although doctors are often overworked, _____ _____ *a rewarding profession.*

medicine is

9N *Bob will ask the managers to support his plan, which I think is foolish.*

The problem with this sentence is that *which* has [no, two] _____ antecedent(s).

two

□ We sometimes use the pronouns *which* and *this* to refer to a whole idea rather than to a word.

> *Sheila gave her month's allowance to charity, which I think was courageous.*

In this sentence *which* refers to the fact that _____ _____.

Sheila gave her month's allowance to charity

□ Using *which* or *this* to refer to a whole idea may cause confusion.

> *The group argued for the conservative policy; this is unrealistic.*

A person reading this sentence may well ask what is un-realistic—the group's arguing or the _____.

conservative policy

□ *The group argued for the conservative policy; this is unrealistic.*

If the writer considers the arguing unrealistic, he should have written the sentence this way:

> *It was unrealistic of the group* _____ _____.

to argue for the conservative policy

□ *The group argued for the conservative policy; this is unrealistic.*

If the writer considers the conservative policy unrealistic, he should have written the sentence this way:

> *The group argued for the* _____.

unrealistic conserva-tive policy

174

□　*He announced the committee's decision publicly, which the members think was unjust.*

If the members consider the public announcement rather than the decision unjust, this sentence should be phrased this way:

The members think that it was _____

_____ .

unjust for him to announce the committee's decision publicly

<hr>

Complete the following frames.

□ Correct this sentence.

Since Lydia wished to converse while she was in France, she decided to study it.

French
~~*it*~~
its
~~*the radio's*~~
the radio
~~*it*~~

□ Correct this sentence.

Although the radio's battery is weak, it still plays.

□　*I told Bob that I had not placed his name on the roster; this was my mistake.*

If the mistake was the telling, this sentence can be clarified by rewriting it this way:

My mistake _____

_____ .

was telling [to tell] Bob that I had not placed his name on the roster

□ Rewrite this sentence to show clearly that it is her own coat that Marianne is giving.

Marianne gave Barbara her coat.

_____

Marianne gave her coat to Barbara.

□ Correct this sentence.

Neither the cola nor the root beer has cyclamates in their formula.

its
~~*their*~~

REFLEXIVE AND INTENSIVE PRONOUNS

reflexive intensive	**90** *They asked themselves the same question.* *They themselves asked the same question.* *Themselves* is [reflexive, intensive] _____ in the first sentence and _____ in the second.

selves	□ The personal pronouns have a form ending in *self* or *selves*. This form of *I* is *myself;* the form of *we* is *our-*_____.
selves	□ The pronoun *you* has two forms, the singular form *your-self* and the plural form *your-*_____.
self selves	□ The third-person pronouns of this kind are similarly formed: *himself, herself, it-*_____, and *them-*_____.
himself *themselves*	□ Most of us have no difficulty forming the pronouns ending in *self* or *selves*. We recognize *hisself* as an incorrect form of _____ and *theirselves* as an incorrect form of _____.
myself *I*	□ A pronoun ending in *self* or *selves* has two uses and is named accordingly. If it repeats the subject to show that the subject acts on itself, it is called a reflexive pronoun. *I hurt myself.* In this sentence the reflexive pronoun _____ expresses the subject _____ acting on itself.
himself	□ Complete this sentence with the appropriate reflexive pronoun. *Bob shot* _____ *in the foot.*

176

□ Sometimes we use a form of the pronoun ending in *self* or *selves* simply for emphasis. When used this way, it is called an intensive pronoun.

Rita herself is to blame.

herself

The intensive pronoun in the sentence is _____ .

□ A simple way to determine whether a pronoun is reflexive or intensive is to omit it mentally. If the sense of the sentence is the same without it but less emphatic, the pronoun is intensive. If omitting it destroys the sense, it is reflexive.

They excused themselves early.
They finished the work themselves.

first
second

Themselves is a reflexive pronoun in the [first, second] _____ sentence; the same pronoun is an intensive pronoun in the _____ sentence.

reflexive
intensive

□ Omitting a(n) [reflexive, intensive] _____ pronoun destroys the sense of a sentence; omitting a(n) _____ pronoun makes a sentence less emphatic.

□   *We visited France ourselves this year.*
    We gave ourselves a vacation in France this year.

intensive
reflexive

Ourselves is a(n) _____ pronoun in the first sentence and a(n) _____ pronoun in the second.

9P Cross out and replace any incorrect word in the following sentences.

him
~~*himself*~~

She cooked dinner for her daughter and herself.
Mrs. Burton invited his father and himself to accompany the family.

□ A pronoun ending in *self* or *selves* should be used only as a reflexive or intensive pronoun.

> *I will do it* [*myself, me*].
> *Bob will do it for* [*myself, me*].

Myself is the correct choice to complete the [first, second]

first second _____ sentence but not the _____ sentence.

□ *Bob will do it for me.*

Ordinarily we would not be tempted to substitute *myself* incorrectly for *me* in a sentence such as this. However, we might in a sentence having *me* as part of a compound element.

> *Bob will do it for my father and* [*myself, me*].

Since we say *for me*, we should also say for *my father*

me *and* _____ .

□ To avoid using a *self* or *selves* form of a pronoun incorrectly as part of a compound sentence element, mentally exclude the other parts of the element.

> *Elliot and* [*myself, I*] *came.*

Since we do not say *myself came*, the correct pronoun

I for this sentence is _____ .

□ Test each pronoun choice by itself before completing these sentences.

> *The Ridleys wondered whether or not the Smiths and*
they > [*themselves, they*] _____ *would be able to go.*
> *Elsa suggested that I help Roger and* [*myself, me*]
myself > _____ *to some sandwiches.*

□ Complete these sentences.

myself

I included Pete, Hal, and [*myself, me*] _____
on the roster.

me

The coach included Pete, Hal, and [*myself, me*] _____
on the roster.

Correct the following sentences where necessary. Mark correct sentences C.

me
~~myself~~

□ *There is considerable misunderstanding between Hawkins and myself.*

C

□ *Helen bought the records and hi-fi equipment for her husband and herself to enjoy.*

C

□ *She will go herself.*

they
~~themselves~~

□ *Both the Lawtons and themselves joined the Country Club.*

TEN
CASE OF PRONOUNS

FORMS OF THE PERSONAL PRONOUNS

(a) subjective

(b) objective

(c) subjective or objective

(d) subjective or objective

(e) objective

(f) subjective

10A Identify the following pronouns according to case.

(a) I _____

(b) us _____

(c) you _____

(d) it _____

(e) him _____

(f) they _____

☐ Personal pronouns—those referring to persons—have different forms to refer to the same person.

> *I hit the ball.*
> *The ball hit me.*

The pronoun *I*, the subject of the first sentence, refers to the same person as the pronoun _____, the direct object of the second sentence.

me

180

□ The form of the pronoun depends on its function.

I hit the ball.
The ball hit me.

The form *I* is used as the _____ of the first sentence. The form *me* is used as the direct_____ of the second sentence.

□ We distinguish the forms of personal pronouns by case. The form of the pronoun used as the subject of a sentence is said to be in the subjective case.

I hit the ball.

I is a pronoun in the _____ case.

□ The form of the pronoun used as an object is said to be in the objective case.

The ball hit me.

Me is a pronoun in the objective _____.

□ A pronoun used as a subject is in the _____ case.
A pronoun used as an object is in the _____ case.

□ *We thanked Sue.*
Sue thanked us.

We is in the _____ case. *Us* is in the _____ case.

□ We can easily identify a pronoun according to its case by trying it as the subject or object of a verb such as *thanked*. Thus *he, she,* and *they* are in the _____ case; *him, her,* and *them* are in the _____ case.

□ The personal pronoun *you* has the same form for both the subjective and objective cases.

> *Bob thanked you.*
> *You thanked Bob.*

objective
subjective

We know from its position rather than its form that *you* in the first sentence is in the _____ case, while in the second sentence it is in the _____ case.

□ The pronoun *it,* like *you,* lacks a distinctive form for the subjective and objective cases.

> *You hit it.*
> *It hit you.*

you
it

These sentences show that both the pronoun _____ and the pronoun _____ lack distinctive subjective and objective forms.

□ Like *you* and *it,* all nouns and pronouns except the personal pronouns lack a distinctive subjective and objective form. When we speak of the subjective and objective cases, we are concerned only with the _____

personal

pronouns—excluding *you* and *it.*

REVIEW

In the following sentences identify the personal pronouns according to case.

I is subjective
him is objective

□ *I found him sleeping.*

she is subjective

□ *On the whole, she was quite uneasy.*

They is subjective
you is objective

□ *They gave you a book.*

he	**10B** Complete these sentences.
him	*It may have been* [*he, him*] _____.
	It may have hit [*he, him*] _____.

☐ A pronoun following an action verb is either a direct or an indirect object. The case of such pronouns is objective.

> *He hit him.*

objective

The pronoun *him* is the direct object of the verb *hit* and is in the _____ case.

☐ A direct object receives the effect of a verb and is normally not identical to the subject.

> *He hit him.*

do not

Here the subject *He* and the direct object *him* [do, do not] _____ refer to the same person.

☐ A pronoun following a form of *be (am, are, is, was, were, be, being, been)* is not its object. The forms of *be* link a pronoun to the subject to show that it is identical to the subject.

> *That man helped you.*
> *That man is you.*

You and *man* refer to the same person in the [first, second]

second   first

_____ sentence but not in the _____ sentence.

☐ A pronoun following a form of *be* is not an object but a subjective complement. In formal writing we should use the subjective pronoun following forms of *be*.

she

> *That person was* [*she, her*] _____.

□ We use a subjective pronoun to follow a form of *be* because the pronoun and the subject can change places without any change in the meaning of the sentence. Complete the second sentence.

They are the men in the front lines.
The men in the front lines are _____.

they

□ Only in a sentence having a form of *be* as the verb can we reverse the subject and the pronoun following the verb without changing the meaning of the sentence.

That girl called her.
That girl is she.

We can reverse the subject and pronoun only of the [first, second] _____ sentence without changing its meaning.

second

□ Since all verbs except forms of *be* are followed by objective pronouns, we tend to choose objective pronouns for the forms of *be* as well. Thus we may tend to say *It was me* or *It's him* even though the forms of *be* require a subjective pronoun as their complement.

It was [I, me] _____.
It's [he, him] _____.

I
he

□ Although objective pronouns are acceptable as subjective complements of the forms of *be* in informal conversation, written English usually requires subjective pronouns.

It may be [he, him] who spoke.

The informally acceptable pronoun to complete this sentence is _____. The formally correct pronoun is _____.

him
he

184

□ Although such forms as *It was her* and *It is them* are beginning to appear in relatively formal writing, some teachers insist that subjective pronouns should follow *be*.

It is [*we, us*] *who are to blame.*

we

The formally correct pronoun to complete this sentence is _____.

□   *It should have been them.*

them   they

To make this sentence formally correct, we would replace the pronoun _____ with the pronoun _____.

□ The forms of *be* are the only verbs requiring subjective pronouns as complements. All other verbs require objective pronouns as complements.

him

The council members should have chosen [*he, him*] _____.

he

The council members' choice should have been [*he, him*] _____.

10C   Complete these sentences.

me

Just between you and [*I, me*] _____, *his case is hopeless.*

we

Neither the Carsons nor [*we, us*] _____, *unless there is a change in plans, can come.*

□ Ordinarily we do not have to think about the case of personal pronouns in order to choose the correct form.

I   her
she
me

[*I, me*] _____ *gave* [*she, her*] _____ *one of the books, and* [*she, her*] _____ *returned it to* [*I, me*] _____ *today.*

□ One of the few difficulties we may have is in choosing the correct case of a pronoun which is part of a compound sentence element.

He and I came.

He

I

Both the pronouns in this sentence, _____ and _____ , are part of a compound sentence element joined by *and.*

□ Choosing pronouns for compound elements often is troublesome because sentences containing them seem more complicated than they are really are. Although we never hear *Him came* or *Me came,* we sometimes hear *Him and me came.* The correct pronouns for this sentence are these:

He I

_____ and _____ came.

□   *He and I came.*

The subjective pronouns *He* and *I* are correct because both are [subjects, objects] _____ of the verb *came.*

subjects

□ We may also hear sentences such as this one:

Frank told he and I the story.

We know that the pronouns in this sentence are incorrect because we would say neither *Frank told he the story* nor *Frank told I the story.* The correct pronouns are these:

him   me

Frank told _____ *and* _____ *the story.*

□   *Frank told him and me the story.*

Because *him and me* is an indirect object in this sentence, the [subjective, objective] _____ pronouns *him* and *me* are correct.

objective

186

□ *Between you and I, the party was a waste of time.*

The two pronouns in this sentence are the objects of the preposition *Between*. We would correct this sentence by substituting the pronoun _____ for the incorrect pronoun _____.

me

I

□ If in doubt about which form of a pronoun to use in a compound sentence part, try each form by itself.

In his talk today the President spoke about you and [I, me].

Since we would not say *The President spoke about I*, we should complete this sentence with the objective pronoun _____.

me

□ *The Snells and [we, us] will live here next year.*

Trying each form of the pronoun apart from its related words shows us that the correct form is _____.

we

□ *Mrs. Silvers won't speak to either you or [she, her].*

We should not let the correlative form *either . . . or* hide the fact that both pronouns in this sentence are objects of the preposition *to*. The correct pronoun to complete this sentence is _____.

her

□ *The new editor will be either [he, him] or [I, me].*

Because both pronouns are subjective complements of the verb *will be*, the formally correct forms are _____ and _____.

he

I

□ Complete these sentences.

Roger will ask either Mr. James or [he, him] _____ to accompany us.
Our companion will be either Mr. James or [he, him] _____.

him

he

10D   Complete these sentences.

Let's you and [*I, me*] _____ *go.*

Two of us, Hank and [*I, me*] _____ , *will go.*

□ We often clarify a noun's meaning by adding other nouns or pronouns to it.

Two brothers, Marty and he, leave today with the team.

The pronoun *he,* together with the noun *Marty,* clarifies the meaning of the noun _____ .

brothers

□ Any noun or pronoun joined to another to clarify it is called an appositive.

Two brothers, Marty and he, leave today with the team.

appositives

The noun *Marty* and the pronoun *he* are both _____ .

□ Pronouns serving as appositives rename in order to clarify the words they follow. Thus a pronoun appositive follow- the subject of a sentence is parallel to the subject and should be in the subjective case.

Two brothers, Marty and he, leave today with the team.

Since *brothers* is the subject, the appositive pronoun *he,*

subjective

in the _____ case, is correct.

□ If in doubt about which case of a pronoun to use as an appositive, substitute the pronoun by itself for the noun which it clarifies.

Their parents gave the boys, Paul and [*he, him*], *an old car to use.*

him

By trying *he* and *him* as substitutes for *the boys,* we can easily determine that the correct form is _____ .

□ Complete these sentences. Remember that forms of the verb *be* are followed by subjective pronouns in formal writing.

Their best friends were the two sisters, Eileen and [*she, her*] _____.

she

They nominated two new members, Harry and [*I, me*] _____.

me

□ We seldom use the contraction *let's* in our formal writing, but we should keep in mind that it is a contraction of *let us.* Since *us* is an objective pronoun, a pronoun appositive following *let's* should be in the _____ case.

objective

□ *Let's you and* [*I, me*] *go.*

The correct form to complete this sentence is _____, the pronoun in the _____ case.

me
objective

□ Occasionally we join a pronoun directly to a noun so that both have a clearer meaning.

We men are ready.

This sentence has a subject composed of the pronoun _____ and the noun _____.

We   men

□ *We men are ready.*

Since it is part of the subject, the [subjective, objective] _____ pronoun *We* is the correct form.

subjective

□ Pronouns joined to nouns should be in the case that they would be if they stood without the noun.

The Liptons gave [*we, us*] *fellows a lift.*

Mentally omitting the noun *fellows* shows us that the correct pronoun for this sentence is _____.

us

□ Omit the noun following the pronoun to determine which form to use in completing these sentences.

us

Some of [we, us] _____ students studied late last night.

we

Some teachers seem to feel that [we, us] _____ students should study late every night.

Correct the following sentences where necessary. Mark correct sentences C.

C

□ *It should have been they.*

he
~~him~~

□ *Three members, Harry, Bob, and him, were fined for skipping meetings.*

me
~~I~~

□ *Just between you and I, Rita is a bore.*

We
~~Us~~

□ *Us girls have formed a basketball team.*

PRONOUNS IN COMPARISONS

10E *The coach expected more from Bob than [he, him].*

If this sentence means that two people expected something of Bob, the coach and the person referred to by the pronoun, the correct pronoun is _____. If it

he

means that the coach expected more from Bob than from the other person, the correct pronoun is _____.

him

190

□ A pronoun following *as* or *than* is part of a comparison.

He is as tall as she.

This sentence compares the height of two persons referred to by the pronouns _____ and _____ .

He she

□ A pronoun following *as* or *than* in a comparison is part of a subordinate clause often not fully expressed.

He is as tall as she [is tall].

Normally we would not express the words in the brackets. However, expressing them shows clearly that the pronoun *she* is the [subject, object] _____ of the clause *as she [is tall].*

subject

□ We do not fully express clauses following *as* or *than* because they would be unnecessarily repetitious.

Earl needs more time than she needs.

Ordinarily we would not express the verb _____ in the subordinate clause *than she needs* because it repeats the verb expressed in the main clause preceding it.

needs

□ *She gave me more than she gave him.*

The meaning of this sentence would be as clear without the subordinate clauses's subject and verb, _____ , which are identical to those in the main clause.

she gave

□ *Bob is less happy about it than she.*

The subordinate clause *than she* lacks two words, unexpressed because they are repetitious: _____ .

is happy

□ *It takes me longer than him.*

The subordinate clause *than him* lacks two unexpressed words which would precede *him*, _____ .

it takes

□ A pronoun following *as* or *than* in a comparison is subjective or objective depending on whether it is the subject or an object of a subordinate clause. Keep in mind that the clause may not be fully expressed.

She is as fat as I.

subject

The subjective pronoun *I* is correct because the pronoun is the [subject, direct object] _____ of the subordinate clause *as I [am fat]*.

□   *Tennis exhausts me as much as him.*

tennis exhausts

Because *him* is the direct object of the subordinate clause *as* [_____] *him*, the objective pronoun used here is correct.

□ If in doubt about which form of a pronoun to use following *as* or *than* in a comparison, supply the unexpressed parts of the clause to which it belongs.

Pete is less clever than [I, me].

I am clever
subject
I

The complete subordinate clause here would be *than* _____. Since the pronoun is its [subject, direct object] _____, the correct form is _____.

□ Complete these sentences.

they
him

The Smiths are as rich as [they, them] _____.
The odds are as much against Jack as [he, him] _____.

□ The case of a pronoun following *as* or *than* in a comparison often indicates the meaning of the sentence.

Mary asked Hal more questions than [he, him].

he asked Hal

If the subjective pronoun *he* is used, the subordinate clause completely expressed will be *than* _____.

192

□ *Mary asked Hal more questions than [he, him].*

she asked him

On the other hand, if the objective pronoun *him* is used, the complete subordinate clause would be *than* _____ _____.

□ *Mary asked Hal more questions than he.*
Mary asked Hal more questions than him.

first

second

These sentences have quite different meanings, indicated by the case of the pronoun following *than*. The [first, second] _____ sentence indicates two questioners, Mary and the person referred to by the pronoun. The _____ sentence indicates that two were questioned, Hal and the person indicated by the pronoun.

□ *I revere General Marshall as much as [he, him].*

I revere him

direct object   *revere*

him

If the meaning here is that General Marshall and someone else are revered, the subordinate clause completely expressed would be _____.
The pronoun would, therefore, be the [subject, direct object] _____ of the verb _____, and the correct pronoun would be _____.

□ Be sure that the case of the pronoun following *as* or *than* is correct according to the meaning of the sentence.

Senator Bruce pays more attention to his career than [she, her].

her

she

If this sentence means that the Senator pays more attention to his career than to the person referred to by the pronoun, the correct pronoun is _____. If it means that he pays more attention to his career than does the person referred to by the pronoun, the correct pronoun is _____.

Correct the following sentences where necessary. Mark correct sentences C.

he
~~*him*~~

□   *Hughes is considerable taller than him.*

C

□   *I am as unhappy as she.*

she
~~*her*~~

□   *I need far less help in math than her.*

he
~~*him*~~

□   *Dr. Rogers expended far more energy on the assignment than him.*

INTERROGATIVE PRONOUNS

Who
Whom

10F   Complete these sentences.

[*Who, Whom*] _____ *do you think will win?*
[*Who, Whom*] _____ *do you want to win the game?*

□ The pronouns *who* and *whom* are also personal pronouns. If used in questions, they are called interrogative pronouns.

Who is coming?

The subject of this sentence is the interrogative pronoun

Who

_____ .

□ The interrogative pronouns have a distinguishable form for each case. *Who* is subjective; *whom* is objective.

Who is coming?

To show that the interrogative pronoun *who* is the subject, it is in the _____ case.

subjective

194

□   *To [who, whom] are you speaking?*

whom

In this sentence the objective pronoun _____ is the correct form because it is the object of the preposition

To

_____ .

□ Interrogative pronouns, both subjective and objective, always come before the verb in a sentence. For this reason we may mistake an object for the subject of the sentence.

Whom are you speaking to?

The pronoun *you* is the subject of this sentence. *Whom,* the interrogative pronoun, is the object of the preposition

to

that comes at the end of the sentence, _____ .

□ A quick way to determine whether to use *who* or *whom* is to rephrase the question as an answer, substituting *he* or *him* for the interrogative pronoun. If *he* is correct, the question requires *who*; if *him* is correct, the question requires *whom.*

[Who, Whom] removed the battery?

We rephrase the question as an answer this way:

He

[He, Him] _____ *removed the battery.*

□   *[Who, Whom] removed the battery?*

Since *He* is correct in this question rephrased as an answer,

Who

the correct interrogative pronoun is _____ .

□ Use the device described in the last two frames to complete these sentences.

Who

Whom

[Who, Whom] _____ *will play in his place?*
[Who, Whom] _____ *will the coach pick to play in his place?*

□ In our informal conversation we may often use *who* in place of *whom* because it sounds less stilted.

[Who, Whom] are you referring to?
[Who, Whom] asked her to come?

second
first

In the [first, second] _____ sentence *Who* is both formally and informally correct. In the _____ sentence *Who* is correct in informal conversation.

□ While *who* is acceptable in all uses in everyday conversations, careful writers usually maintain the distinction between *who* and *whom* in their writing. Complete these sentences with the form of the pronoun required in formal writing.

Who
Whom

[Who, Whom] _____ helped Mrs. Green?
[Who, Whom] _____ did you see helping Mrs. Green?

REVIEW

Choose the formally correct pronoun to complete the following sentences.

Whom

□ *[Who, Whom] _____ did the committee pick to act in his place?*

Whom

□ *[Who, Whom] _____ should the police question in the Folger case?*

Who

□ *[Who, Whom] _____ do you think you are?*

196

who

who

10G   Complete these sentences.

I'll bet I know [*who, whom*] _____ *the winner will be.*

Harry Fish is the candidate [*who, whom*] _____ *we feel is the best choice.*

□ We use the pronouns *who* and *whom* to introduce subordinate clauses.

> *We avoid a person who talks too much.*

In this sentence *who* introduces the four-word subordinate clause _____ .

who talks too much

□ *Who* and *Whom* are called relative pronouns when they relate a subordinate clause to the main clause.

> *He asked who was coming.*

relative

who was coming

In this sentence the _____ pronoun *who* introduces the subordinate clause _____ .

□ The relative pronouns *who* and *whom* are also subject, subjective complement, or object in the subordinate clauses they introduce.

> *Peter knew who saw me.*
> *Peter knew whom I saw.*

who

whom

In the first sentence the relative pronoun _____ is the subject of the clause it introduces. In the second sentence the relative pronoun _____ is the direct object of the verb *saw*, even though it appears before the verb.

☐ *Who* is the relative pronoun of the subjective case; *whom* is the relative pronoun of the objective case.

> *Peter knew who saw me.*
> *Peter knew whom I saw.*

The subjective pronoun *who* is used in the first sentence because it is the [subject, direct object] _____ in its clause. The objective pronoun *whom* is used in the second sentence because it is the _____ of the verb *saw*.

subject

direct object

☐ Whether subject, subjective complement, or object, the relative pronoun always precedes the verb in its clause. For this reason choosing between *who* and *whom* for some sentences may be difficult.

> *Peter knew whom I saw.*

Normally the direct object in a sentence follows the verb. This sentence illustrates, however, that the direct object in a subordinate clause, if it is a relative pronoun, always comes [before, after] _____ the verb.

before

☐ In order to choose the correct case of a relative pronoun, it is necessary to know what function the pronoun has in its clause. Perhaps the best help is to view the clause as an independent sentence.

> *Earl writes well. He is our associate editor.*
> *Earl, who is our associate editor, writes well.*

These examples show that the subordinate clause *who is our associate editor* can be expressed as an independent sentence, _____ *our associate editor*.

He is

☐ *Earl writes well. He is our associate editor.*
Earl, who is our associate editor, writes well.

Changing the sentence *He is our associate editor* to a subordinate clause requires the substitution of the relative pronoun in the subjective case, _____, for the subjective pronoun *He*.

who

□   *There is the girl who won the contest.*

Changing the subordinate clause *who won the contest* to an independent sentence requires substituting the subjective pronoun *she* for the subjective relative pronoun *who:* _____ *the contest.*

She won

□   *Dr. Jordan, whom I met yesterday, is chairman of the history department.*

Changing the subordinate clause *whom I met yesterday* to an independent sentence requires the objective pronoun *him:* I _____ .

met him yesterday

□ If in doubt about whether to use *who* or *whom*, test the subordinate clause as an independent sentence. If it requires a subjective pronoun (*he, she, they*), the relative pronoun should be *who*. If it requires an objective pronoun (*him, her, them*), the relative pronoun should be _____ .

whom

□   *The children* [*who, whom*] *I enjoy least are playing in the flower beds.*

Since rewriting the subordinate clause [*who, whom*] *I enjoy least* as an independent sentence requires the objective pronoun _____ , the correct relative pronoun is _____ .

them
whom

□   *Mr Hicks frowned at those* [*who, whom*] *laughed at his jokes.*

Since rewriting the subordinate clause in this sentence as an independent sentence requires the [subjective, objective] _____ pronoun *they*, the correct relative pronoun is _____ .

subjective
who

199

□ A relative pronoun may be the object of a preposition.

Senator Niles, to whom I sent that letter, voted against the measure today.

When the relative pronoun follows its preposition directly —as it does in this sentence—choice of the [subjective, objective] _____ pronoun *whom* is automatic.

objective

□ A relative pronoun which is the object of a preposition may be separated from its preposition.

Senator Niles, whom I sent that letter to, voted against the measure today.

The relative pronoun *whom* is the object of the preposition _____, even though it appears apart from it.

to

□ We can easily determine whether or not a relative pronoun is the object of a preposition separated from it by testing the subordinate clause as an independent sentence.

Senator Bundy, whom I voted for, was absent during the balloting.

The subordinate clause expressed as an independent sentence is *I* _____. *Whom*, then, is the object of the preposition _____.

voted for him

for

□   *There is the girl [who, whom] I came with.*

Testing the subordinate clause as an independent sentence shows that the correct form of the relative pronoun is _____.

whom

200

□ A relative pronoun may sometimes be the subjective complement of its clause.

I know [who, whom] that man is.

Remember that strict formal usage requires the subjective pronoun following forms of *be*. The subordinate clause expressed as an independent sentence is *That* _____ _____. Since the subjective pronoun *he* takes the place of the relative pronoun, the correct form of the relative pronoun is _____.

man is he

who

□ Complete these sentences. If necessary, test the subordinate clauses as independent sentences before choosing the relative pronoun.

whom

who

The four salesmen [who, whom] _____ *he hired sold the most products last month.*
The four salesmen know [who, whom] _____ *their customers are.*

□ Complete these sentences.

who

whom

A man [who, whom] _____ *is willing to work is a valuable employee.*
A woman [who, whom] _____ *my mother knew in college married Professor Gordon.*

□ Occasionally we use short qualifying clauses such as *I think* and *we feel* within subordinate clauses. These normally appear directly after the relative pronoun.

Ellis is the accountant who they believe is the best bet for promotion.

The qualifying clause added to the subordinate clause in this sentence is _____.

they believe

201

□ A short qualifying clause included in a subordinate clause does not affect the choice of the relative pronoun. We should mentally omit such clauses when determining which case of the relative pronoun to use.

Bob is dating a girl [who, whom] he says has an attractive sister.

When choosing the form of the relative pronoun for this sentence, we should mentally omit the qualifying clause

he says

_____.

□ *Bob is dating a girl [who, whom] he says has an attractive sister.*

Mentally omitting the qualifying clause *he says* helps us to see that the relative pronoun is the [subject, direct

subject   object] _____ of the verb *has*. The
who   correct relative pronoun is _____.

□ While completing these sentences, identify and mentally omit any qualifying clauses.

who   *The man [who, whom] _____ the editors believe is the most newsworthy is given the prize.*
The editors are careful to nominate only those men
whom   *[who, whom] _____ they have faith in.*

Correct the following sentences where necessary. Mark correct sentences C.

□ *The people whom we remember from high school seem*
C   *to have changed when we meet them later in life.*

C   □ *This is the girl who the judges felt was the most attractive.*

whom ~~who~~	☐ *When he asked me who Roger was dancing with, I couldn't answer him.*
who ~~whom~~	☐ *You cannot always tell whom your friends are.*

PRONOUNS WITH PARTICIPLES AND GERUNDS

me *my*	**10H** Complete these sentences. *The boss caught [my, me] ——————— napping on the job.* *The boss disliked [my, me] ——————— napping on the job.*
	☐ The personal pronouns have possessive forms which we use to identify nouns. *I lost my umbrella.*
my *umbrella*	The possessive form of *I* in this sentence is ———————. It identifies the noun ———————.
you	☐ All personal pronouns have possessive forms. *Our* is a possessive form of *we*; *your* is the possessive form of ———————.
nouns	☐ *His, her, its,* and *their* are possessive forms of the personal pronouns *he, she, it,* and *they*. Like *my, our,* and *your,* these are used to identify ———————.
	☐ *I loaned my car to your friend.*
my *your*	In this sentence the possessive form ——————— identifies *car*, and the possessive form ——————— identifies *friend*.

□ Using possessives correctly is automatic except before gerunds. Recall that a gerund is the *ing* form of a verb used as a noun.

My skiing has improved.

In this sentence the possessive form _____ identifies the gerund _____.

□   *We awaited his arrival.*
   We awaited [his, him] coming.

The gerund *coming* in the second sentence has the same function as the noun *arrival* in the first sentence. Since we use the possessive to identify *arrival*, the correct form to identify *coming* is _____.

□ Use only the possessive form of a pronoun to identify a gerund. Cross out the error in the following sentence and substitute the correct form.

Him grabbing the brake saved us.

□ Complete this sentence.

[*Their, Them*] _____ coming early was quite a surprise.

□ If we hesitate to use a possessive instead of a pronoun before a gerund, it is probably because we recall that participles, identical in form to gerunds, often modify pronouns which they follow.

He found me talking.

In this sentence *talking* is not a gerund but a participle modifying the pronoun it follows, _____.

□ What is the difference between the possessive-gerund pattern and the pronoun-participle pattern?

> *He enjoyed my playing.*
> *He watched me playing.*

The difference is in the meaning suggested. In the first sentence it is the playing rather than the person that is enjoyed. In the second sentence it is the [person, playing]

person   playing

_____ rather than the _____ that is watched.

□ If our concern is with the person's action rather than the person, we use the possessive-gerund pattern:

his

> *The family awaited [his, him] _____ coming.*

□ If our concern is with the person rather than the action, we use the pronoun-participle pattern:

him

> *The family saw [his, him] _____ coming.*

□ Complete these sentences.

him

> *Four youths had seen [his, him] _____ taking the radio.*

his

> *The youths reported [his, him] _____ taking the radio.*

□ Complete these sentences.

my

> *The director approved of [my, me] _____ taking a leave of absence.*

me

> *The director watched [my, me] _____ taking the books off my desk.*

Correct the following sentences where necessary. Mark correct sentences C.

my
~~me~~

☐ *He disapproved of me keeping such late hours.*

C

☐ *He appreciated my keeping the matter to myself.*

me
~~my~~

☐ *He watched my painting the house.*

my
~~me~~

☐ *He felt that me holding the box was wrong.*

206

ELEVEN

MODIFIERS

CHOOSING ADJECTIVES AND ADVERBS

11A *Unusually large crowds may gather very quickly at scenes of trouble.*

large

crowds

unusually large

very quickly quickly

gather

This sentence contains one adjective, _____, which modifies _____. It also contains three adverbs: _____ modifies _____; _____ modifies _____; and _____ modifies _____.

☐ Adjectives and adverbs, the one-word modifiers, serve different pruposes. An adjective always modifies either a noun or a pronoun.

Loud brakes squealed.

Loud   brakes

The adjective _____ modifies the noun _____.

□ Adjectives modify by describing the noun or pronoun to which they are related.

Loud brakes squealed.

We say that the adjective *Loud* modifies *brakes* because it _____ that noun.

describes

□ Unlike adjectives, adverbs modify verbs, adjectives, or other adverbs.

A really good sailboat handles very easily.

In the above sentence the adverb *easily* modifies the verb _____; the adverb *really* modifies the adjective _____; and the adverb *very* modifies the adverb _____.

handles
good
easily

□ Adverbs modify by expressing *how, when,* or *where.*

He walked here quickly then.

Of the three adverbs in this sentence, *here* expresses _____; *quickly* expresses _____; and *then* expresses _____.

where   how
when

□ Adjectives and adverbs, then, have distinct uses. Adjectives modify only _____ and _____ in a way that describes them. Adverbs modify by expressing *how, when,* or *where*; they modify verbs, adjectives, or other _____.

nouns   pronouns

adverbs

11B Complete these sentences.

We heard that the Masque Club put on a [real, really] _____ *fine show.*

I answered the questions as [good, well] _____ *as I was able in those circumstances.*

really
well

208

□   *The late edition of the paper arrived late.*

The first *late* in this sentence is an _____ be-cause it describes the noun _____. The second *late* is an _____ because it expresses *when* in regard to the verb _____.

□   *A fast miler normally runs the first quarter-mile fast.*

Fast is an adjective in its first use because it describes the noun _____. This same word is an adverb in its second use because it expresses _____ in regard to the verb *runs.*

□ Modifiers such as *fast* and *late* have the same form whether they are adjectives or adverbs. The majority of adverbs, however, are distinguished from adjectives by an *ly* end-ing.

The attractive gift was wrapped attractively.

The adverb _____ in this sentence is the ad-jective _____ with *ly* added.

□ Notice the effect of adding *ly* to an adjective.

The attractive gift was wrapped attractively.

The adjective *attractive* describes the noun _____; the adverb *attractively* expresses _____ the gift was wrapped.

□ While some modifiers do not have distinctive forms for their use as adjectives or adverbs, we form most of our adverbs by adding *ly* to adjectives. The adverb form of

fast is _____. But the adverb form of *pure* is _____.

□ Certain adjectives are formed from nouns by the addition of *ly*. *Lovely* is formed from the noun *love*, and *manly*

from the noun _____.

□ Generally speaking, a word with an added *ly* is an adjective if formed from a noun and an _____ if formed from an adjective.

adverb

□ If a modifier has two forms such as *happy* and *happily*, we use the adjective form to modify a noun or pronoun. Otherwise, we use the adverb form.

We drove [*bad, badly*].

Since the modifier in this sentence expresses *how* in regard to the verb *drove*, the adverb form, _____, is correct.

badly

□ *A* [*real, really*] *good tire should last for 30,000 miles.*

Since the modifier expresses how good, it affects the meaning of the adjective _____, not of the noun *tire*. The correct form is _____.

good

really

□ If in doubt about which word an adjective or adverb modifies, mentally omit the modifier to see which word is affected.

The stream ran [*rapid, rapidly*] *when it reached the bottom of the canyon.*

Omitting the modifier here affects the meaning of [*stream, ran*] _____. The correct form is _____.

ran rapidly

□ Complete these sentences.

We will spend the rest of the day [*quiet, quietly*] _____.
We look forward to a [*quiet, quietly*] _____ *day.*

quietly

quiet

□ *Good* is an adjective; *well* is an adverb.

I did [*good, well*] *on the exam.*

The modifier in this sentence affects the meaning of [*I, did*] _____. The correct completion, therefore, is _____.

did

well

210

□ Decide which word the modifier affects before completing this sentence.

well

The choir didn't sing very [good, well] _____ *today.*

□ *Well* is an adjective only when it means healthy.

A [good, well] child is a blessing.

well

good

If this sentence refers to a child in good health, the correct adjective is _____. If it refers to a well-behaved child, the correct adjective is _____.

□ Complete these sentences.

well

Only [good, well] _____ *patients are released from this hospital.*

well

Paul didn't do very [good, well] _____ *in physics last semester.*

REVIEW

Correct the following sentences where necessary. Mark correct sentences C.

quickly
~~*quick*~~

□ *Get well quick!*

really
~~*real*~~

□ *You'll find this bed real comfortable.*

well
~~*good*~~

□ *He planted the new grass really good.*

C

□ *The children behaved really badly today.*

CHOOSING COMPARATIVE
AND SUPERLATIVE MODIFIERS

11C *Saying that Dave is brighter than Bob is saying only that he is not the least bright person in the class.*

The above sentence contains the comparative adjective _____ and the superlative adjective _____.

brighter
least bright

□ Adjectives and adverbs modify by attributing some quality or characteristic to persons, things, or actions.

   Ralph is strong.

The adjective *strong* expresses a quality of the person named by the noun _____.

Ralph

□ Modifiers can express more or most of a quality.

   Ralph is stronger than Ed.
   Ralph is the strongest member of the team.

The adjective _____ expresses more of the quality of strength; the adjective _____ expresses most of the quality.

stronger
strongest

□ There are three ways in which a modifier can attribute a quality. It can express the quality in itself (*strong*), more of the quality (*stronger*), or _____ of the quality (*strongest*).

most

□ The form of the modifier indicates the degree to which a quality is attributed. For instance, the *er* ending of *stronger* indicates more of the quality. The _____ ending of *strongest* indicates most of the quality.

est

□ Modifiers attributing more or most of a quality are used in comparisons.

Ralph is stronger than Ed.

The key word in this comparison is the adjective *stronger*. We know from its form that Ralph has [more, most] _____ of the quality of strength when compared to Ed.

more

□ Adjectives attributing more of a quality to one person or thing in comparison to another are comparative adjectives.

Ralph is stronger than Ed.

Stronger is a _____ adjective.

comparative

□ Adjectives attributing most of a quality to one person or thing in comparison to two or more others are superlative adjectives. Complete this sentence with the superlative adjective based on *strong*.

Ralph is the _____ *member of the team.*

strongest

□ The ending *er* makes an adjective comparative; the ending *est* makes it superlative. The comparative form of *great* is _____ ; the superlative form is _____ .

greater   greatest

□ *Easier* is a _____ adjective, and *easiest* is a _____ adjective.

comparative
superlative

□ Generally, if an adjective has more than two syllables, we do not use the *er* and *est* endings to form the comparative and superlative. Instead, we use *more* with the adjective to form the comparative and *most* with the adjective to form the superlative. Thus the comparative form of the four-syllable adjective *intelligent* is *more intelligent*; the superlative form is _____ *intelligent*.

most

□ We form the comparative adjective in one of two ways.

He is _____ *than I.*

The comparative form of *sad* to complete this sentence

is _____. The comparative form of *miserable*

is _____.

□ *He is the* _____ *man I know.*

The superlative form of *happy* to complete this sentence

is _____. The superlative form of *charitable*

is _____.

□ Adverbs, too, have comparative and superlative forms. Normally, one-syllable adverbs have a comparative form ending in *er* and a superlative form ending in *est*. The comparative form of the one-syllable adverb *fast*, then, is

_____; the superlative form is _____.

□ Most adverbs with two or more syllables end in *ly*. The comparative and superlative forms of these are made by adding them to *more* and *most*. Thus the comparative

form of *easily* is _____ *easily*; the superlative

form is _____ *easily*.

□ Any adjective or adverb ending in *er* or preceded by *more*

is _____; any ending in *est* or preceded by *most*

is _____.

□ *Brightest* is a _____ adjective. *More brightly*

is a _____ adverb.

□ Adjectives and adverbs have, in addition, a comparative form expressing less of a quality and a superlative form expressing least of a quality.

This house is less expensive than the other; it may be the least expensive house on this street.

Less expensive is [comparative, superlative] _____;

least expensive is _____.

214

□ Joining *less* to any modifier makes it comparative; joining *least* to it makes it superlative. Thus the comparative of *simple*, attributing less of that quality, is _____;
the superlative of the same word, attributing least of that quality, is _____.

less simple

least simple

□ We recognize as comparative any adjective or adverb ending in *er* or preceded by *more* or _____.

less

□ We recognize as superlative any adjective or adverb ending in *est* or preceded by _____ or _____.

most   least

□ English has a few modifiers with irregularly formed comparatives and superlatives. The adjective *good*, for instance, has the comparative *better* and the superlative *best*. Complete these sentences with the correct form of *good*.

better

best

This is a _____ movie than that.
This is the _____ movie we have seen.

□ The adverb *well* has comparative and superlative forms identical to those of the adjective *good*.

better

best

Harris writes _____ than I do.
Of the three of us, Harris writes _____.

□ The adjective *bad* and the adverb *badly* have identical comparative and superlative forms. The comparative of both is *worse*; the superlative is *worst*.

She is a worse student than he.
She acts worse than you.

Worse in the first sentence is the comparative of the adjective *bad*. This same modifier in the second sentence is the _____ of the adverb *badly*.

comparative

□ Whether it is regularly or irregularly formed, a modifier is comparative if it attributes more or less of a quality; it is _____ if it attributes most or least.

superlative

215

□   *He is the least awkward of the dancers.*
    He is a better dancer than his partner.

Least awkward in the first sentence is a [comparative, superlative] _____ adjective;   *better* in the second sentence is a _____ adjective.

□ Any modifier, no matter what its form, is comparative if it attributes more or less of a quality and superlative if it attributes _____ or _____ of a quality.

11D   Replace any incorrect word in the following sentences with the correct form.

The men seem to work happier under the new manager than they did under the former one.
These men are the least easiest pleased of any I know.

□ Comparative and superlative adjectives, like other adjectives, modify nouns or pronouns.

He is quicker than I.

The comparative modifier *quicker* in this sentence is an adjective attributing more of the quality of quickness to a person named by the pronoun _____.

□ Comparative and superlative adverbs modify verbs, adjectives, and other adverbs.

He thinks more quickly than I.

The comparative modifier *more quickly* is an adverb attributing more of the quality of quickness to an action expressed by the verb _____.

216

□ Since many comparative and superlative modifiers are identical in form whether adjectives or adverbs, use determines what they are.

Ben tries harder than Ned.
Ned has a harder time than Ben.

Harder in the first sentence is a comparative [adjective, adverb] _____ because it attributes the quality to the action of trying. In the second sentence it is a comparative [adjective, adverb] _____ because it attributes the quality to a thing, time.

adverb

adjective

□ Choosing modifiers which have the same form for use as either adjective or adverb involves no difficulty. *Hard* is one such modifier; *high* is another.

This car has a higher roof than that.
This flag should be raised higher than that.

We know from its use that *higher* is an _____ in the first sentence and an _____ in the second.

adjective
adverb

□   *This car has a higher roof than that.*
This flag should be raised higher than that.

Higher is an adjective in the first sentence because it attributes the quality to [a thing, an action] _____.
It is an adverb in the second sentence because it attributes the quality to [a thing, and action] _____.

a thing

an action

□ Many comparative and superlative modifiers, however, are adjectives or adverbs according to their form. *Happier* is a comparative adjective; *more happily* is a _____ adverb.

comparative

□ *Easiest* is a superlative _____; *most easily* is a superlative _____.

adjective
adverb

□ If a comparative or superlative modifier has separate adjective and adverb forms, our choice depends on whether the quality expressed by the modifier is attributed to a person or thing or to an action. If it is attributed to a person or thing, the [adjective, adverb] _____ form is correct; if attributed to an action, the _____ form is correct.

adjective

adverb

□   *This package is the [most attractive, most attractively] one we have.*
This package is the [most attractive, most attractively] wrapped of all.

Since the modifier in the first sentence attributes the quality to a thing, the correct form is _____.

most attractive

Since the modifier in the second sentence attributes the quality to an action, the correct form is _____.

most attractively

□ Complete these sentences, basing your choice of modifier on whether a person or thing or an action is modified.

steadier

I have a [steadier, more steadily] _____ hand now than I used to.
I am pleased that I can work [steadier, more steadily]

more steadily

_____ *now than I used to.*

□ Complete these sentences.

Charlie is [less forceful, less forcefully] _____

less forceful

_____ *than his father.*
Charlie speaks [less forceful, less forcefully] _____

less forcefully

_____ *than his father.*

greater
~~*greatest*~~

least
~~*less*~~

When we compare the two stock issues, we see that the first has the greatest real value.

Left to his own devices, John would buy the stock on this list of ten which had the less value.

□ We use a comparative modifier only when comparing one person, thing, or action to one another.

Your date is prettier than mine.

comparative

Since this is a comparison of one person with one other, the [comparative, superlative] _____ adjective *prettier* is correct.

□ A comparison of one person, thing, or action with two or more others requires a superlative modifier.

Of the eight men in the department, Jones is the [worse, worst] choice for promotion.

worst
superlative

Since this is a comparison of one man to several others, the correct modifier is _____, the [comparative, superlative] _____ form.

□   *Which brand of cola is [stronger, strongest]?*

strongest

stronger

If we are comparing three or more brands of cola, we will complete this sentence with _____. If we are comparing only two, we will complete the sentence with

_____.

□ Most sentences clearly require either the comparative or the superlative modifier. Select the correct modifier for each of these.

heavier

Of our two starting tackles, Bob is the [heavier, heaviest] _____.

best

Of our three starting quarterbacks, Jim is the [better, best] _____ passer.

219

□ Cross out the incorrect modifier and replace it with the correct one.

largest
~~larger~~

better
~~best~~

Which is the larger city, Cleveland, Omaha, or Dallas?

Which color do you like best, red or white?

REVIEW

Correct the following sentences where necessary. Mark correct sentences C.

C

□ *Mr. Jones is the more talkative of the two teachers.*

efficiently
~~efficient~~

□ *I am able to work more efficient now that my office is air-conditioned.*

fastest
~~faster~~

□ *Of the four cars entered in the first race, Roswell's is the faster.*

prettier
~~prettiest~~

□ *Which model has the prettiest hair, Jane or Ellen?*

more easily
~~easier~~

□ *The power mower will allow you to mow your lawn easier than the conventional type.*

CHOOSING ADJECTIVES
AS SUBJECTIVE COMPLEMENTS

11F Complete these sentences.

bad

The judge felt [bad, badly] _____ about the young criminal's sentence.

worthy

The judge proved [worthy, worthily] _____ in his appointed position.

220

□ Choosing the correct form of a modifier to follow a verb will be difficult if we do not know what it modifies.

> *Henry behaved foolishly.*
> *Henry was foolish.*

Foolishly in the first sentence is an adverb modifying the action verb *behaved*. *Foolish* in the second sentence is an adjective modifying the subject, the noun _____.

Henry

□ A linking verb joins an adjective to the subject which it modifies.

> *Henry was foolish.*

was

foolish

In this sentence the linking verb _____ joins the adjective _____ to the subject it modifies, *Henry*.

□ Linking verbs plus their adjective complements express a condition rather than an action of the subject.

> *She looks happy.*

Happy, the adjective modifying the subject *She*, is joined to the subject by the linking verb *looks*. Together, the verb and the adjective express [an action, a condition] _____ of the subject.

a condition

□ English has four kinds of linking verbs which, together with an adjective as complement, can express a condition rather than an action of the subject.

> Being: *be, remain, stay, keep, prove*
> Becoming: *become, get, turn, grow*
> Seeming: *seem, look, appear, act*
> Sensing: *feel, taste, smell, sound*

adjective

All of these verbs have this in common: they can link an [adjective, adverb] _____ to the subject which it modifies.

□ *Yesterday I felt [bad, badly].*

Since *felt* expresses a condition rather than an action of the subject, the correct modifier is the adjective _____.

bad

□ Many verbs such as *feel* can express either an action or a condition of the subject. Only if a verb expresses a condition do we use an adjective as its complement.

awkward

Mr. Smith felt [awkward, awkwardly] _____ *in front of the large audience.*

awkwardly

Mr. Smith felt [awkward, awkwardly] _____ *through his pockets in search of his notes.*

□ When choosing a modifier to follow a verb, determine whether the verb expresses an action or a condition of the subject.

suddenly

The truck appeared [sudden, suddenly] _____.

sudden

His action appeared [sudden, suddenly] _____.

□ Complete these sentences, keeping in mind that *good* is always an adjective and the *well* is an adverb unless it means in good health.

good

Bob felt [good, well] _____ *in his tuxedo.*

well

Bob felt [good, well] _____ *after a few days in the hospital.*

□ *Prove* is another verb that can link an adjective to the subject, but only if it expresses a condition of the subject rather than an action. Complete these sentences.

ably

The lawyer proved his case [able, ably] _____.

able

The lawyer proved [able, ably] _____ *in presenting his case.*

222

□ Always determine whether a verb expresses an action or condition of the subject before choosing a modifier to follow it.

silent

> The prisoner remained [silent, silently] _____ throughout the questioning.

worthless

> In all, over half of the corn crop looked [worthless, worthlessly] _____.

REVIEW

Correct the following sentences where necessary. Mark correct sentences C.

C

□ I really felt bad about his losing the match.

bad
~~badly~~

□ The weather turned badly almost as soon as we left.

good
~~well~~

□ My speakers sound well now that I have installed them in a new enclosure.

uneasily
~~uneasy~~

□ Bob felt uneasy around the wall for the light switch.

PLACING MODIFIERS

Only should be placed before *one* in the first sentence and *hardly* before *any* in the second.

11G Correct the position of any misplaced modifier in these sentences.

> Barnes only received one job offer.

> That used car lot hardly has any cars left to sell.

223

□ The placement of modifiers often affects the meaning of a sentence.

Only Smith borrowed her pen.
Smith only borrowed her pen.

second

The position of *only* in the [first, second] _____ sentence indicates that Smith did not intend to keep the pen. The position of *only* in the _____ sentence

first

indicates that no one except Smith borrowed her pen.

□ *Only* and *almost* are two modifiers whose position in a sentence may affect its meaning.

Only Smith borrowed her pen.
Smith only borrowed her pen.

Smith

borrowed

In the first sentence *Only* modifies the noun _____ ; in the second sentence *only* modifies the verb _____ .

□   *Smith borrowed only her pen.*
    Smith borrowed her only pen.

first

The position of *only* in the [first, second] _____ sentence indicates that Smith did not borrow anything

second

else from her. Its position in the _____ sentence indicates that she had no other pen but the one he borrowed.

□   *The chairman [only] asked [only] for silence.*

Adding the modifier *only* to such sentences as this requires care. If we wish the sentence to mean that the chairman did not ask for anything except silence, we will place

after

only [before, after] _____ *asked*. If we wish it to mean that the chairman did not insist on silence, but only

before

requested it, we will place *only* _____ *asked*.

224

□ Like *only*, *almost* is another modifier requiring careful placement.

He [almost] lost [almost] all his money.

If we wish this sentence to mean that he came close to losing his money, we will place *almost* [before, after] _____ *lost*. If we wish it to mean that he lost a large portion of his money, we will place *almost* _____ *lost*.

before
after

□ *Hardly* is another adverb whose position may affect a sentence's meaning.

Al [hardly] expects [hardly] any help from his father.

If we wish this sentence to mean that Al expects some help from his father, but very little, we will place *hardly* [before, after] _____ *expects*. If we wish it to mean that Al strongly doubts that he will receive any help at all from his father, we will place *hardly* _____ *expects*.

after

before

□ Modifiers such as *only, almost,* and *hardly* may be misleading if carelessly placed. They will be correctly placed if joined to the words they modify.

I only made one basket all night.

Only is incorrectly placed here. It does not modify *made*, but rather _____.

one

□ *I only made one basket all night.*

Correct the placement of *only*.

I _____ one basket all night.

made only

□ Place the bracketed modifier correctly in each sentence. Be sure each modifier is joined to the word it modifies.

... took almost all ...

[almost] *He* —————— *took* —————— *all the cake.*

... remember hardly any ...

[hardly] *I* —————— *remember* —————— *any of the story.*

□ Place the bracketed modifiers correctly.

, ... fell only ...

[only] *The workman* —————— *fell* —————— *ten feet.*

... deliberated only ...

[only] *In all, the jury members* —————— *deliberated* —————— *three hours.*

11H *The press secretary who had insulted the reporters' intelligence thoughtlessly apologized later.*

thoughtlessly insulted

Correcting this sentence requires that the word ———— be moved to precede the word —————.

□ We are more likely to misplace adverbs than adjectives because adverbs modifying verbs can appear in several positions within a sentence.

Then we / saw / his difficulty /.

can

The adverb *then* [can, cannot] —————— be moved to any of the positions marked by the slanted lines.

□ Although we normally have a choice in positioning adverbs, a sentence will be misleading if an adverb appears between two verbs which it could modify.

The dog that barked viciously snapped at us.

barked   snapped

In this sentence the adverb *viciously* can modify either of two verbs, —————— or ——————.

□ If an adverb could modify more than one verb, place the adverb nearer the verb it modifies, away from any other verb it could modify.

The dog that viciously barked snapped at us.

The position of *viciously* in this sentence shows that it modifies the verb _____.

barked

□   *The dog that barked viciously snapped at us.*

If we wish *viciously* to modify *snapped*, we can place it after the verb _____ or after the pronoun _____.

snapped   us

□   *The child I was watching carefully edged toward the deep end of the pool.*

If we wish *carefully* to modify *was watching*, we should place it before _____.

watching

□   *The child I was watching carefully edged toward the deep end of the pool.*

If we wish *carefully* to modify *edged*, we can place it in one of two positions—either after _____ or after

edged
pool

_____.

REVIEW

Correct the following sentences where necessary.   Mark correct sentences C.

□   *Mr. Bruno hardly gave me any help at all.*

Mr. Bruno gave me hardly any help at all.

_____

_____

227

Whatever we strongly desire . . .
 	
        or
. . . affects strongly . . .
        or
. . . other desires strongly.
	☐ *Whatever we desire strongly affects our other desires.*
	
	_____
	_____

C	☐ *When he runs rapidly, he gets out of breath.* _____ _____
She has tried Chinese food only once in her life.	☐ *She has only tried Chinese food once in her life.* _____ _____

PLACING PREPOSITIONAL PHRASES

The phrase *with a shout* should follow *bus*. The phrase *with new fringe benefits* should follow *contract*.	**11I** Correct these sentences by shifting any misplaced phrase to its proper place. *Hank tried to stop the bus as it passed him with a shout. The managers thought that the union contract for assembly workers with new fringe benefits was quite realistic.*

□ Modifiers may be phrases rather than single words. Prepositional phrases, for instance, function like the one-word modifiers, adjectives and adverbs.

The quality of his playing improved from the beginning.

This sentence contains two phrases introduced by prepositions. The phrase *of his playing* modifies the noun _____, and the phrase *from the beginning* modifies the verb _____.

quality
improved

□ *In the kitchen you will find a stove with four burners.*

Of the two prepositional phrases in this sentence, *in the kitchen* functions as an [adjective, adverb] _____ phrase expressing *where,* and *with four burners* functions as an _____ phrase describing the stove.

adverb

adjective

□ Prepositional phrases functioning as adjectives normally follow the nouns they modify. Those functioning as adverbs may appear in any of several positions in the sentence.

In the kitchen you will find / a stove with four burners / .

The phrase *in the kitchen,* which functions as an adverb, [can, cannot] _____ be moved to either of the positions marked by the slanted lines.

can

□ We have to be careful when placing prepositional phrases.

You will find a stove with four burners in the kitchen / .

If we moved the phrase *with four burners* to the position marked by the slanted line, the phrase would appear to modify the noun _____ instead of the noun it modifies, _____.

kitchen
stove

□ Separating a phrase from the noun it modifies may make a sentence difficult to understand.

This store sells sweaters for collegians in all popular sizes.

In this sentence the phrase *in all popular sizes* seems to modify the noun _____ instead of the noun it should modify, _____.

collegians
sweaters

□ Rewrite the sentence in the last frame, placing the modifying phrase in the correct position.

This store sells sweaters _____
_____.

in all popular
sizes for collegians

□ *The girl in the car with red hair is Ron's date.*

Since a car cannot have red hair, we would rewrite the sentence this way:

The girl _____ *is Ron's date.*

with red hair
in the car

□ *I enjoy hunting large animals like my father.*

To show that *like my father* modifies *I* rather than *animals*, we can place the phrase next to *I* by beginning the sentence with it.

_____, *I enjoy hunting large animals.*

Like my father

□ Prepositional phrases which function as adverbs can also be in positions which make the sentence awkward or misleading.

Allen watched as the dog ran away with a smile.

In this sentence the phrase *with a smile* modifies the verb _____, not the verb *ran*, which it seems to modify.

watched

230

□ To avoid ambiguity, place a prepositional phrase near the verb it modifies. Rewrite the sentence in the last frame to make its meaning clear.

with a smile as the dog ran away

    Allen watched _____.

□   *The Governor pointed out that our state had made great progress during his speech.*

The progress that the Governor mentioned did not occur only during his speech. Rewrite this sentence, placing the prepositional phrase by the verb it modifies.

during his speech that our state had made great progress

    The Governor pointed out _____

_____.

□ Rewrite this sentence to clarify its meaning.

He drank his coffee in a hurry while the others watched.

    He drank his coffee while the others watched in a hurry.

_____

_____

REVIEW

Rewrite the following sentences where necessary, shifting any misplaced phrase to its proper position. Mark correct sentences C.

Without a word the other Congressmen listened to Brewster speak.

*   or*

The other Congressmen listened without a word to Brewster speak.

□   *The other Congressmen listened to Brewster speak without a word.*

_____

_____

_____

That chair with a decorative cushion in the living room has to be reupholstered.

☐ *That chair in the living room with a decorative cushion has to be reupholstered.*

_____

_____

_____

☐ *The sailboat docked at the pier with its sails furled is a yawl.*

_____

_____

_____

The sailboat with its sails furled docked at the pier is a yawl.

MISPLACED AND DANGLING VERBAL PHRASES

We admired the beautiful statuary made with great skill and care on display at the Palace of Fine Arts.

11J Rewrite the following sentence, placing in its correct position any misplaced word or word group.

Made with great skill and care, we admired the beautiful statuary on display at the Palace of Fine Arts.

_____

_____.

□ Any form of a verb used as an adjective is called a participle.

The cracking sound of the breaking ice fills our ears.

In this sentence the participle *cracking* modifies the noun _____, and the participle *breaking* modifies the noun _____.

sound
ice

□ A participle ending in *ing* is a present participle. A participle ending in *ed* is a past participle.

The cracking ice floats down the clotted river.

In this sentence the present participle _____ modifies the noun *ice*. The past participle _____ modifies the noun *river*.

cracking
clotted

□ Although the present participle of all verbs ends in *ing,* the past participle of some verbs does not end in *ed. Learned* is the part participle of *learn*, but *taught* is the past participle of _____ .

teach

□ Although we cannot always recognize the past participle as the form of the verb ending in *ed,* we can recognize it as the form we use with the auxiliary verb *have.* The past participle of *steer* is [*have*] _____; the past participle of *go* is [*have*] _____.

steered
gone

□ A third form of the participle is the perfect participle. This form is composed of *having* plus the past participle of the verb. The perfect participle of *break* is *having broken;* the perfect participle of greet is _____.

having greeted

□ Verbs, then, have three participles—the present, the past, and the perfect participles. The present participle of *see* is _____; the past participle is _____; the perfect participle is _____.

seeing   seen
having seen

□ Any participle may serve as an adjective.

Having finished, the smiling, wrinkled old man departed.

smiling   wrinkled
Having finished

In this sentence three participles modify *man*: the present participle _____; the past participle _____; and the perfect participle _____.

□ Although used as an adjective, a participle keeps certain characteristics of a verb: it can take an object and have adverb modifiers.

Having finally finished his work, the man departed.

finally
work

In this sentence *Having finished* has a modifier, the adverb _____, and a direct object, the noun _____.

□ A participle together with the words related to it is called a participial phrase. Such phrases serve as adjectives.

Happily singing an old ballad, the entertainer strolled among the guests.

Happily singing an
old ballad

In this sentence the participial phrase _____ _____ modifies the noun *entertainer.*

□ To avoid ambiguity, we should keep participles and participial phrases close to the nouns or pronouns they modify.

I saw an old stone fort rowing down the river.

fort
I

In this sentence the participial phrase *rowing down the river* is misplaced. It seems to modify the noun _____ instead of the pronoun it really modifies, _____.

□   *I saw an old stone fort rowing down the river.*

We can place the participial phrase next to the pronoun *I* by moving the phrase to the beginning of the sentence.

_____

_____

Rowing down the
river, I saw an old
stone fort.

234

we

jewelry

□   *Made by the Mexican craftsman, we thought that the silver jewelry was exquisite.*

In this sentence the participial phrase *Made by the Mexican craftsmen* seems to modify the pronoun _____ instead of the noun it modifies, _____.

□   *Made by the Mexican craftsmen, we thought that the silver jewelry was exquisite.*

that the silver jewelry
made by the Mexican
craftsmen was ex-
quisite

Rewrite this sentence, placing the participial phrase next to the word it modifies.

   We thought _____

_____.

□   *I watched the puppies chasing each other sitting in the shade.*

Correct the position of the participial phrase in this sentence.

Sitting in the shade,
I watched the puppies
chasing each other.

_____

_____

□ Participles and participial phrases that can logically modify more than one noun or pronoun require careful placement.

   Susan saw Harry climbing the stairs.

In this sentence the participial phrase *climbing the stairs* modifies the noun _____.

Harry

□   *Susan saw Harry climbing the stairs.*

If we wish this sentence to mean instead that Susan was climbing the stairs at the time she saw Harry, we would move the modifying phrase to the beginning of the sentence.

Climbing the stairs,
Susan saw Harry.

_____

□ *Visiting the city, the Mayor of Danville spoke briefly to the officials.*

The Mayor of Danville spoke briefly to the officials visiting the city.

If the officials rather than the Mayor were the visitors, we would rewrite the sentence this way:

_____

_____

11K   Correct the following sentence.

[*As, When,* or *While*] *I was trying to follow my father's car closely*

Trying to follow my father's car closely, a truck blocked my way.

_____ ,

a truck blocked my way.

□ Participial phrases normally modify a noun or pronoun.

Arriving late, I apologized to the host profusely.

I

In this sentence the participial phrase *Arriving late* modifies the pronoun _____ .

□ Normally, a participial phrase introducing a sentence modifies the subject.

Tacking against the wind, the crew just missed the bell buoy.

Tacking against the wind

In this sentence the introductory participial phrase _____ _____ modifies *crew,* the subject.

□ Indroductory participial phrases which do not modify the subject are said to be dangling.

Writing carefully, the assignment was finished in time to hand in.

is

Since *Writing carefully* cannot modify *assignment,* it [is, is not] _____ dangling.

236

□ Dangling participial phrases may cause misreading.

Driving over the hill, the ocean came into view.

On first reading, this sentence seems to mean that the _____ was driving over the hill.

ocean

□ One way to correct a dangling participial phrase is to re-write it as a subordinate clause.

Driving over the hill, the ocean came into view.
As we _____, the ocean came into view.

[were driving] drove over the hill

□ *Standing by the tower, the bells seemed unusually loud to Mary.*

Rewrite the dangling participial phrase in this sentence as a subordinate clause.

Since _____, the bells seemed unusually loud to her.

Mary was standing by the tower

□ *Wearing a pink dress, Henry was able to spot Martha in the crowd.*

Rewrite this sentence.

_____,
Henry was able to spot her in the crowd.

Since Martha was wearing a pink dress

□ An introductory infinitive phrase, like a participial phrase, should modify the subject of the sentence.

To learn shorthand, practice is needed.

The infinitive phrase *To learn shorthand* is dangling be-cause it does not modify the subject, the noun _____.

practice

237

□ One of the ways we can correct the problem created by a dangling infinitive phrase is to give it a subject it can modify.

To learn shorthand, a student must practice.

The infinitive phrase *To learn shorthand* now has a subject to modify, _____.

student

□ *To choose a political candidate wisely, the important issues should be studied.*

Complete the revision of this sentence using *a voter* as the subject of the sentence.

To choose a political candidate wisely, _____ _____ the important issues.

a voter should study

□ *To remain in good health, a sound diet should be followed.*

Complete the revision of this sentence, using *a person* as the subject.

To remain in good health, _____ _____ .

a person should follow a sound diet

11L *To be precise, Hank is just a day over twenty.*

To be precise, a watch does not need twenty-one jewels.

The infinitive phrase *To be precise* is dangling in [the first, the second, neither] _____ sentence(s).

neither

238

□ Normally, introductory participial and infinitive phrases modify the subject of their sentences. Occasionally, however, we use such phrases only to express our attitude toward the statements that follow them.

Generally speaking, the pioneers conquered the West by hard work rather than by shooting each other.

In the above sentence the introductory participial phrase

Generally speaking

_____ expresses the writer's attitude.

□ Since a participial or infinitive phrase expressing a writer's attitude toward his statement is not a modifier, it is not dangling.

Considering the effects, nuclear test are dangerous in many ways.
Considering the effects, scientists have publicized the dangers of nuclear tests.

second

first

In neither sentence is *Considering the effects* dangling. It modifies the subject of the [first, second] _____ sentence and expresses the writer's attitude toward his statement in the _____ sentence.

□ The difference between a participial or infinitive phrase expressing the writer's attitude and one that is dangling is this: a phrase expressing a writer's attitude is not a modifier; a dangling phrase is a modifier without a word to modify.

To be precise, this car cost $1,600.
To be precise, careful measurements were made.

first

second

To be precise expresses the writer's attitude in the [first, second] _____ sentence; the same phrase is dangling in the _____ sentence because it does not have a word to modify.

second first	☐ *Judging from his appearance, Mr. Snell refused to hire the man.* *Judging from his appearance, Hal must be over forty.* *Judging from his appearance* is used correctly in both sentences. In the [first, second] _____ it expresses the writer's attitude; in the _____ sentence it modifies the subject following it.
is not	**11M** *The audience having been seated, the speaker took the podium.* The introductory phrase in the above sentence [is, is not] _____ dangling.
Roger *sun*	☐ One way to avoid a dangling participial phrase is to give the participle a subject of its own. *Having left, we waited for Roger in vain.* *Roger having left, we waited for him in vain.* These examples show that giving the dangling participial phrase *Having left* a subject, the noun _____, helps clarify its relationship to the sentence. ☐ A participial phrase with its own subject is an independent unit instead of a modifier. Hence, it is not dangling if it does not modify the subject of the sentence. Such phrases are called absolute phrases. *The sun being bright, Hank wore his dark glasses.* *The sun being bright* is an absolute phrase; it is not dangling since the participle *being* has its own subject, the noun _____ .

240

□   *Having been painted recently, I was unable to close the door completely.*

We can make this dangling element into an absolute phrase by giving it a logical subject.

door

The _____ having been painted recently, I was unable to close it completely.

□   *Being dry, the workmen found that the glue was unusable.*

Rewrite this sentence, making the dangling participial phrase an absolute phrase.

The glue being dry

_____, the workmen found that it was unusable.

The car needing repairs, we were afraid to drive it the long distance to Chicago.

□   *Needing repairs, we were afraid to drive the car the long distance to Chicago.*

Rewrite this sentence correctly, using an absolute phrase.

_____

_____

REVIEW

Revise the following sentences which require correction. Mark correct sentences C.

Driving along Highway 40, we saw a serious automobile accident.

□   *We saw a serious automobile accident driving along Highway 40.*

_____

_____

241

C	☐ Strictly speaking, a politician's future depends on his loyalty to a party.
	_____
	_____
The stumps being old and rotten, the gardeners were able to remove them easily.	☐ Being old and rotten, the gardeners were able to remove the stumps easily.
or	
Since the stumps were old and rotten, the gardeners were able to remove them easily.	_____
	_____
C	☐ Weather permitting, we'll hold the picnic outdoors.
	_____
	_____

TWELVE
OMITTED PARTS

ADDING NECESSARY NOUN DETERMINERS
AND VERBS

12A Add any necessary word to the following sentence.

His advisor and political speechwriter first met the Senator when the three men were law students in New York.

His should be added
before *political.*

□ We often omit words and phrases not necessary to the meaning of our sentences.

Bob made a chair and [a] table.

is not

The bracketed *a* [is, is not] _____ necessary to the meaning of this sentence.

□ Omitting *a*, *an*, and *the* is often possible.

The electricians and the plumbers have finished their work.

plumbers

We can omit the *the* before the noun _____ without affecting the meaning of this sentence.

□ *A, an,* and *the* are called noun determiners because they indicate to the reader that he is approaching a separate noun. If two or more related nouns clearly refer to different persons or things, it is not necessary to use a separate noun determiner before each noun.

The electricians and the plumbers have finished their work.

Since *electricians* and *plumbers* clearly refer to separate persons, the noun determiner *the* before *plumbers* [is, is not] _____ necessary.

is not

□ Occasionally, two or more related nouns can refer to the same person or thing.

The teacher and lecturer addressed the group.

Here the nouns *teacher* and *lecturer* [could, could not] _____ refer to the same person.

could

□ Always repeat the noun determiner *a, an,* or *the* before related nouns which refer to separate persons or things if they could refer to only one person or thing without it.

The teacher and the lecturer addressed the group.

Repeating *the* before *lecturer* makes it clear that the nouns *teacher* and *lecturer* refer to [the same, two different] _____ person(s).

two different

□   *The cat and [the] dog played happily.*
  The strawberries and [the] cream spilled.

If there are two distinct subjects intended in each of these sentences, the *the* before *dog* [is, is not] _____ necessary; the *the* before *cream* _____ necessary.

is not
is

□   *The transmitter and receiver will be finished tomorrow.*

If *transmitter* and *receiver* refer to separate instruments, it is necessary to repeat the noun determiner _____ before the noun _____.

the
receiver

244

□ *The ham and cheese loaf had been ordered.*
The cheese loaf and ham had been ordered.

If *ham* and *cheese loaf* refer to different objects, we need no additional noun signal in the [first, second] _____ sentence. However, we should repeat *the* before _____ in the _____ sentence.

second
cheese
first

□ The possessive forms of the personal pronouns—*my, our, your, his, her, its,* and *their*—function as noun determiners and should be repeated whenever required for clarity.

He lost his wallet and cardholder.

If *wallet* and *cardholder* refer to different objects, we should repeat the possessive _____ before *cardholder.*

his

□ *Her father and mother offered to help her.*
Her friend and classmate offered to help her.

Only one of these sentences requires an additional *her* as a noun determiner: to make it clear that there are two separate subjects, we should repeat the possessive form _____ before the noun _____.

her   classmate

12B   Add any necessary word to the following sentence.

The living room was painted gray, the dining room papered in yellow, and the den and playroom paneled in oak.

Were should be added before *paneled.*

□ We can often improve a sentence by omitting auxiliaries and verbs which are merely repetitious.

Bob can [go] and should go.

Omitting the bracketed verb go [will, will not] _____ harm the sentence's clarity.

will not

245

□ *The sandwiches are hot and the drinks are cold.*

are
cold

Since it is a repetition of the verb expressed in the first part of the sentence, we can omit the verb _____ before the adjective _____ .

□ When they are clearly understood even though unexpressed, we can omit auxiliaries and verbs which would be repetitious.

He was working when I left and will be for at least another week.

be

In this sentence *working,* expressed once, is clearly understood after _____ .

□ *The audience was seated and the curtain drawn.*

was
drawn

The auxiliary verb _____ , expressed before *seated,* is understood before _____ .

□ Normally we should not omit words which are not expressed elsewhere.

The applause was warm and the shouts for an encore repeated loudly.

were

The omission of the auxiliary verb _____ before the verb *repeated* is not correct because it is not expressed elsewhere in the sentence.

□ Correct this sentence.

Insert *were* before
repeated.

The applause was warm and the shouts for an encore repeated loudly.

□ To be omitted, the auxiliary or verb must be identical to one expressed. If it is not, it should be expressed.

Henry plays golf on Saturday and his brothers on Sunday.

play

Although *plays* is expressed, the verb understood after *brothers,* _____ , is not identical and should also be expressed.

246

received	☐ *Paul never has and never will receive poor grades.* To correct this sentence, we must add the verb _____ incorrectly omitted after the auxiliary *has*.
second *first*	☐ *The books were stacked and the work finished.* *The trumpet was sounding and the loudspeaker blaring.* Both of these sentences lack an auxiliary verb, *was*. It is correctly omitted from the [first, second] _____ sentence but not from the _____ sentence.
Insert *remembers* after *Bob*.	☐ Correct this sentence. *You remember everything you hear, but Bob nothing.*

REVIEW

	Add any words necessary to the following sentences. Mark correct sentences C.
The should be added before *writer*.	☐ *The political scientist and writer who signed a contract to write a text on modern Chinese history have a common interest in Sun Yat-sen's influence on the Kuomintang.*
Was should be added after *one*.	☐ *Four windows were broken yesterday and one broken today.*
Lecture should be added after *will*.	☐ *Professor Fine lectured Wednesday and Thursday; Professor Alberts will today.*

ADDING NECESSARY RELATIVE PRONOUNS

That should be added before *Barnes*.	**12C** Add any necessary word to the following sentence. *I prefer Elliot's design, even though I know Barnes, the local architect, has submitted one.*

☐ *That* often introduces subordinate clauses.

I know that he's good.

In this sentence *that* introduces the subordinate clause

that he's good

_____.

☐ *That* is sometimes the subject of the clause it introduces.

The Wendells owned the house that burned.

burned

That introducing the subordinate clause *that burned* is the subject of the verb _____.

☐ If *that* is not the subject of the clause it introduces, we can often omit it without loss of clarity.

I told him [*that*] *I had finished.*

can

Since *I* rather than *that* is the subject of the subordinate clause [*that*] *I had finished*, we [can, cannot] _____ omit *that*.

☐   *The radio that I bought works beautifully.*

The radio that was here has been stolen.

first

second

That can be omitted from the [first, second] _____ sentence but not from the _____ sentence.

☐ Occasionally *that,* even though it is not the subject of its clause, is necessary for clarity.

He remembered the girl he had dated was away for the summer.

remembered

The *that* omitted after *remembered* is not the subject of its clause; however, it is necessary because without it *girl* seems on first reading to be the direct object of the verb _____ rather than the subject of the clause.

□ *He remembered that the girl he had dated was away for the summer.*

Using *that* to signal the beginning of the clause makes it clear that girl [is, is not] _____ the direct object of the verb *remembered*.

is not

□ *Everyone knows the Smiths who visited last year have moved to St. Paul.*

To show clearly that *Smiths* is the subject of the clause rather than the direct object of the verb *knows*, we should insert *that* between _____ and _____.

knows   the

□ *Ellen saw that the papers taken from the table were returned.*

Ellen hoped that the papers taken from the table would be returned.

Although *that* is not the subject of the subordinate clause in either sentence, we can omit it without loss of clarity only from the [first, second] _____ sentence.

second

Which or *that* should be added following *model* and following *but.*

12D Add any necessary word to the following sentence.

This is a model the designers originally had great faith in but the consumer refused to buy.

□ *Whom, which,* and *that* introducing subordinate clauses are often inessential to a sentence's clarity and can be omitted.

Wally is one player whom all the others admire.

Dropping *whom* from this sentence [would, would not] _____ make it less clear.

would not

□   *The paper which I wrote last week was about the Renaissance.*

The clarity of this sentence would not be impaired if we dropped the word _____.

which

□ *Whom, which,* and *that* signal the beginning of subordinate clauses. We should omit them only if the signal they provide is unnecessary.

There is the car which I bought.

Since *which* is not necessary to signal the subordinate clause *which I bought,* we [can, cannot] _____ omit it.

can

□ If two or more subordinate clauses come in succession, *whom, which,* or *that* should be used to signal the beginning of each subordinate clause.

The hi-fi set which Hank assembled last summer and which someone stole recently is worth $500.

Each of the clauses modifying *set* is clearly distinguished because _____ is used to signal the beginning of both, even though it would be unnecessary if either one were alone.

which

□   *He asked only that the trophy be presented to the entire student body and it be displayed in the student union.*

This sentence would be clearer if *that* were added before the pronoun _____.

it

□ Use *whom, which,* or *that* to signal the beginning of subordinate clauses whenever two or more such clauses appear in sequence.

The company Steve worked for this summer and I work for now is going out of business.

This sentence would be clearer if *which* or *that* were added after _____ and after _____.

company   and

250

Whom should be added after *writer* and after *and*.	☐ Add the clause signal *whom* where necessary. *This young novelist is a writer critics have noted many times with favor and readers have enjoyed greatly.*
That should be added after *suggested* and after *and*.	☐ Add the necessary clause signals to this sentence. *The director suggested the committee report their findings as soon as possible and the other members prepare to discuss the implications of the report.*

REVIEW

	Add any word necessary for clarity in the following sentences. Mark correct sentences C.
That should be added after *learn*.	☐ *Some diplomats learn the lessons contained in the history of other nations cannot be ignored.*
Which or *that* should be added after *car* and after *and*.	☐ *The car my father bought from Bob Gordon last year for $100 and my brother rebuilt had a good motor.*
C	☐ *I understand he can be persuaded.*
That should be added after *remembered*.	☐ *I just remembered the house we lived in at Cape May was painted blue.*

AVOIDING INCOMPLETE CONSTRUCTIONS

For should be added after *concern*.	**12E** Add any necessary word to the following sentence. *Although Helen objected, her fiance showed his concern and interest in her by escorting her both to and from school.*

□ Certain verbs in English require certain prepositions. We say *His action adds to his honor* and *His action detracts from his honor.* As these examples show, the verb *adds* is normally followed by the preposition *to,* the verb *detracts* by the preposition _____.

□ Although we say *He asked for his share,* we say *He insisted* _____ *his share.*

□ Notice, too, that we often let two or more prepositions share the same object.

His action detracts from rather than adds to his honor.

The prepositions *from,* related to the verb *detracts,* and *to,* related to *adds,* share the same object, the noun _____.

□ If two or more prepositions sharing the same object are different, we should express each one. Since we say *He did not ask for his share* and *He insisted on his share,* we should also say *He did not ask* _____ *but insisted on his share.*

□ Complete this sentence.

We believed _____ *and hoped for eventual success.*

□ Add the preposition missing from this sentence.

We remembered too late that Stanley was arriving, not departing from, Chicago at 9 A.M.

□ Add the preposition missing from this sentence.

When working with a wood plane, remember to push it away, not pull it toward you.

12F Correct this sentence by adding necessary words.

While sleeping off yesterday's exertions, the alarm clock rang noisily just out of my reach.

Add *I was* after *While.*

□ To avoid unnecessary repetition, we often omit parts of subordinate clauses.

While I was studying, I ate two candy bars.
While studying, I ate two candy bars.

The second sentence shows that omitting *I was* from the subordinate clause *While I was studying* in the first sentence [does, does not] _____ make the sentence less clear.

does not

□ Clauses with parts missing but clearly understood are called elliptical clauses.

When traveling in London, Ellen lost her luggage.

The words missing but clearly understood in the elliptical clause *When traveling in London* are _____ *was.*

she [Ellen]

□ *While he was campaigning, Nevins gave more than thirty speeches.*

The subordinate clause in this sentence will be just as clear if it is elliptical:

While _____, Nevins gave more than thirty speeches.

campaigning

□ The words omitted from an elliptical clause introducing a sentence are clearly understood only if the subject of the clause is the same as the subject of the sentence.

While he was working for the Rand Company, Cargill received a bonus every Christmas.

The words *he was* can be omitted from the introductory clause in this sentence because *he* and *Cargill* [refer, do not refer] _____ to the same person.

refer

□ Using an elliptical clause whose omitted subject is different from the subject of the sentence makes a sentence
confusing.

While bathing, the doorbell rang twice.

Since we expect the subject of an elliptical clause to refer
to the same person or thing as the subject of the sentence,
this sentence seems to suggest that the _____
was bathing.

doorbell

□ To avoid confusing your reader, supply the missing parts of
elliptical clauses whose omitted subjects are different from
the subjects of their sentences. Rewrite the sentence in the
last frame, using *Carol* as the subject of the clause.

While _____ bathing, the doorbell rang twice.

Carol was

□ *When opening the can, Bob spilled its contents on the
floor.*
When opening the can, the contents spilled on the floor.

The elliptical clause in the [first, second] _____
sentence requires the missing words *Bob was.* The same
clause in the _____ sentence does not.

second

first

□ *When opening the can, the contents spilled on the floor.*

Correct the error in this sentence, giving the elliptical clause
the subject *Bob.*

_____,

the contents spilled on the floor.

When Bob was open-
ing the can

□ *When ten years old, my father moved our family to California.*

Correct this sentence, supplying the elliptical clause with
the logical subject.

_____,

my father moved our family to California.

When I was ten years
old

□ Correct this sentence.

When running for the bus, a car almost hit me.

_____ ,

a car almost hit me.

12G *The French are far more interested in attracting tourists to their country than Americans.*

*are
Americans*

This sentence will make sense only if _____ is added after _____ .

---

is not

□ We often omit words from comparisons in order to avoid unnecessary repetition.

This gear turns faster than that wheel turns.

Repeating *turns* after *wheel* [is, is not] _____ necessary.

□ *Ralph runs the quarter-mile as fast as Bob runs the quarter-mile.*

will

If we remove *runs the quarter-mile* repeated after *Bob,* this sentence [will, will not] _____ be just as clear.

□ Cross out the words unnecessarily repeated in this sentence.

. . . television
~~*provides.*~~

Some say that radio provides better news coverage than television provides.

□ We can omit from comparisons those words which are clearly understood.

Water boils at a lower temperature in higher altitudes than at sea level.

[water] it boils

The omitted words clearly understood after *than* are

_____ .

□ Omitting words from comparisons without causing ambiguity is possible only if the missing words are clearly understood.

Mr. Blake offered me more money than John.

This comparison is ambiguous because we do not know which words are missing. Either *he gave* is missing after *than* or *gave me*—or simply *did*—is missing after _____.

John

□ If words omitted from a comparison are not clearly understood, we should supply them.

Dan helps Peter more often than Art.

If this sentence means that Dan helps both Peter and Art, we should add the words _____ between *than* and *Art.*

he helps

□ *Dan helps Peter more often than Art.*

If this sentence means instead that Dan and Art both help Peter, we should add the two words _____ or the single word _____ after *Art* .

helps him
does

□ *Phillip is more concerned with business success than his family.*

To make it clear that this sentence expresses a comparison between Phillip's concern and his family's concern, we should add the word _____ after *family* .

is

□ *Phillip is more concerned with business success than his family.*

If this comparison is instead between Phillip's concern for business success and his concern for his family, we should add the preposition _____ before _____.

with his

In the following sentences, add any necessary words and cross out any unnecessary words. Mark correct sentences C.

☐ Before studying the problem, Baker was less able to see its complexities than Norton.

☐ While he was trying on the suit, John ripped open a seam on the coat.

☐ I can write as well as anyone else in my class can write.

☐ When keeping track of your bank balance, remember that you add all deposits and subtract all checks from the current figure.

☐ I admire Hank much more than Bob.

C

~~he was~~

... my class ~~can write~~

To should be added after *deposits*.

I admire should be added before *Bob* or *admires him*—or simply *does*—should be added after *Bob*.

THIRTEEN
MIXED AND
ILLOGICAL
CONSTRUCTIONS

AVOIDING FAULTY SUBJECT-PREDICATE COMBINATIONS

The price of a Rolls
Royce is relatively
high.
or
A Rolls Royce is rel-
atively expensive.

13A *The price of a Rolls Royce is relatively expensive.*

Rewrite this sentence to clarify the logical relationship of its parts.

_____

_____

☐ The most important relationship in any sentence is that between the subject and the predicate. If the predicate is not a logical assertion about the subject, a sentence will be ambiguous.

   Al's height is six feet.

The predicate *is six feet* can be logically asserted about

[Al's] height

the subject, _____.

258

□ Through carelessness we may occasionally write sentences such as this:

Al's height is six feet tall.

The predicate *is six feet tall* is illogical because it is not Al's height but _____ who is six feet tall.

Al

□   *The cost of living nowadays is extremely expensive.*

This sentence is illogical because *is extremely expensive* cannot be asserted about the subject, the noun _____.

cost

□   *The cost of living nowadays is extremely expensive.*

Costs logically are not expensive but high. Complete the revision of this sentence.

The cost of living nowadays is _____.

extremely high

□   *My opinion of the movie is abominable.*

This sentence is illogical because it is not the opinion but the _____ which the writer feels is abominable.

movie

□   *My opinion of the movie is abominable.*

The predicate *is abominable* will be logical only if the subject of the sentence is *movie*.

In my opinion, _____.

the movie is abominable

□   *Mr. Elkins' job is a teacher.*

This sentence is illogical because it is not the job but _____ who is a teacher.

Mr. Elkins

□   *Mr. Elkins' job is a teacher.*

Rewrite this sentence logically.

_____ *is a teacher.*

Mr. Elkins

□ *That phone call late last night was Rudy.*

A phone call cannot be a person but rather from a person:

That phone call late last night _____.

was from Rudy

REVIEW

Rewrite any illogical sentence in the following group. Mark any sentence not needing revision C.

□ *Before becoming political editor for the* Examiner, *Harold Rapke's profession was an economics teacher at Arizona State University.*

... Harold Rapke was
an economics teacher
...

_____

_____

□ *That wild cheering which broke out during the candidate's speech was the California delegation.*

... was from the California delegation.

_____

_____

□ *The choice of the name for our boat was selected by my sister.*

... was made by my
sister.

_____

_____

AVOIDING ILLOGICAL COMPARISONS

13B Replace any incorrect word in this sentence.

ape's
~~ape~~

When he climbs the rope, Hal's arms seem as powerful as an ape.

□ Expressing comparisons requires care to ensure that the persons or things compared are logically related.

Ralph is a better student than Pete.

This sentence is logical because it compares the abilities of two persons, _____ and _____.

Ralph   Pete

□ *Ralph's scholastic record is better than Pete.*

This sentence is not logical because it compares a thing, _____, to a person, _____.

scholastic record
Pete

□ *Ralph's scholastic record is better than Pete.*

This sentence would be logical if it compared Ralph's scholastic record to _____ scholastic record.

Pete's

□ *Ralph's scholastic record is better than Pete's.*

This comparison is logical. Although *scholastic record* is not understood to follow Pete in the previous sentence, it is understood to follow the possessive form of that noun used in this sentence, _____.

Pete's

□ *Her skin is as smooth as a child.*

This comparison is illogical because it compares a thing, _____, with a person, _____.

skin   child

□ *Her skin is as smooth as a child.*
Her skin is as smooth as a child's.

Although *skin* is not expressed, it can be understood to follow the final word in the [first, second] _____ sentence, but not the final word in the _____ sentence.

second
first

□ *Some have said that a newspaperman's responsibilities are graver than a doctor.*

Correct this comparison.

Some have said that a newspaperman's responsibilities are graver _____.

than a doctor's

□ *The shape of the football used in the early days of the sport is different from the football now used.*

The error in this comparison is fairly well concealed. However, the sentence is illogical because it compares two unlike things, the _____ of the football formerly used and the _____ now used.

shape
football

□ Add the words necessary to make the comparison in the last frame logical.

The shape of the football used in the early days of the sport is different from the _____ *football now used.*

shape of the

□ *The shape of the football used in the early days of the sport is different from the shape of the football now used.*

If we wish to avoid repeating *the shape*, we can substitute the pronoun *that* for it in its second appearance:

The shape of the football used in the early days of the sport is different from _____ *football now used.*

that of the

□ *The ship traffic on the Great Lakes is equivalent to any large American harbor.*

Correct this comparison, using the pronoun *that*.

The ship traffic on the Great Lakes is equivalent to _____ *any large American harbor.*

that in

than that of	□ *The plot of this play is far less complex than the novel upon which it is based.* Correct this comparison. *The plot of this play is far less complex* _____ *the novel upon which it is based.*

13C Correct this comparison.

Other should be added after *any*.	*After reading Disraeli's biography, I'm convinced that he had more political insight than any man of his era.*
	□ A comparison is illogical if it compares a person with himself or a thing with itself. *This movie is better than any movie I have seen.* Since the better movie obviously belongs to the group of all the movies with which it is compared, the comparison
is not	[is, is not] _____ logical.
	□ *This movie is better than any movie I have seen.* Using *other,* we can make this comparison logical:
any other	*This movie is better than* _____ *movie I have seen.*
	□ *New York City is more populous than any city in the United States.*
other *city*	This comparison will be logical only if we add _____ before _____.

263

□ In some comparisons *else* rather than *other* is necessary.

> *He is faster than anyone.*
> *He is faster than anyone else.*

These examples show that adding *else* separates the person compared from the group with which he is compared. The second comparison [is, is not] _____ logical.

is

□ *My camera is more valuable than anything I own.*

This comparison will be logical if we add *else* following _____.

anything

□ Make these comparisons logical by adding *other* or *else*.

> *My brother Ralph is more successful than anyone I know.*

. . . anyone else . . .

> *Alaska has fewer inhabitants per square mile than any state in the Union.*

. . . any other state . . .

□ Make these comparisons logical.

> *Plate glass has fewer surface flaws than any kind of glass.*

. . . any other kind . . .

> *After a month in Paris, Bob realized that his wash-and-wear shirts were more practical than anything he took with him to Europe.*

. . . anything else . . .

13D Correct this comparison by adding any word necessary.

> *This apartment is as good, if not better than, any other apartment we have looked at.*

. . . as good as . . .

□ We occasionally use two kinds of comparisons in the same sentence. For instance, we join comparisons such as *He is as happy as she* and *He is happier than she:*

> *He is as happy as, if not _____, she.*

happier than

264

□ When using two kinds of comparisons in the same sentence, we should be certain that each kind is logically complete.

> *The weather here is as good, if not better than, the weather in Florida.*

The first kind of comparison is incomplete. Since we say *The weather here is as good as the weather in Florida,* we should not omit the second *as* when we combine this kind of comparison with another.

as

> *The weather here is as good* _____, *if not better than, the weather in Florida.*

□ *Bob is as strong, if not stronger than, his brother George.*

To complete the first kind of comparison, we should add

as   strong

_____ after _____.

□ One way to ensure that a two-part comparison is logically complete is to finish one part before beginning the second:

strong as

> *Bob is as* _____ *his brother George, if not stronger.*

□ *The final movement of the Fourth Symphony was as dull, if not duller than, any movement preceding it.*

To be logically complete, the first part of this comparison requires *as* after *dull.* Alternatively, we can complete the first part of the comparison before beginning the second:

as any movement
preceding it

> *The final movement of the Fourth Symphony was as dull* _____ *, if not duller.*

□ *The Asian people are as hungry as, if not hungrier than, the people of any other continent.*

Rewrite this sentence, completing the first part of the comparison before beginning the second.

the people of any
other continent, if
not hungrier

> *The Asian people are as hungry as* _____
> _____
> _____.

Correct the following sentences by adding words where necessary. Mark correct sentences C.

Other should be added after *any*.	☐ *This TV antenna is superior in sensitivity to any antenna selling at a comparable price.*
Those on or *hemlines on* should be added after *than*.	☐ *Hemlines on women's dresses and skirts are a good deal higher now than the dresses and skirts worn by women in the last century.*
C	☐ *The bridegroom was as nervous as the bride, if not more nervous.*
As should be added after *high*.	☐ *That last jump seemed as high, if not higher than, any Brooks has made all day.*

MIXED FORMS WITH THIS, THAT, THESE, AND THOSE

This ~~*These*~~	☐ **13E** Replace the incorrect word in this sentence. *These kind of slacks once was very popular.*

☐ The noun determiners *this*, *that*, *these*, and *those*, traditionally called demonstrative adjectives, are often misused in certain kinds of sentences.

This kind of knife is useful for cutting linoleum.

In this sentence, *This* is related to the noun _____.

kind

This and *that* are singular and are used only with singular nouns.

That sort of tactic is dangerous.

is

Because *sort* is a singular noun, *That* [is, is not] _____ the correct form.

□   *These* and *those* are plural forms, used only with plural nouns.

    [*This, these*] *kinds of fish are poisonous.*

Since *kinds* is a plural noun, the correct form to complete the sentence is _____, the plural form.

□   *These sort of chairs used to be popular.*

Since *sort* is [singular, plural] _____, the plural form *These* [is, is not] _____ correct.

□   *These sort of chairs used to be popular.*

We often hear the plural forms *these* and *those* used incorrectly with the singular nouns *kind, sort,* and *type.* In this sentence we should use the singular form _____ in place of *These.*

□ We might tend to use the plural form *these* and *those* with *kind, sort,* and *type* because these singular nouns are often directly followed by the preposition *of* with a plural noun as its object.

    These sort of chairs used to be popular.

The preposition and the plural noun following *sort* in this sentence are _____.

□   *These sort of chairs used to be popular.*

Choosing *these* for sentences such as this is an effort to use a suitable form for the singular noun *sort* and the plural noun *chairs.* However, since *These* is related to *sort,* not *chairs,* the correct form is the singular one, _____ .

□ *This sort of chairs used to be popular.*

Since *This* and *sort* are singular, the noun following *of* should also be singular.

    This sort of _____ *used to be popular.*

□ The noun following *of* connected to the singular nouns *kind*, *sort*, and *type* should be singular. Those following *of* connected to the plural nouns *kinds*, *sorts*, and *types* should be plural. Complete these sentences.

attitudes

> *These kinds of [attitude, attitudes] _____ are not healthy.*

remark

> *That kind of [remark, remarks] _____ can cause trouble.*

□ When choosing *this*, *that*, *these*, or *those* to modify the singular nouns *kind*, *sort*, and *type*, remember that they require a singular form *this* or *that*. Complete this sentence.

This

> *[This, These] _____ type of furniture is out of style now.*

□ The plural nouns *kinds*, *sorts*, and *types* require a plural form, *these* or *those*. Complete this sentence.

Those

> *[That, Those] _____ kinds of racquets will be on display tomorrow.*

□ Complete these sentences.

these

> *Criminologists have difficulty explaining [this, these] _____ sorts of crimes.*

that

> *I find [that, those] _____ kind of reminder helpful.*

268

Complete the following sentences.

this

☐ *He warned me that [this, these]* _____ *kind of fun could be dangerous.*

These

☐ *[This, These]* _____ *sorts of research may open new possibilities in treatment for cancer.*

that

☐ *Say what you will, the reason he refused was that he didn't care for [that, those]* _____ *type of politics.*

FOURTEEN
WORDINESS

AVOIDING REDUNDANCIES

—ink— with my own two eyes —in size—	**14A** Cross out any redundant word in these sentences. *I saw him stealing your ink pen with my own two eyes.* *For a fullback, he is quite small in size.*

☐ One important quality of good prose is economy of expression. Generally speaking, therefore, we should express our ideas in as few words as possible.

Draw a round circle on the blackboard.

This sentence contains an unnecessary word, the adjective *round*. The idea of roundness is adequately expressed in

circle

the noun which *round* modifies, ⎯⎯⎯⎯⎯⎯ .

☐ Words that unnecessarily repeat ideas are said to be redundant.

Draw a round circle on the blackboard.

redundant

The adjective *round* is ⎯⎯⎯⎯⎯⎯ and should be omitted.

270

tall

□   *The tall skyscrapers were brilliant with light.*

Since a skyscraper is a tall building, the adjective _____ is redundant and should be omitted.

□   *This text contains the basic essentials.*

basic
essentials

The adjective _____ is redundant because it repeats the idea expressed by _____, the noun it modifies.

□   *The party slowly descended down the steep slope.*

down

Since descend means to go down, the preposition _____ is redundant in this sentence.

□ Cross out the redundant word in this sentence.

—*hot*—

The hot boiling water dissolved the chemical easily.

□ Phrases as well as single words may be redundant.

The design was square in shape.

shape

Since a square is a definite kind of shape, the phrase *in* _____ is redundant and should be omitted.

□   *Mary's evening gown is blue in color.*

Since *blue* obviously refers to a color, the phrase _____

in color

_____ is redundant.

□   *Elliot arrives in the morning at 8* A.M.

in the morning

Since the abbreviation A.M. has the same meaning as the phrase _____, this sentence should have either the abbreviation or the phrase, but not both.

□ *Mr. Randall will be traveling in Europe during the month of April.*

In this case, *April* can refer only to a month. This sentence should be shortened:

April

Mr. Randall will be traveling in Europe during _____.

□ Cross out the unnecessary phrase in this sentence.

~~of today~~

Our contemporary scientists of today are less hampered by prejudice than their forerunners.

REVIEW

Cross out any redundant words and phrases in the following sentences. If the sentence is correct, mark it C.

~~up~~

□ *The jack would raise the flat tire no more than one inch up from the ground.*

~~in size~~

□ *The aggregate pile just off the highway near Hoberg's is larger in size today than yesterday.*

~~with her hand~~

□ *She stroked the furniture lovingly with her hand.*

AVOIDING WORDY CONSTRUCTIONS

14B Cross out any unnecessary words in this sentence.

~~that was~~

From Russian Hill we could see the fog that was rolling in from the sea.

□ In order to express ourselves economically, we should learn to avoid wordy constructions.

The car which is blue is mine.

We can express this sentence more economically:

blue

The _____ *car is mine.*

□ *The car which is blue is mine.*

The subordinate clause *which is blue* is an unnecessarily wordy construction because it serves only to relate the adjective _____ to the noun _____.

blue   car

□ Using a clause merely to relate an adjective to a noun is generally wordy.

I prefer a tie that is narrow.

The subordinate clause *that is narrow* is an unnecessarily wordy construction to relate the adjective _____ to the noun _____.

narrow
tie

□ *I prefer a tie that is narrow.*

We can shorten this sentence by two words if we place the adjective in front of the noun.

I prefer a _____.

narrow tie

□ *Sidewalks which are icy are dangerous.*

Rewrite this sentence, shortening it.

_____ *are dangerous.*

Icy sidewalks

□ Phrases as well as clauses may be uneconomical devices to relate an adjective to a noun.

The dress of silk sold for $98.

This sentence should be shortened.

silk

The _____ *dress sold for $98.*

□ *The police department offers lessons in driving.*

Shorten this sentence.

driving lessons

The police department offers _____.

□ *Clouds of gray stood out against a sky of blue.*

Shorten this sentence.

Gray clouds
a blue sky

_____ *stood out against*

_____.

□ A subordinate clause may contain a prepositional phrase which would be adequate to express the idea by itself.

The bottle which is on the sink is empty.

In the subordinate clause *which is on the sink* the prepositional phrase *on the sink* is the only part that is necessary. The sentence should be shortened.

on the sink

The bottle _____ *is empty.*

□ Examine every subordinate clause to see if it contains a phrase that would be adequate without the other words in the clause.

Mr. Allen called to the man who was on the corner.

In the clause *who was on the corner* only the prepositional

on the corner

phrase _____ is necessary.
Therefore, the sentence could be rewritten this way:

Mr. Allen called to
the man on the
corner.

_____

_____

□ *Those books which are in my locker belong to a girl who is in my math class.*

Shorten this sentence.

in my locker
in my math class

Those books _____ *belong to*
a girl _____.

274

□ A subordinate clause may contain a participial phrase that would be adequate by itself to express the idea contained in the clause.

The parts which were exposed to the weather rusted badly.
The parts exposed to the weather rusted badly.

These examples show that the subordinate clause *which were exposed to the weather* contains a participial phrase which expresses the same idea more economically,

exposed to the weather

_____ .

□ *The car struck the light post which was mounted on the corner.*

The participial phrase *mounted on the corner,* contained in the subordinate clause *which was mounted on the corner,* [can, cannot] _____ take the place of the clause in which it occurs.

can

□ Cross out the unnecessary words in this sentence.

The car struck the light post which was mounted on the corner.

~~which was~~

□ Cross out the unnecessary words in this sentence.

The shortstop was unable to tag the runner who was sliding into second base.

~~who was~~

□ Cross out the unnecessary words.

The janitor who was making his rounds turned off the light which was burning in my room.

~~who was~~
~~which was~~

14C *The hall was decorated by the prom committee.*

Rewrite this sentence, shortening it.

_____

The prom committee decorated the hall.

□   *The car was driven by my father.*

     My father drove the car.

These examples show that the idea in the first sentence is expressed more economically but [less, just as] _____ clearly in the second sentence.

just as

□   *The car was driven by my father.*

     My father drove the car.

The difference between these two sentences is that the verb of the first, *was driven,* is in the [active, passive] _____ voice, while the verb of the second, *drove,* is in the _____ voice.

passive
active

□ Sentences having passive verbs are wordier than sentences having active verbs.

    The runner was tackled by two opposing linemen.
    Two opposing linemen tackled the runner.

Since its verb is in the active voice, the second sentence requires [one, two] _____ less word(s) to express the same idea contained in the first sentence.

two

□ Sentences having passive verbs are always wordier than those having active verbs. As often as possible, we should rewrite such sentences, rearranging their parts in order to use active verbs.

    Hank was caught speeding by an alert policeman.

Rewrite this sentence, using an active verb.

An alert policeman _____.

caught Hank
speeding

□   *"The Rich Boy" was written by F. Scott Fitzgerald after he himself had become wealthy.*

Rewrite this sentence, using an active verb.

_____

after he himself had become wealthy.

F. Scott Fitzgerald
wrote "The Rich Boy"

□ *A picture of the warehouse fire was snapped by an alert amateur photographer.*

Rewrite this sentence more economically.

_____

_____

_____

An alert amateur photographer snapped a picture of the warehouse fire.

REVIEW

Shorten the following sentences by rewriting them or by crossing out superfluous words they contain. If a sentence is economically written as it stands, mark it C.

~~the year of~~

□ *By the year of 1970, the population of this city will have grown to half a million.*

_____

_____

~~to the eye~~

□ *The building and its grounds were very attractive to the eye.*

_____

_____

~~which were~~

□ *All the homes which were damaged in last year's flood are completely restored.*

_____

_____

□ *The two old refrigerators were hauled away by the workmen.*

_____

_____

The workmen hauled away the two old refrigerators.

~~who are~~

□ *The men who are responsible for personnel recruitment met today.*

_____

_____

277

AVOIDING EMPTY-WORD CONSTRUCTIONS

It was   who

There are   who

14D Cross out any unnecessary words in the following sentences.

It was Herman rather than George who left early.

There are three Senators who have actively opposed the new bill.

□ Introducing a sentence with *there* plus a form of *be (there is, there are, there was,* etc.) is often unnecessarily wordy.

There was only one piece of cake that remained.
Only one piece of cake remained.

There

that

The second sentence has three fewer words than the first: the two-word introductory phrase _____ *was* and the relative pronoun _____.

□ Before using the introductory word *there*, we should look for a more economical way to express the same idea.

There are several girls whom I date.

This sentence can be more economically expressed:

several girls

I date _____.

□ Although in certain limited situations we may prefer the wordier *there* construction because it provides the kind of emphasis we need, we should remember that the indiscriminate use of such constructions will weaken the expressive power of our prose. At least we should be aware that more economical constructions are available to us. For instance, we can omit three words from this sentence.

There were

who

There were a number of gate-crashers who managed to get in.

□ We can omit four words from this sentence.

There have been

which

There have been several crucial injuries which have hampered the team's chances this year.

278

□ *It*, like *there*, is often unnecessarily used as an introductory word.

> *It was Senator Eldridge who proposed the bill.*
> *Senator Eldridge proposed the bill.*

These examples show that dropping *It was* and *who* from the first sentence [would, would not] _____ change its meaning.

would not

□ *It is the water pump that needs replacement.*

This sentence would be just as clear with three words omitted.

> *The* _____.

water pump needs replacement

□ Cross out the superfluous words in this sentence.

> *It has been Bruce's hard work that has held the club together.*

~~It has been~~ ~~that~~

□ Cross out the superfluous words in this sentence.

> *It was the newspaper strike that showed me how much we rely on the press for our information.*

~~It was~~ ~~that~~

14E   Cross out the unnecessary words in these sentences.

> *One factor we should consider is how important a thing good water is to public health.*
>
> *My Uncle Henry is a person who really enjoys fishing.*

~~One factor is~~
~~a thing~~
~~is a person who~~

□ Certain words that we commonly use lead almost automatically to uneconomical expression. One such word is *thing*.

> *The thing we should consider is our budget.*
> *We should consider our budget.*

These examples show that dropping *The thing* and *is* from the first sentence [would, would not] _____ make it any less clear.

would not

□ *Thing* is often an empty word signaling a weak, wordy construction.

> *The thing Mrs. Albert asked for was her purse.*

The idea expressed here can be expressed far more concisely:

> *Mrs. Albert* _____.

asked for her purse

□   *The thing I approve of is his attitude.*

Rewrite this sentence, shortening it.

_____

I approve of his attitude.

□ The empty word *thing* can appear almost anywhere in a sentence. At times we may prefer the less economical construction involving *thing* because it provides a certain kind of emphasis. But generally we can omit it along with other words it requires and improve the sentence.

> *The radio he built was a beautiful thing.*

Only one word need appear after *was*.

> *The radio he built was* _____.

beautiful

□ Cross out the superfluous words in this sentence.

> *He admitted that our arrival was a fortunate thing.*

a̶ t̶h̶i̶n̶g̶

280

□ When used as s substitute for *thing, one* is also an empty word that leads to uneconomical expression.

   The one Henry liked best was the Ford.

Rewrite this sentence more economically.

liked the Ford best

   Henry _____.

□ Cross out the superfluous words in this sentence.

a~~ one~~

   Braddock's catch was a spectacular one.

□ Writers who understand that *thing* and *one* are empty words may mistakenly substitute in their place other empty words such as *factor* or *aspect.*

   The thing scholars should examine is Swift's art.
   The factor scholars should examine is Swift's art.

These examples show that substituting *factor* for *thing*

would not

[would, would not] _____ improve the first sentence.

□ *Factor* and *aspect* are attractive as substitutes for *thing* or *one* because they suggest that a statement is important, profound. However, *factor* and *aspect* are often used simply as elegant versions of *thing*. Cross out the superfluous words in this sentence.

~~The factor~~ ~~is~~

   The factor scholars should examine is Swift's art.

□ Cross out the unnecessary words in this sentence.

~~The aspect~~ ~~is~~

   The aspect we will now consider is the atom's relation to the molecule.

□ Cross out the unnecessary words in this sentence.

~~an~~ ~~factor~~

   The rise of industrialism was an important factor in developing political attitudes among the poor.

281

□ Cross out the unnecessary words in this sentence.

One aspect he stressed was that fear led to hatred, and hatred to violence.

□ *Person* may be an empty word leading to uneconomical expression in sentences about people.

The person who helped me was my father.

We can rewrite this sentence using half the number of words it now contains:

My _____ .

□ We can often omit *person* and related words. Cross out the superfluous words in this sentence.

My father is a helpful person.

□ Cross out the superfluous words in this sentence.

Mr. George is the person responsible for my going to college.

~~One aspect~~ ~~was~~

father helped me

~~a~~ ~~person~~

~~the person~~

Cross out any superfluous words you find in the following sentences. If a sentence has none, mark it C.

~~there were~~
~~who~~

☐ One authority estimated that there were eighty thousand workers in the area who were unemployed.

~~It was~~ ~~who~~
~~a~~ ~~thing~~

☐ It was Mr. Peters who convinced me that education was a necessary thing.

~~A factor~~ ~~was~~

☐ A factor he did not allow for was the waste resulting from the arrangement of the pattern on the material.

~~One person~~ ~~is~~

☐ One person I really don't care for is Ed.

FIFTEEN
COORDINATION; PARALLELISM; SUBORDINATION

FORMING COMPOUND SENTENCES

15A   *The huge jet rolled to a stop. The dignitaries descended into a mob of waiting reporters.*

The reporters had been waiting since midnight. General DeGaulle was due to arrive from Paris.

Decide which group of sentences would make a good compound sentence. Using the appropriate coordinating conjunction, join the sentences in a compound sentence.

_____

_____

The huge jet rolled to a stop, and the dignitaries descended into a mob of waiting reporters.

☐ Joining closely related sentences with a coordinating conjunction such as *and* or *but* helps to stress their relationship.

> *I liked her. She liked me.*
> *I liked her, and she liked me.*

The relationship between the consecutive ideas is stressed in the [first, second] _____ example.

second

284

□ A sentence in which two or more independent clauses are joined by a coordinating conjunction such as *and* or *but* is a compound sentence.

I liked her, and she liked me.

compound

This is an example of a _____ sentence.

□ Join the following closely related sentences in a compound sentence.

The weather cooled. The leaves began to fall.
The weather cooled, _____.

and the leaves began
to fall

□ Form a compound sentence from the following sentences, using *but* as the coordinating conjunction.

My left eye is perfect. My right eye requires correction.
My left eye is perfect, _____
_____.

but my right eye
requires correction

□ Use the appropriate coordinating conjunction, *and* or *but*, in the following compound sentences.

Hank agreed to help, _____ John refused.

but

The chairman took the vote, _____ the res-olution passed.

and

□ Sentences should be combined in a compound sentence only if they are closely related.

The waves were choppy. The wind was cold.
The waves were choppy. Lights flickered on the moored boats.

first

Only the [first, second] _____ group of senten-ces would make a good compound sentence.

first

☐ *The house is on a large lot. Its rooms are spacious.*
The house is on a large lot. The school is nearby.

Only the [first, second] _____ group of sentences would make a good compound sentence.

☐ *The abandoned car had a smashed fender. Two of its*
tires were flat.

The abandoned car had a smashed fender. The police
towed it away.

Form a compound sentence from the one group of sentences that is closely related.

and two of its tires
were flat

The abandoned car had a smashed fender, _____
_____.

Make a compound sentence of each of the following sentence groups which is closely related. Indicate which group
or groups would not make a good compound sentence.

Judy will be fifteen in
August, and Hank
will be eighteen in
November.

☐ *Judy will be fifteen in August. Hank will be eighteen in*
November.

_____

_____

I was quite anxious to
become a member
of the committee,
but the board refused
to accept my
candidacy.

☐ *I was quite anxious to become a member of the com-*
mittee. The board refused to accept my candidacy.

_____

_____

This group would not
make a good com-
pound sentence.

☐ *These lights were left on all day. Tomorrow, make sure*
that they are turned off promptly at 8 A.M.

_____

_____

15B *Four civilians were wounded during the rioting in Caracas. Two soldiers were also wounded.*

These sentences should be combined:

Four civilians _____

_____.

and two soldiers were wounded during the rioting in Caracas

□ We can often combine two sentences in one.

Harry went to a movie last night. Al went with him.
Harry and Al went to a movie last night.

The second, more economical expression of identical ideas [is, is not] _____ as clear as the first.

is

□ Two successive sentences with different subjects but similar predicates can often be combined in one sentence without loss of clarity.

The Ford is for sale. So is the Chevrolet.

The ideas expressed in these two sentences can easily be combined in one sentence.

The Ford _____ *are for sale.*

and the Chevrolet

□ *The Harrells live in Oceanside. The Randalls live in that same city.*

These sentences can be combined in one sentence having a compound subject.

The Harrells _____ *live in Oceanside.*

and the Randalls

□ *These letters can be mailed today. That package can be mailed too.*

Combine these sentences in one.

These letters _____

_____ .

and that package can be mailed today

□ Two sentences with subjects that refer to the same person or thing and with different predicates can often be combined in one sentence with a compound predicate.

Perkins called room service. He ordered a club sandwich.

Combine these sentences in one.

Perkins called room service _____ .

and ordered a club sandwich

□ *This television set has the usual front tuning devices. It has an additional fine tuner in back.*

These sentences can be made into one having a compound direct object.

This television set has the usual front tuning devices

_____ .

and an additional fine tuner in back

REVIEW

Form a single sentence from each of the following sentence groups.

□ *The Martins visited us yesterday. So did the Caldwells.*

_____

_____

The Martins and the Caldwells visited us yesterday.

The chemist added sulfuric acid carefully to the water and then poured the mixture into a large beaker.	☐ *The chemist added sulfuric acid carefully to the water. He then poured the mixture into a large beaker.* _____ _____
The new humanities building and the law school will be built during the years 1973-1974.	☐ *The new humanities building will be constructed during the years 1973-1974. The law school will be built during those years also.* _____ _____

MAINTAINING PARALLELISM

to allow ~~*allowing*~~	**15C** Strengthen the parellelism in this sentence by careful revision. *To maintain adequate security and at the same time allowing appropriate information to be made public are requirements which many governmental agencies have difficulty satisfying.*

☐ The coordinating conjunctions such as *and, but,* and *or* join words and word groups of equal importance.

Milk and cheese are considered dairy products.

This sentence has a compound subject composed of two nouns equally important, _____ and _____ .

Milk   cheese

☐ *He may go or stay.*

This sentence has a compound predicate composed of two verbs of equal importance, _____ and _____ .
They are joined by the coordinating conjunction _____ .

go   stay
 or

□ We often use compound elements in our sentences to express two or more closely related ideas of equal importance. Normally, parts of a compound sentence element have the same grammatical form.

Milk and cheese are considered dairy products.
He may go or stay.

The compound subject of the first sentence is composed of two [nouns, verbs] _____. The compound predicate of the second is composed of two _____.

nouns
verbs

□ Parts of a compound sentence element having the same grammatical form are said to be parallel.

Missing a train and losing a sure bet are distressing experiences.

The parts of the compound subject in this sentence, the participial phrases *Missing a train* and *losing a sure bet,* [are, are not] _____ parallel.

are

□ Maintaining parallelism—that is, using the same grammatical form in compound sentence elements—is not an exercise in decorative symmetry. Rather, it stresses the equality of the ideas expressed.

The child plays happily and with vigor.

Here two ideas of equal importance joined by *and* lack parallelism. One part is an adverb, _____; the other is a prepositional phrase, _____.

happily
with vigor

□ *The child plays happily and with vigor.*

Although some might think that calling this sentence incorrect is undue faultfinding, this sentence will be smoother and the relationship between the modifiers clearer if we use a one-word adverb in place of *with vigor:*

The child plays happily and _____ly.

vigorous

□ *Blond-haired and with blue eyes, Mary catches men's attention easily.*

Stressing the parallelism between the adjective and the prepositional phrase joined by *and* requires converting the phrase *with blue eyes* to a hyphenated modifier like *Blond-haired.*

eyed

Blonde-haired and blue-_____, Mary catches men's attention easily.

□ *His favorite recreations were making furniture and to sail his sloop.*

The breakdown in parallelism here is fairly obvious. *To sail* should be a gerund rather than an infinitive to be parallel to the gerund *making.*

sailing

His favorite recreations were making furniture and _____ his sloop.

□ *To be ready with a quip and having a fund of tall stories at hand were his secret ambitions.*

Correct the parallelism in this sentence.

to have

To be ready with a quip and _____ a fund of tall stories at hand were his secret ambitions.

□ The correlatives such as *either ... or, neither ... nor,* and *not only ... but also* join the parts of compound sentence elements.

Neither radio nor television provides the careful voter with adequate information.

Neither ... nor

Two nouns, *radio* and *television,* are joined by the correlative _____.

□ Parts joined by correlatives should be parallel.

Henry was not only a skilled physician but also ambitious.

Not only ... but also joins the noun *physician* to the adjective *ambitious.* By rearranging the sentence parts slightly, we can put the adjectives *skilled* and *ambitious* in parallel positions.

skilled but also ambitious

Henry was a physician not only _____
_____ .

□ *We spent those relaxed hours either strolling along the quiet streets or in the swimming pool.*

Strengthen the parallelism in this sentence.

We spent those relaxed hours either strolling along the quiet streets or _____.

swimming in the pool

□ *His leg is neither healing nor much worse.*

Neither ... nor in this sentence joins a verb, *healing,* and an adjective, *worse.* Adding an appropriate verb after *nor* will strengthen the parallelism:

becoming [*getting*]

His leg is neither healing nor _____ *much worse.*

15D Strengthen the parallelism in the following sentences.

Add *on* before *the low hills* in the first sentence Add *that* before *Mr. Harris* in the second.

Whether on the beach's gray sand cleared by the shifting tide or the low hills rolling eastward, the relics of D-Day are now few indeed.
We respectfully request that Mr. Gunther be granted full power of attorney and Mr. Harris be named executor.

292

□ Repeating a preposition in short parallel constructions is often unnecessary.

He is in the kitchen or [in] the basement.

Omitting the bracketed preposition *in* [would, would not] _____ make this sentence less clear.

would not

□ Repeating prepositions in longer parallel constructions stresses the parallelism and prevents misreading.

He is on the beach sunning himself or the pier fishing.

We can stress the parallelism between the two nouns joined by *or*, *beach* and *pier*, by repeating the preposition *on* after _____ .

or

□ *The government has made some effort to provide work for older people unemployed by technological advances and young people inadequately trained in the higher skills.*

The parallelism between the two parts of this sentence following *work* will be clearer if we repeat the preposition _____ after the word _____ .

for   and

□ Add the preposition necessary to strengthen the parallelism in this sentence.

Bach's complex musical structures are beyond the comprehension of the casual listener—and even that of some serious students of music.

Add *beyond* after *and* or *even*.

□ We often omit *whom*, *which*, and *that* introducing subordinate clauses in short parallel constructions.

This is a record that Ralph likes and [that] I abhor.

Omitting the bracketed *that* from this sentence [would, would not] _____ make it less clear.

would not

would

□ If parallel subordinate clauses are relatively long, it is wise to repeat *whom, which,* or *that* to introduce each clause.

> *This is the record that Ralph likes more than any of the others he owns and* [*that*] *I abhor.*

Here, repeating *that* following *and* [would, would not] _____ help show the parallelism between the two subordinate clauses.

which

and

□ *The truck which broke down yesterday and had been repaired several times was scrapped.*

To stress the parallelism between the two subordinate clauses in this sentence, we should repeat _____ after _____ .

whom

and

□ *This is the pilot whom you perhaps remember meeting in London and you flew back to New York with.*

To stress the parallelism between the subordinate clauses in this sentence, we should repeat _____ after _____ .

Add *that* after *and*.

□ Add the word necessary to stress the parallelism between the subordinate clauses in this sentence.

> *I suggest that the committee find a remedy for our lack of funds and John Nevins be appointed the committee chairman.*

□ Add the word necessary to stress the parallelism in this sentence.

Add *which* after *or*.

> *The persimmon trees which the harvesters injured with their trucks last autumn or the frost injured last winter will require special care.*

Strengthen the parallelism in the following sentences where necessary. Mark any sentence not requiring changes C.

digging
~~*to dig*~~

☐ The child seemed to prefer playing on the gym equipment and to dig in the sand pile.

unsuccessfully
~~*without success*~~

☐ In his efforts to make the varsity, John tried valiantly but without success.

Add *that* after *and.*

what
~~*the things*~~

☐ This is the route that is best in bad weather and takes you through less mountainous terrain.

☐ We are often known by what we say rather than the things we think.

SUBORDINATION

Because I had a flat tire, I was late.
or
I was late because I had a flat tire.

15E Revise the following sentence, logically subordinating one of its ideas.

I had a flat tire and I was late.

_____

☐ Although the coordinating conjunction *and* is useful in joining two or more closely related ideas, it is the most misused connective in our language.

We didn't water the lawn, and it dried up.
The lawn dried up because we didn't water it.

Of these two sentences, which express the same ideas, only the [first, second] _____ adequately expresses the relationship between the ideas.

second

295

□ *We didn't water the lawn, and it dried up.*
The lawn dried up because we didn't water it.

Comparing these examples shows the weakness of the first. We should never use the coordinating conjunction *and* carelessly as a substitute for the subordinating conjunction _____.

because

□ The relationship between ideas is often better expressed with a subordinating conjunction such as *because* than with a coordinating conjunction such as *and.*

The chair was weak, and the table had a broken top.
The chair was weak, and it collapsed.

The relationship between the ideas in one of these sentences would be clearer if expressed with *because:*

it collapsed

Because the chair was weak, _____.

□ The grammatical effect of a subordinating conjunction on a clause it introduces is that it makes the clause a dependent—a subordinate—unit.

Because the chair was weak, it collapsed.

Because

In this sentence the subordinating conjunction _____ subordinates its clause to the main clause, *it collapsed.*

□ Often the relationship between two or more ideas is clear only if one idea is subordinated.

She behaved rudely, and Pete didn't ask her out again.

This sentence contains a clause requiring subordination:

because she behaved rudely

Pete didn't ask her out again _____.

□ Normally, a cause-and-effect relationship is clearer if the statement of the cause is subordinated to the statement of its effect. *Because* and *since* are the subordinating conjunctions we use for this.

The workman failed to fasten his safety belt, and he fell.

Subordinate the idea of cause in this sentence, using *since*.

_____ ,

he fell.

Since the workman failed to fasten his safety belt

□ *We made two calls to New Orleans, and our phone bill was unusually high.*

Rewrite this sentence, logically subordinating one idea to the other.

_____

_____

Since [Because] we made two calls to New Orleans, our phone bill was unusually high.
or
Our phone bill was unusually high because we made two calls to New Orleans.

15F Rewrite the following sentence, logically subordinating one idea to the other.

Either the painters finish within a week, I told him, or we can't move in on time.

_____

_____

Unless the painters finish within a week, I told him, we can't move in on time.

□ Two kinds of statements often linked together are a conditional statement and a statement of its consequences.

If he helps, we'll finish early.

The statement of the consequences, *we'll finish early*, is qualified by a conditional statement, _____ .

If he helps

□ Making a conditional statement an independent clause in a compound sentence is often unsatisfactory.

> *You hit me, and I'll hit you.*
> *If you hit me, I'll hit you.*

These examples show that the relationship between the condition and its consequence is clearer if the condition is expressed as a subordinate clause introduced by _____.

If

□ Normally, a condition should be subordinated to the consequence, using *if* or *unless*.

> *You get that bridge straightened, or you'll have trouble with the rest of your teeth.*

Unless you get that bridge straightened

Subordination will improve this sentence:

_____,

you'll have trouble with the rest of your teeth.

□ *You work tonight, and I'll examine your progress later. You work tonight, and you'll be paid overtime.*

The first part of one of these sentences is a condition that should be subordinated:

you'll be paid over time

If you work tonight, _____.

□ *Either the Senate passes the bill by November, or the House of Representatives will not be able to discuss it this term.*

Unless the Senate passes the bill by November, the House of Representatives will not be able to discuss it this term.

Subordinate the idea of condition in this sentence.

_____

_____

298

15G Rewrite the following sentence, logically subordinating one idea to the other.

> Mr. Jenkins has spent over $500 on repairs, but his car still gives him trouble.

_____

_____

Although [Though] Mr. Jenkins has spent over $500 on repairs, his car still gives him trouble.

□ We sometimes find it necessary to add to a statement some qualifying statement conceding that an opposite or contrary fact is true to some extent.

> *Although he plays well, he is no All-American.*

Although he plays well

The statement *he is no All-American* is linked to a statement of concession, _____.

□ Using the overworked coordinating conjunction *but* to join a concession to the statement it qualifies often results in a weak sentence.

> *Speed can kill, but poor driving is the greatest single cause of traffic fatalities.*
> *Although speed can kill, poor driving is the greatest single cause of traffic fatalities.*

These illustrations show that the concession—speed's ability to kill—is more forcefully expressed as a subordinate clause introduced by the subordinating conjunction

Although

_____.

□ Whenever expressing a concession related to a contrary statement, we should remember that subordination is the most forceful way.

> *This car is cheaper, but that one is a better value.*

Subordinate the concession expressed in this sentence, using *although.*

Although this car is cheaper

_____, *that one is a better value.*

299

□ *Although*, the basic subordinating conjunction of concession, has close synonyms we often use in its place: *though*, *while*, and *whereas*.

Some thought that Mr. Rogers was a poor choice, but many favored his appointment.

Subordinate the idea of concession in this sentence, using *while*.

While some thought that Mr. Rogers was a poor choice

_____ ,

many favored his appointment.

□ *Bob is good in math, but he has a poor grasp of science.*

Subordinate the idea of concession, using *though*.

Though Bob is good in math

_____ , *he has a poor grasp of science.*

15H Rewrite the following sentence, stressing by subordination the time relationship between the two events.

A child has to develop his leg muscles, and then he can learn to walk.

_____

_____

A child has to develop his leg muscles before he can learn to walk.

□ Using *and* to stitch together ideas which are related in time often produces sentences which are crudely inexact.

I was running for the bus, and he tried to stop me.
While I was running for the bus, he tried to stop me.

These examples show that the time relationship of the two events [is, is not] _____ expressed more clearly in the second example.

is

□ The expression of two events related in time is usually clearer if one event is expressed as a subordinate clause.

He had finished his work, and he called me.

This sentence will be clearer if the first event is expressed in a subordinate clause.

After _____, he called me.

he had finished his work

□ English has a variety of subordinating conjunctions useful in expressing time relationships: *before, when, while, as, after, since,* and *until.* Normally we should use one of these to link our expressions of events related in time and thus avoid the clumsiness resulting from the use of *and.*

We waited, and the motor finally died.

Rewrite this sentence, using *until* as the subordinating conjunction.

We waited _____.

until the motor finally died

□ *The pilot learned that his fuel was low, and he tried to land immediately.*

Rewrite this sentence, using *when.*

_____

_____

When the pilot learned that his fuel was low, he *tried to land immediately.*

□ *The car turned into the steep street, and it skidded.*

Rewrite this sentence, using *as.*

_____

_____

As the car turned into the steep street, it skidded.

□ *The electrician found that he had to clean the wires, and then he could join them.*

Rewrite this sentence, subordinating the second part.

The electrician found that he had to clean the wires

_____.

before he could join them

301

151 Rewrite these sentences as one, stressing by subordination Mr. Ellis' presidency.

Mr. Ellis is the president of our cooperative. He owns four acres of lemon trees.

_____

_____

Mr. Ellis, who owns four acres of lemon trees, is the president of our cooperative.

□ The relative pronouns and adjectives, *who, whose, whom, which,* and *that,* are useful in combining closely related ideas which would be crudely expressed as independent clauses or sentences.

> *Charlie is my cousin. He lives with us.*
> *Charlie, who lives with us, is my cousin.*

The relationship between the ideas here is better expressed in the [first, second] _____ example.

second

□ *Charlie is my cousin. He lives with us.*
Charlie, who lives with us, is my cousin.

By substituting *who* for *He,* the second sentence in the first example becomes an adjective clause modifying the noun _____.

Charlie

□ *The sewage plant cost $500,000. It serves Elk County.*

By substituting *which* for *It,* we can use the second sentence as an adjective clause modifying plant:

The sewage plant _____ cost $500,000.

which serves Elk County

□ *Marge has an attractive brother. Liz dates him regularly.*

We can make the second sentence into an adjective clause modifying *brother.*

Marge has an attractive brother whom _____
_____.

Liz dates regularly

302

□ *Lee Construction won the road improvement contract.*
It will soon be the largest firm of its kind in the state.

The second sentence can serve as an adjective clause in the first:

which will soon be

Lee Construction, _____ the
largest firm of its kind in the state, won the road improve-
ment contract.

□ *Elliot McGill has become General Sales Manager. He*
had been the West Coast representative.

Combine these sentences in one, making the second an adjective clause.

who had been the
West Coast rep-
resentative, has
become General
Sales Manager

Elliot McGill, _____
_____

□ When we subordinate with an adjective clause, we should express the more important idea as the main clause, the less important as the subordinate clause.

The camping trailer which sleeps three costs $1,200.
The camping trailer which costs $1,200 sleeps three.

The more important idea in the first sentence is the [cost, size] _____ of the trailer. The more important idea in the second is its _____.

cost
size

□ *Burns worked here three years. He was fired yesterday.*

Join these sentences in one, stressing the firing.

who worked here
three years, was fired
yesterday

Burns, _____.

□ *Burns worked here three years. He was fired yesterday.*

Now join these sentences in a way that stresses the length of employment.

who was fired yester-
day, worked here
three years

Burns, _____.

□ *The medical building is ten stories tall. It has fifty offices.*

Join these sentences in a way that stresses the height of the building.

The medical building, _____

_____.

which has fifty offices, is ten stories tall

□ *Mack had worked with me in Hawaii. He visited us last week.*

Join these sentences in a way that stresses the visit.

Mack, _____

_____.

who had worked with me in Hawaii, visited us last week

REVIEW

Rewrite the following sentences, logically subordinating one idea to the other in each.

Unless you pay your bill by next Tuesday, we will turn the matter over to our lawyers.

□ *Either you pay your bill by next Tuesday or we will turn the matter over to our lawyers.*

_____

_____

Because [Since] the tanks on gasoline trucks are vented, they cannot explode.

□ *The tanks on gasoline trucks are vented, and they cannot explode.*

_____

_____

304

| Ralph Jones, who worked for me last year, is now working in the engineering department.

 or

 Ralph Jones, who is now working in the engineering department, worked for me last year. | ☐ Ralph Jones worked for me last year; he is now working in the engineering department.

 _____
 _____ |
| Although [Though, While] Pete began mowing the lawn at 9 A.M., he is not finished yet. | ☐ Pete began mowing the lawn at 9 A.M., but he is not finished yet.

 _____
 _____ |

SIXTEEN
END PUNCTUATION

USING PERIODS, QUESTION MARKS, AND
EXCLAMATION MARKS

16A Add the punctuation necessary to complete the following quotations of the kind indicated.

(a) "1316 14th St." (a) [Statement] "1316 14th St "

(b) "1316 14th St.**?**" (b) [Question] "1316 14th St "

(c) "1316 14th St.**!**" (c) [Exclamation] "1316 14th St "

☐ We end our sentences with one of three punctuation marks:
a period (.), a question mark(**?**), or an exclamation mark (!).
A period marks the close of a statement. Punctuate this
sentence.

*fights***.**   *He went to the fights*

☐ *He went to the fights.*

This sentence could be a question in certain circumstances.
If it were, we would use a question mark:

*fights***?**   *He went to the fights*

□   *He went to the fights?*

In still different circumstances this sentence could be an exclamation—of a speaker's outrage, for instance. It would then require an exclamation mark:

fights!

    He went to the fights

□ Normally, question and exclamation marks are used only at the ends of sentences. Periods, however, are used also to indicate an abbreviation—*Dr.* (Doctor), *Mr.* (Mister), *Ave.* (Avenue). Punctuate this sentence.

Dr.   Mrs.   party.

    Dr and Mrs Bell will attend the party

□ If an abbreviation comes at the end of a sentence requiring a period, one period will serve to indicate the abbreviation and to end the sentence:

St.

    He lives on Blair St

□ If an abbreviation comes at the end of a sentence requiring a question mark or an exclamation mark, we must use a period to indicate the abbreviation. Complete the punctuation of this sentence.

St.?

    He lives on Blair St ?

□ Add the necessary punctuation to the following sentences.

(a) Main St.?
(b) Main St.

    (a)   *Can you deliver this to the address on Main St*
    (b)   *I already delivered it to that address on Main St*

16B   *"What a wonderful party"*

It was a wonderful party

Normally, an exclamation mark will end [the first, both]

the first

_____ sentence(s).

□ The normal use of the exclamation mark is to show that a speaker's voice is unusually loud. For instance, we punctuate a shout with an exclamation mark:

"Hey!"

    "Hey "

□ An exclamation mark is useful in direct quotations to indicate that a speaker has shouted or spoken loudly. Complete the punctuation of this sentence.

"Ouch!"

    "Ouch " he said.

□ In writing, we cannot shout at our readers. Forceful expression in prose is a matter of word choice and word order rather than voice level.

□   *These are the times that try men's souls.*
    Wow, these are really rough times.

will not

Closing the second sentence with an exclamation mark [will, will not] _____ make it as forceful as the first.

□   *These are the times that try men's souls.*
    Wow, these are really rough times.

exclamation

The first sentence, written by Thomas Paine, is vigorous without an exclamation mark. The second sentence, in contrast, is feeble even though ended with an _____ mark.

□ Just as shouting will not make an argument more convincing, ending a statement with an exclamation mark will not make it more vigorous. As a general rule, we should reserve the exclamation mark for direct quotations of shouted words or sentences.

    "Look at that car"
    The car we saw was painted shocking pink

first

Ordinarily we would end only the [first, second] _____ sentence with an exclamation mark.

Add the necessary punctuation to the following sentences.

Dr. Mrs. party.

☐ *Dr and Mrs Rogers will attend the party*

"Ouch!"

☐ *"Ouch "*

10th St.?"

☐ *"Does he live on 10th St "*

AVOIDING SENTENCE FRAGMENTS

16C Correct this example.

We decided that both of the girls had swelled heads. And that, if they didn't improve their attitude, we would ignore them.

swelled heads and that, if

☐ One of the most confusing experiences in reading the prose of careless writers is to find part of a sentence after the period or question mark which signals the sentence's close.

She left. And returned later with Harry.

Since in reading this we would ignore the period after *left*, it should be written without it:

She left and

_____ *returned later with Harry.*

☐ Parts of sentences cut off from the sentences to which they belong are called sentence fragments.

He said he would try. A little harder.

is

A little harder [is, is not] _____ a sentence fragment.

□ *He said he would try. A little harder.*

Since the sentence fragment *A little harder* belongs to the sentence preceding it, we should not separate it from that sentence with a period:

try a little harder

He said he would _____.

□ Normally, we punctuate a word group as a sentence only if it has a subject and a predicate.

He came alone.
And came alone.

first

He

Although both of these word groups have a predicate, *came alone,* only the [first, second] _____ has a subject, the pronoun _____.

□ *And came alone.*

Seeing this sentence fragment, we can guess that it is part of a compound predicate cut off erroneously from a preceding sentence.

He left Helen downtown. And came alone.

The fragment should be joined to the sentence:

and came alone

He left Helen downtown _____.

□ We should make sure that all the parts of a compound predicate are included in the sentence.

The plane landed. The passengers got off.
The plane landed. And taxied to the terminal.

second

The second part of a compound predicate is cut off from its sentence in the [first, second] _____ example.

□ *The plane landed. And taxied to the terminal.*

The detached part of the compound predicate should be joined to the sentence.

landed and taxied
to the terminal

The plane _____.

310

□ *Hank waxed his skis, Bob weatherproofed his boots.*
Hank waxed his skis. And weatherproofed his boots.

Make a single sentence of the group having a part of its compound predicate detached.

and weatherproofed his boots

Hank waxed his skis _____.

□ We should be careful not to detach part of a compound direct object or subjective complement from the sentence to which it belongs.

Pigs make poor pets. And worse roommates.

Both *pets* and *roommates* are complements of the verb *make*. The fragment should be joined to the sentence:

poor pets and worse roommates

Pigs make _____.

□ *Mrs. Sims lost her purse. And her hat.*

Rewrite this sentence correctly.

purse and her hat

Mrs. Sims lost her _____.

□ Sentence fragments are often modifying phrases which have been erroneously detached from their sentences.

He left his camera. At the beach.

The modifying phrase *At the beach* [should, should not] _____ be detached.

should not

□ *Jones slipped and fell. Trying to reach the top shelf.*

The participial phrase *Trying to reach the top shelf* is a modifier belonging to the sentence it follows:

fell trying to reach the top shelf

Jones slipped and _____.

□ A subordinate clause, because it has a subject and a predicate, may seem to have a claim to independence that a phrase does not have.

If I were there.

Although this clause has a subject, *I*, and a predicate, *were there*, it [is, is not] _____ a complete expression by itself.

is not

□ *I could help. If I were there.*

Since the clause *If I were there* does not make sense except with the sentence it follows, it should be part of that sentence:

I could help _____.

if I were there

□ We should be sure that a clause beginning with a subordinating conjunction or a relative pronoun is not detached from the sentence to which it belongs.

Here is the watch. Which I bought yesterday.

The second clause, having a subject and predicate of its own, [is, is not] _____ independent in meaning from the sentence it follows.

is not

□ *We are to deliver the piano. Which one did the customer buy?*
We are to deliver the piano. Which the customer bought.

One of these examples has a detached subordinate clause. Join it to the sentence.

We are to deliver the piano _____.

which the customer bought

□ *I didn't care for the book. Because you asked for it, you can have it.*
I didn't care for the book. Because the illustrations are so poorly drawn.

Join the sentence fragment to its sentence.

I didn't care for the book because _____.

the illustrations are so poorly drawn

312

☐ *The driver veered sharply. When he saw the stalled truck ahead.*

The driver veered sharply. When he put on his brakes, he skidded.

he saw the stalled truck ahead

Join the sentence fragment to its sentence.

The driver veered sharply when _____.

Rewrite correctly the following sentence groups which contain fragments. Mark correct groups C.

☐ *I saw him quite clearly. Standing in the darkness by the door.*

I saw him quite clearly standing in the darkness by the door.

_____

_____

☐ *The President was forthright in stating his position. On the question of atomic weapon control, he was particularly direct.*

C

_____

_____

The child removed his shoes and without warning threw them into the pool.

☐ *The child removed his shoes. And without warning threw them into the pool.*

_____

_____

After the speech one person stood and asked a question which was gauged to embarrass the speaker.

☐ *After the speech one person stood and asked a question. Which was gauged to embarrass the speaker.*

_____

_____

SEVENTEEN

COMMAS AND SEMICOLONS WITH COMPOUND ELEMENTS

USING COMMAS AND SEMICOLONS IN COMPOUND SENTENCES

17A Add any necessary punctuation to the following sentences.

(a) labeled; his

    (a) *His grips were packed and labeled his passport was in order.*

(b) labeled, and

    (b) *His grips were packed and labeled and his passport was in order.*

□ A semicolon (;) or a comma (,) signals the division between independent clauses in a compound sentence. If the clauses are joined by a coordinating conjunction, a comma is the normal signal.

The clerk rang up the sale, and his helper packed the groceries.

and

Since the two independent clauses are joined by the coordinating conjunction _____, a comma signals the division between them.

314

□ If independent clauses are not joined by a coordinating conjunction, a semicolon normally signals the division between them. Punctuate this sentence.

sale; *his*

> *The clerk rang up the sale his helper packed the groceries.*

□ Punctuate these sentences.

(a) paint, and

(a) The bedroom requires five quarts of paint and the bathroom requires two.

(b) soil; Ed

(b) Kelley turned over the soil Ed planted the bulbs.

□ Correct the punctuation in these sentences if it is incorrect.

(a) house; its

(a) Four old oak trees screened the house, its roof was scarcely visible from the street.

(b) Jane may carry the flowers, or she may give them to the maid of honor if she wishes.

□ Add the necessary punctuation to the following sentences.

(a) loud, and the

(a) The conversation was unbearably loud and the laughter was boisterous.

(b) well-dressed; they

(b) The guests were well-dressed they all seemed in a party mood.

17B If necessary, correct the punctuation in the following sentences.

(a) November; nevertheless,

(a) The house was not quite finished by November, nevertheless, we moved in.

(b) The kitchen was bare and the bedrooms were unpainted.

(c) strenuously; and

(c) Bob dashed to the front door, laughing and panting strenuously, and Harry, unable to keep up, followed a distance behind.

□ If the clauses joined by a coordinating conjunction in a compound sentence are relatively short and have only a single subject and predicate, a comma marking their division is unnecessary.

The wind blew and the waves crashed.

would not

A comma before *and* [would, would not] _____ be necessary.

□ Only if clauses are relatively short and only if each has a single subject and predicate should we omit the comma dividing them.

He left early, and I followed him.

is not

Although helpful to the reader, the comma in this sentence [is, is not] _____ necessary.

□ Add any necessary punctuation to the following sentences.

(a) *Rita and Paul,*

    (a) *Carl invited Rita and Paul and I invited myself.*
    (b) *Carl invited Rita and I invited myself.*

□ Independent clauses in compound sentences are often joined by conjunctive adverbs: *however, moreover, nevertheless, consequently,* and the like.

I won't go today; moreover, I'll never go with him.

moreover

The relationship between the independent clauses in this sentence is expressed by the conjunctive adverb _____.

□ Conjunctive adverbs are different from coordinating conjunctions. As its name indicates, a conjunctive adverb is a modifier as well as a connective; and like other adverbs it can appear in several positions within its clause.

The girl wouldn't tell me her name; nevertheless, she did / give me her phone number / .

can

Nevertheless [can, cannot] _____ appear in the other positions marked by the slanted lines.

316

□ Unlike a conjunctive adverb, a coordinating conjunction cannot appear in other positions but only at the division between clauses.

The girl wouldn't give her name, but she did / give her phone number / .

cannot

The coordinating conjunction *but* [can, cannot] _____ be moved to the positions marked by the slanted lines.

□ A conjunctive adverb's mobility within its own clause distinguishes it from a coordinating conjunction. It belongs to one clause within a compound sentence, not both, and to show this we use a semicolon rather than a comma preceding it.

He was outraged; however, he calmed down later.

is not

Substituting a comma for the semicolon in this sentence [is, is not] _____ possible.

□ *And, but, or, for,* and *yet* are coordinating conjunctions. *However, moreover, nevertheless,* and *consequently* are conjunctive adverbs. Punctuate these sentences.

(a) *times*; *never-theless*
(b) *repairs*, *but*

    (a)   *The motor stalled three times nevertheless, we were able to get home.*
    (b)   *The motor was due for major repairs but we delayed them because of the expense.*

□ If necessary, correct the punctuation in these sentences.

(a) *days*; *never-theless*

    (a)   *We invited him to stay for three days, nevertheless, he stayed for eight.*
    (b)   *We invited him to stay for three days, but he stayed for eight.*

□ Of course if we use a coordinating conjunction with a conjunctive adverb, a comma is adequate.

*The weatherman predicted rain for Wednesday, and con-
sequently the skies cleared by noon.*

should not

Since the conjunctive adverb *consequently* is preceded by
the coordinating conjunction *and*, the comma in this sentence [should, should not] _____ be changed
to a semicolon.

□ Add the necessary punctuation to these sentences.

(a) weeks, but

(a)   *I hadn't studied for three weeks but nevertheless
I took the test.*

*(b) carefully;
however*

(b)   *The trees were planted carefully however, three of
them failed to take root.*

□ If clauses joined by a coordinating conjunction have other
commas, it is a good practice to mark the division between
them with a semicolon rather than a comma.

*If this paint remover works, I won't regret paying that
much for it, but if it doesn't, I'll demand my money back.*

but

It would be helpful to substitute a semicolon for the comma
preceding _____.

□ A comma dividing clauses which have other commas is
easily overlooked.   A semicolon will help the reader find
the division between the clauses more readily. Correct the
punctuation in this sentence.

be late; and

*Unless you're ready, we'll be late, and if we're one minute
late, we won't get in the door.*

□ Correct the punctuation where necessary in these sentences.

(a) it; but

(a)   *If you recommend it, I'll buy it, but even so, I won't
promise to like it.*

(b)   *Along the lakefront is a low range of hills, and behind
that the Blue Ridge is distantly visible.*

17C If necessary, correct the punctuation in this sentence.

Dr. Bronson examined Mr. Burns carefully, and after-wards recommended a long rest.

☐ Coordinating conjunctions are used to join compound sentence elements as well as independent clauses in compound sentences.

She cut the vegetables and cooked the stew.

This is not a compound sentence but a sentence with a compound predicate. Its parts, *cut the vegetables* and *cooked the stew*, are joined by a coordinating conjunction,

and

_____.

☐ The division between two parts of a compound sentence element is not punctuated with a comma or a semicolon.

Both his backstroke and his crawl needed improvement.

A comma before *and* in this sentence would be [correct, incorrect] _____ because it joins parts of a compound subject.

incorrect

☐ Before placing a comma before *and*, we should make sure that it joins independent clauses in a compound sentence and not compound sentence elements.

He took his football and went home.
He took his football and the team went home.

A comma before *and* would be incorrect in the [first, second] _____ sentence because it joins the parts of a compound predicate.

first

☐ Add any necessary punctuation to these sentences.

(a) *We take Math 1 this semester and Solid Geometry the next.*

(b) *Our gym class meets on Tuesdays and Thursdays and on Thursdays we swim.*

(b) Thursdays, and on Thursdays

□ Add any necessary punctuation to these sentences.

(a) *He felt that trying hard didn't pay off and simply quit.*

(b) can, but

(b) *He thought he had tried as hard as a person can but he could have tried harder.*

Change or add punctuation where necessary in the following sentences. Mark sentences correctly punctuated C.

C

□ *She is here and he is there.*

properly;
consequently

□ *He didn't undercoat the wood properly, consequently, the paint began flaking off after three months' exposure.*

blocker; and

□ *Roberts is, on the whole, a fine passer and blocker and he runs as well on option plays as any other quarterback in the league.*

The comma after *oil* should be omitted.

□ *He added a friction-proofing compound to the oil, and made it a habit to change the oil every 1,000 miles.*

numerous, and

□ *The tales of woe he had to tell were numerous and, therefore, people tended to avoid him.*

PUNCTUATING COORDINATE SENTENCE ELEMENTS

17D Add the necessary punctuation to this sentence.

valley, climbed
hill, and

We hiked across the valley climbed the steep hill and descended to the town.

320

□ Three or more words, phrases, or clauses joined in a sentence comprise a series.

Paine lettered in football and basketball.
Paine lettered in track, gymnastics, and swimming.

the second

A series of nouns is illustrated by [the second, both] _____ sentence (s).

□ A series, although composed of three or more separate parts, normally has only one coordinating conjunction. A comma replaces conjunctions between the remaining parts of the series.

We grow apples and oranges and pears.

Only in exceptional cases would we find the *and* after *apples* expressed as it is here. A comma usually replaces it:

,oranges and pears

We grow apples _____.

□ *We grow apples, oranges and pears.*

Although this sentence is now adequately punctuated, most writers prefer to place another comma before *and* in sentences such as this to stress the division of the series' parts:

,and pears

We grow apples, oranges _____.

□ Punctuate this sentence, using a comma before the coordinating conjunction.

Babylon, Egypt, and

These lectures will deal with the ancient civilizations of Babylon Egypt and India.

□ A sentence may contain a series composed of three or more phrases.

We found him dashing around in circles waving his arms and shouting wildly.

three

This sentence has a series composed of [three, four] _____ participial phrases.

□ Phrases in series are punctuated in the same way that words in series are. Punctuate this sentence.

circles, waving arms, and

> *We found him dashing around in circles waving his arms and shouting wildly.*

□ Subordinate clauses as well may be joined in series of three or more. Punctuate this sentence.

been, what doing, and

> *Mr. Blake asked Bob where he had been what he had been doing and why he was late.*

□ If a compound sentence has three or more short independent clauses, we can punctuate them as a series:

door, Al door, and

> *I tried the front door Al tried the back door and Harry tried the window.*

□ If three or more independent clauses in a compound sentence are long and have commas within them, use semicolons to mark the divisions between them. Correct the punctuation in this sentence.

good; the better; and

> *On the whole, this paper is good, the next, I hope, will be better, and the one after that will rate an A.*

□ Correct the punctuation in these sentences where necessary.

(a) order; the note; and

> (a) *The meeting was called to order, the chairman, Mr. Hockins, read a brief note, and the meeting adjourned.*
>
> (b) *The secretary typed the letter, Mr. Hockins signed it, and the mail clerk delivered it that day.*

□ A series of long subordinate clauses with other punctuation marks should be separated by semicolons rather than commas so that the divisions between the parts of the series are clear. Correct the punctuation in this sentence.

office; that draft; and

> *Burke informed the newsman that he would not run for office, that he would not submit to a draft, and that, in addition, he intended to retire from public office entirely.*

□ Correct the punctuation in these sentences where necessary.

(a) He saw that she resented the question, that she was unhappy, and that she might cry.

(b) crime; that citizen; and

(b) The lawyer told the jury that this was the accused person's first crime, that he had, in fact, been a model citizen, and that he would, if freed, continue to be one.

17E Add any necessary punctuation to this sentence.

small, well-kept

Our family moved to a small well-kept house in a large northern industrial city.

□ We often use two or more adjectives to modify the same noun.

He makes large portable signs.

signs

The adjectives *large* and *portable* modify the noun _____.

□ *He makes large portable signs.*

However, it is not precisely true that both *large* and *portable* modify *signs* in the same way. If this were true, we could reverse the positions of the two adjectives without altering the sense.

He makes portable large signs.

does not

This sentence [does, does not] _____ have the same sense as the previous one.

☐ *He makes large portable signs.*

That the adjectives *large* and *portable* cannot be reversed shows that the adjective *large* modifies the adjective and noun following it, *portable signs*, and that *portable* modifies the noun *signs* alone.

This machine stamps out clear plastic containers.

plastic containers
containers

In this sentence the adjective *clear* modifies the adjective and noun following it, _____; *plastic* modifies the noun _____ alone.

☐ In modifying nouns, we often build up such levels of adjectives, each modifying everything ahead of it.

Small bright green particles covered the table.

bright green particles
green particles
particles

Small modifies _____; *bright* modifies _____; and *green* modifies _____.

☐ Occasionally, however, two or more adjectives we use are not on separate levels of modification. We know this because we can reverse their positions without changing the sense conveyed.

Handsome, successful men attract women.

does not

Reversing the position of the adjectives modifying *men*, *Handsome* and *successful*, [does, does not] _____ destroy the sense conveyed.

☐ *Handsome, successful men attract women.*

The sign of reversible adjectives is the comma that separates them. This comma takes the place of *and*, which can be substituted for it.

Handsome and successful men attract women.

does not

Replacing the comma in the previous sentence with *and* [does, does not] _____ change the sense.

324

□ Adjectives which can be reversed in position are called coordinate adjectives, or adjectives of equal rank.

Handsome, successful men attract women.

Handsome and *successful*, then, are _____ adjectives.

coordinate

□ If we do not express the *and* between coordinate adjectives, we should separate them with a comma.

Hernshaw was an able willing employee.

There should be either an *and* or a comma between the two coordinate adjectives in this sentence, _____ and _____.

able
willing

□ By far the best way to determine whether a comma goes between two adjectives is to try reversing their positions. If this is possible, they are coordinate adjectives and should be separated by a comma—or *and*, if the writer prefers.

A gentle chilly rain greeted us.

The adjectives *gentle* and *chilly* [should, should not] _____ be separated by a comma.

should

□ Remember that adjectives which cannot be reversed in position are not coordinate and are not separated by commas. Add any necessary comma to these sentences.

    (a) *In the bowl were four beautiful bright green eating apples.*
    (b) *A frowning muscular guard blocked our path.*

(b) frowning,
muscular

□ Add any necessary comma to this sentence.

We shuddered as the greasy unkempt mechanic slid behind the wheel of our brand new hardtop convertible.

greasy, unkempt

325

Change or add punctuation where necessary in the following sentences. Mark sentences correctly punctuated C.

The comma after *small* should be omitted.

☐ A rather small, metallic object caused extensive damage to the computer's storage system.

dollars; that additions
dollars; and that

☐ The report stated that reserve capital was at a new high, two million dollars, that additions to buildings and equipment cost two hundred thousand dollars, and that a new subassembly factory was planned for immediate construction.

vigorous, aggressive

☐ Haskins is a vigorous aggressive sales director.

dressing, Sue
cake, and

☐ Carol mixed the salad dressing Sue baked the cake and Dad poured the punch.

PUNCTUATING DATES AND ADDRESSES

(a) *Sunday, December 7, 1941, Japanese*
(b) *William Burke, 1517 Bay St., San Diego, California, immediately*

17F Add any necessary punctuation to the following sentences.

(a) On Sunday December 7 1941 Japanese carrier planes bombed Pearl Harbor.
(b) Please send your reply to William Burke 1517 Bay St. San Diego California immediately.

□ Punctuating dates is simply a matter of separating the parts with commas and closing the final part with a comma if it is not the final item in the sentence.

On Tuesday, May 1, 1960, she returned to this country.

This sentence is correctly punctuated. The three parts—day, date of month, and year—are separated by commas; and a final comma [does, does not] _____ indicate the close of the series.

does

□ Add the necessary punctuation to this sentence.

Saturday, August 14,
1864, the

On Saturday August 14 1864 the Grant Hotel burned to the ground.

□ We follow the same basic principle when only two of the three parts of a date are expressed:

March 14, 1963, this

After March 14 1963 this store will be closed.

□ If only one part of a date is expressed, it does not require punctuation.

I leave on June 11 for Madrid.

would not

A comma [would, would not] _____ be correct after *June 11*.

□ Add any necessary commas to these sentences.

(a) Monday, August
7, I

(a) *On Monday August 7 I go to work.*

(b) July 4, 1914, his

(b) *Until July 4 1914 his grandfather lived in Syracuse.*

□ Add any necessary commas to these sentences.
(a) *We moved in 1954 to Omaha.*

(b) Friday, January
24, 1946, my

(b) *On Firday January 24 1946 my brother Harry was born.*

□ We use the same principles in punctuating addresses that we use in punctuating dates. An address may have as many as five parts—name, street address, city, state, and country. Add the necessary punctuation to this sentence.

Ship this order to Ralph Paul 3411 Hazel St. Vancouver British Columbia Canada as soon as possible.

□ If only one part of an address is given, it does not require special punctuation.

We lived on Western Avenue until the war.

This sentence [does, does not] _____ require commas.

□ Two or more parts of an address require the same punctuation as two or more parts of a date. Add the necessary commas to this sentence.

He came all the way from Clint Texas this fall.

□ Add any necessary commas to the following sentences.

(a) *This letter is to be sent to Russel Arne 73 Novato Way Elko Nevada immediately.*

(b) *Colorado is the right state, and 1163 is the right street number.*

Add punctuation where necessary in the following sentences. Mark correct sentences C.

Fresno, California, this

☐ *The convention is to be held in Fresno California this year.*

Sunday, August 20, 1862, a

☐ *On Sunday August 20 1862 a platoon of Confederate cavalry raided this town.*

C

☐ *I returned in 1959 from the Eniwetok Proving Grounds to San Francisco.*

June, 1959, we
Syracuse, New York,
to Hollister, California

☐ *In June 1959 we moved from Syracuse New York to Hollister California.*

EIGHTEEN

COMMAS WITH SUBORDINATE ELEMENTS

PUNCTUATING ADVERB CLAUSES

18A Add any necessary punctuation to these sentences.

(a) *We cannot ship your order until the factory supplies us with the model you requested.*

(b) requested, we

(b) *Until the factory supplies us with the model you requested we cannot ship your order.*

☐ As a general rule, adverb clauses —those introduced by subordinating conjunctions such as *if, while,* and *until*— are not separated from the main clause by a comma if they follow the main clause.

I'll go when you go.

A comma would be incorrect before *when* because the adverb clause *when you go* [precedes, follows] _____ the main clause *I'll go.*

follows

□ If an adverb clause comes before the main clause, we separate the two clauses with a comma. Punctuate this sentence.

go, I'll

> *When you go I'll go.*

□ Add a comma where needed.

(a) repaired, we

> (a) *Until the refrigerator is repaired we cannot store frozen food.*
> (b) *We cannot store frozen foods until the refrigerator is repaired.*

□ Punctuate these sentences.

> (a) *You have a good memory if you can remember that.*

(b) that, you

> (b) *If you can remember that you have a good memory.*

□ Many writers prefer not to use a comma to separate from the main clause an adverb clause introducing a sentence if the separation between the clauses is clear without it.

> *Until the refrigerator is repaired, we cannot store frozen foods.*

Because the division between the introductory clause and the main clause is clear, the comma in this sentence [is,

is not

is not] _____ necessary.

□ However, omitting the comma following an introductory adverb clause may cause trouble.

> *While Tom was fighting Harry and Bob were running away.*

We have to read this sentence at least twice to make sense of it. A comma signaling the end of the subordinate clause

fighting

—that is, after the verb _____—will make misreading impossible.

□ If you wish to omit the comma after introductory adverb clauses, be sure that the omission will not cause a reader difficulty.

> *Until he had returned the package remained on the table.*
> *Until he called for it the package remained on the table.*

A comma following the introductory adverb clause is optional in the [first, second] _____ sentence. It is necessary in the _____ sentence.

second
first

□ Add any comma necessary in the following sentences.

(a) appointed, the

(a) *When I am appointed the company representative will get my help.*

(b) discharged, the

(b) *When the gun discharged the remaining bullet struck the floor.*

□ It is always possible that our reader will have to hunt for the end of an introductory adverb clause. Perhaps the best practice is to use a comma at the end of all such clauses. Punctuate these sentences accordingly.

(a) lies, we

(a) *If we forget where our duty lies we are faithless to ourselves.*

(b) certain, some

(b) *Since we cannot always be certain some say we learn nothing.*

18B Add any necessary punctuation to the following sentences.

(a) man, although

(a) *We feel that he is the best man although we cannot be sure.*

(b) sure, we

(b) *Although we cannot be sure we feel he is the best man.*

332

□ One kind of adverb clause which should always be set off from the main clause by a comma is one introduced by *although.*

I was unable to make the team although I tried.

This sentence requires a comma between the words _____ and _____ .

team   although

□ *Although* (and its close synonyms *though, while,* and *whereas*) introduces an adverb clause that expresses an idea contrasted to the idea of the main clause. When speaking, we mark this contrast with a pause; when writing, we mark it with a comma to signal the pause:

This machine works well now though it hasn't been repaired lately.

now, though

□ Our ear helps us distinguish between adverb clauses introduced by *although* (*though, while,* and *whereas*) and other adverb clauses. Speak these sentences aloud before adding the necessary punctuation.

(a) *He offered to help when he had the time.*
(b) *He offered to help although he had little time.*

(b) help, although

□ Although a comma following most introductory adverb clauses is optional, it is necessary following such clauses beginning with *although* (*though, while,* and *whereas*).

(a) *When the firemen finally arrived, the fire was already out of control.*
(b) *Though the fire was out of control when they arrived, the firemen were able to protect the nearby property.*

Although the comma after *arrived* is optional in the [first, second] _____ sentence, it is necessary in the _____ sentence.

first
second

333

<table>
<tr><td>(a) Mary, whereas</td><td>(a) Hanna is a faster typist than Mary whereas Mary is neater.

(b) Mary is neater in her work than Hanna because she takes greater pains.</td></tr>
</table>

REVIEW

Change or add punctuation where necessary in the following sentences. Mark correct sentences C.

relax, although	□ He found he could not relax although he certainly tried hard.
C	□ The advance mechanism of his camera jammed because he had threaded the film improperly.
permissive, the	□ Whereas the child's father was permissive the mother was overly strict.
A comma after *left* is optional.	□ When he left we felt a good deal better.

PUNCTUATING RESTRICTIVE AND NONRESTRICTIVE CLAUSES

	18C Add any necessary punctuation to these sentences.
	(a) The jacket which I am wearing now was a gift from my mother.
(b) San Francisco, which water, is	(b) San Francisco which is surrounded on three sides by water is an important banking center.

□ The relationship between an adjective clause and the noun it modifies is often signaled by commas. If the clause is not essential in identifying the noun, it is set off with commas—that is, a comma appears at both ends of the clause.

Henry, who had a cold last week, is now well.

Since the clause *who had a cold last week* is not essential in identifying Henry, it is set off with _____.

commas

□ *The student who had a cold last week is now well.*

In this sentence the adjective clause *who had a cold last week* [is, is not] _____ essential in identifying which student is referred to.

is

□ Adjective clauses essential to identify the nouns they modify are called restrictive clauses. Those which are not, but which merely add information, are called nonrestrictive clauses.

Henry, who had a cold last week, is now well.
The student who had a cold last week is now well.

The adjective clause *who had a cold last week* is restrictive in the [first, second] _____ sentence and nonrestrictive in the _____ sentence.

second
first

□ Restrictive clauses are not set off with commas. Nonrestrictive clauses are set off with commas to show that the information they contain is additional rather than essential.

The boat which sank cost $800.
The boat, which I cherished because of its price, sank yesterday.

The adjective clause *which sank* is [restrictive, nonrestrictive] _____; *which I cherished because of its price* is _____.

restrictive
nonrestrictive

□ Add the necessary commas to these sentences. Remember that we use a comma both before and after a nonrestrictive clause.

(a) Nevada, which country, has

(a) *Nevada which attracts tourists from all over the country has a small permanent population.*

(b) *The California that I remember was a good deal different from the California of today.*

□ If a nonrestrictive clause comes at the end of a sentence, only one comma is necessary to set it off. Add any necessary comma to these sentences.

(a) husband, who

(a) *She loves her husband who gambles more than a poor man should.*

(b) *Beware of marrying a man who gambles more than he should.*

□ Many adjective clauses are restrictive or nonrestrictive, depending on meaning.

The witness who was stubborn refused to discuss the matter.
The witness, who was stubborn, refused to discuss the matter.

restrictive

To identify one witness among several, *who was stubborn* is [restrictive, nonrestrictive] _____ in the first sentence. To show that *who was stubborn* is simply additional information about the only witness, the clause is

nonrestrictive

_____ in the second sentence.

□ *Students, who seldom read, cannot expect their education to mean much.*
Students who seldom read cannot expect their education to mean much.

first
second

The punctuation of *who seldom read* in the [first, second] _____ sentence indicates that no student reads much. The punctuation of this same clause in the _____ sentence indicates only that some students do not read much.

336

□ *People, who ask too many questions, irritate me.*

all

The punctuation of this sentence suggests that [some, all] _____ people ask too many questions.

□ Be sure that your commas signal the meaning you intend.

I respect teachers who are tough-minded.

will not

will

If we want this sentence to refer to only some teachers, we [will, will not] _____ add a comma before *who*. If we wish it to refer to all teachers, we [will, will not] _____ add a comma before *who*.

REVIEW

Change or add punctuation where necessary in the following sentences. Mark correct sentences C.

Sterling, *who*
Greece, *began*

□ *Charles Sterling who was with our tour group in Greece began graduate school this semester.*

Both commas should be omitted.

□ *All cars, which have cracked windshields, will not receive certification from the Department of Motor Vehicles until the windshields are replaced.*

C

□ *Members who become inactive forfeit their voting rights.*

jig, *which*

France*, *was*

□ *Hitler's famous jig which he supposedly performed before newsreel camermen to celebrate the surrender of France was faked during processing by a Canadian film technician.*

PUNCTUATING APPOSITIVES

18D Add any necessary punctuation to the following sentences.

(a) Brutus, one characters, was

(a) Brutus one of Shakespeare's most complex characters was Caesar's friend and assassin.

(b) Ceasar's friend Brutus joined the conspirators only after lengthy reflection.

□ We often follow nouns with appositives—words or phrases that add information about the nouns.

Hal, my friend, was with me.

appositive

In this sentence *my friend* is an _____ that adds information about *Hal.*

□ *The car, a large Cadillac, pulled up to the gate.*

a large Cadillac

car

In this sentence, _____ is an appositive adding information about the noun _____.

□ Appositives are set off from the rest of the sentence with commas. Add the necessary punctuation to this sentence.

Pauline, an friend, arrived sari, an

Pauline an old school friend arrived wearing her sari an Indian dress.

□ An appositive is usually a noun, but it can be accompanied by a number of modifying words and phrases. When punctuating appositives, be sure to set off all the related words together.

Gomez, the St. Louis, returns

Hurricane Gomez the middleweight contender now living in St. Louis returns to the Garden for tonight's fight.

□ Punctuate this sentence.

The spinnaker, a mast, drove

The spinnaker a large balloon-like sail puffing forward from the mast drove the boat along at high speed.

338

□ In certain constructions an explanatory noun may come before the noun to which it is related.

> George, *my pal*, came with me.
> My pal George came with me.

In the second sentence the explantory noun *pal* comes before the noun to which it is related in both sentences,

George

_____.

□ An explanatory noun preceding the noun to which it is related is not an appositive, and normally it is not set off with commas.

> Nancy my wife arrived yesterday.
> My wife Nancy arrived yesterday.

Commas are required to set off *my wife* in the [first, second] _____ sentence but not in the _____ sentence.

first   second

□ Add the necessary punctuation to these sentences.

> (a) Congressman Lawrence W. Adams spoke on housing problems.
> (b) Lawrence W. Adams our Congressman spoke on housing problems.

(b) Adams, our Congressman, spoke

□ In using two related nouns, we may occasionally have difficulty deciding whether one is an appositive. To solve this problem, remember that an appositive follows a noun and adds explanation.

> Faulkner, *the novelist*, wrote screenplays and short stories also.

We know that *the novelist* is an appositive in this sentence because it explains the noun _____.

Faulkner

<table>
<tr><td></td><td>☐   *The novelist Faulkner wrote screenplays and short stories also.*</td></tr>
<tr><td>should not</td><td>Since the explanatory noun *novelist* precedes the related noun in this sentence, it [should, should not] _____ be set off with commas.</td></tr>
<tr><td></td><td>☐ Add the necessary punctuation to these sentences.</td></tr>
<tr><td>(b) *Jones, road-racing champion, was*</td><td>(a)   *Road-racing champion Floyd Jones was injured today.*
(b)   *Floyd Jones road-racing champion was injured today.*</td></tr>
</table>

<h2 style="background:black;color:white">REVIEW</h2>

Correct or add punctuation where necessary in the following sentences. Mark correct sentences C.

<table>
<tr><td>Both commas should be omitted.</td><td>☐   *Heavyweight champion, Rocky Marciano, retired undefeated.*</td></tr>
<tr><td>*Duncan, a photographer, is*
Nikon, a</td><td>☐   *David Douglas Duncan a* Life *photographer is credited with introducing to his profession the Nikon a truly fine Japanese-made camera.*</td></tr>
<tr><td>C</td><td>☐   *The candidates's trademark, a wide, double-armed wave of greeting and affection, brought renewed cheers from his supporters.*</td></tr>
<tr><td>Both commas should be omitted.</td><td>☐   *My friend, Harry, went with me.*</td></tr>
</table>

18E *Lately we have had other problems.*

A comma after *Lately* is [optional, necessary] _____ .

optional

☐ Single adverbs introducing sentences are most often the free-floating kind that can be in other positions within the sentence.

Frantically he searched his pockets / for a dime / .

Frantically [can, cannot] _____ appear in the other positions marked by the slanted lines.

can

☐ An introductory adverb that can appear in other positions does not require a comma to separate it from its sentence.

Sadly he walked away without the apple.

A comma after *Sadly* is not necessary because this adverb [can, cannot] _____ appear in other positions within a sentence.

can

☐ Occasionally writers use a comma to separate an introductory adverb from its sentence in order to emphasize it.

Angrily the clerk stalked off.

Only if he wished to emphasize the adverb would a writer place a comma after _____ .

Angrily

☐ *Graciously Mr. Carr asked me in.*

This sentence [is, is not] _____ correct as it stands.

is

☐ Punctuate this sentence to stress the introductory adverb.

Graciously Mr. Carr asked me in.

Graciously, Mr. Carr

□ Sometimes a comma separating an introductory adverb from its sentence is necessary to prevent misreading.

Indignant editors righteously cried out against the abuse.
Righteously indignant editors cried out against the abuse.

To assure that the second sentence has the same meaning as the first, a comma is required after _____.

Righteously

□   *Typed copies have become available recently.*
    Recently typed copies have become available.

If the second sentence is to have the same meaning as the first, a comma after *Recently* [is, is not] _____ necessary.

is

□ Punctuate the second sentence to give it the same meaning as the first.

Moving clouds rapidly covered the blue sky.
Rapidly moving clouds covered the blue sky.

Rapidly, moving

□   *Outside Mr. John felt better.*
    Outside the house looked bleak.

A comma after *Outside* would be superfluous in the [first, second] _____ sentence but necessary in the _____ sentence to prevent misreading.

first
second

18F Add the necessary punctuation to the following sentences.

(a) *However we decide to go, we should try to be there by morning.*

(b) However, by

(b) *However by taking Highway One, we will be able to to see the scenery along the coast.*

342

□ A certain kind of introductory adverb called a conjunctive adverb normally requires a comma. *However, moreover, nevertheless,* and *consequently* are conjunctive adverbs we commonly use. Punctuate this sentence.

Moreover, he

> *Moreover he refuses to return.*

□ As their name suggests, conjunctive adverbs have a dual function. In addition to being adverbs, they join the idea expressed in their own sentence to an idea expressed in a previous sentence.

> *Our overall productivity this year was unusually low. Nevertheless, we expect our profits to be substantial.*

Without the sentence preceding it, the conjunctive adverb *Nevertheless* [would, would not] _____ be meaningless.

would

□ When we set them off with commas, we show that introductory conjunctive adverbs serve the dual function of modifying and connecting. Add the necessary comma to this sentence.

> *Moreover this year's stock dividend will be higher than last year's.*

Moreover, this

□ We can see clearly the dual function of a conjunctive adverb if we move it to another position in a sentence.

> *This year's stock dividend, moreover, will be higher than last year's.*

The pull which we feel *moreover* to have toward preceding ideas makes the word an interruption when it appears farther along in the sentence. To mark this interruption, we set *moreover* off from the sentence by placing a _____ before and after it.

comma

□ A comparison of the following sentences shows the difference between an introductory adverb and an introductory conjunctive adverb.

> *Suddenly he shouted to his teammates.*
> *However, he shouted to his teammates.*

The adverb *Suddenly* can be moved to follow *shouted* without becoming an interruption requiring commas, while *However* [can, cannot] _____.

cannot

□ Add any comma necessary in these sentences.

> *(a)   Finally we left.*
> *(b)   However we left.*

(b) However, we left

□ *However* and *then* are two conjunctive adverbs which can function simply as adverbs. If *however* means *nevertheless*, it is a conjunctive adverb; if it means *no matter how,* it is an adverb.

> *However hard she tried, she could not finish.*
> *However, she could not finish.*

However is a conjunctive adverb in the [first, second] _____ sentence and an adverb meaning *no matter how* in the _____ sentence.

second

first

□ Add any necessary comma to these sentences.

> *(a)   However we do it, let's do it now.*
> *(b)   However we should do it correctly.*

(b) However, we

□ When *then* means *consequently*, it is a conjunctive adverb. When it means *at that time*, it is an adverb.

> *You will, then, remember me in your will.*
> *You will remember then that I am your loving nephew.*

In the first sentence *then* is [a conjunctive adverb, an adverb] _____; in the second sentence it is a(n) _____.

a conjunctive adverb

adverb

344

□ Add any necessary commas to these sentences. Remember that a conjunctive adverb appearing within a sentence is an interrupter requiring commas before and after it.

(a) We have, then,

    (a)   *We have then only four chairs.*

    (b)   *We had only four chairs then.*

□ Add any comma necessary in these sentences.

    (a)   *Do it however you wish.*

(b) it, however, my

    (b)   *Do it however my way.*

18G   Add only necessary punctuation to these sentences.

    (a)   *On the assembly line we make car radios.*

(b) On the whole, we

    (b)   *On the whole we make a fine product.*

□ Introductory prepositional phrases are adverb phrases. It is characteristic of them that they can appear in other positions within their sentences.

    At this time we cannot / hire you / .

can

The adverb phrase *At this time* [can, cannot] _____ be moved to either of the positions marked by the slanted lines.

□ Since adverb phrases can be placed in any one of several positions in a sentence, they are not interrupters and do not need to be set off with commas.

    In his work he is extremely conscientious.

is not

A comma following *work* [is, is not] _____ necessary.

345

□ Introductory adverb phrases are often followed by other phrases related to them. Normally, commas setting off such groups are unnecessary.

Before the date of the flood Noah built his ark.

is not

A comma following *flood* [is, is not] _____ necessary.

□ If an introductory adverb phrase, together with its related phrases, is so long that it might obscure the beginning of the main clause, a comma should follow it to mark where the subject of the sentence begins.

In addition to barking dogs and screaming children we heard a passing fire truck blaring its siren.

children

We should place a comma after _____.

□ Add any comma necessary in the following sentences.

(a) After a while he began to enjoy his work immensely.

(b) cannery, he

(b) After a long time on the night shift at the cannery he decided to quit.

□ Certain introductory adverb phrases, like conjunctive adverbs, serve both as modifiers and as connectives. Such phrases are set off with commas for the same reason that conjunctive adverbs are.

Moreover, the rifle jammed.
In addition, the rifle jammed.

In addition

These examples show that, since it can replace the conjunctive adverb *Moreover*, the adverb phrase _____ serves as a connective as well as an adverb.

□ *After all, for example, in addition, on the whole,* and *on the contrary* are a few of the introductory adverb phrases which also function as connectives. We should normally set these off with commas from the sentences they introduce. Add the necessary comma to this sentence.

whole, he's

On the whole he's not very pleased with me.

346

□ Adverb phrases which function as connectives as well as modifiers are set off by commas wherever they appear in a sentence.

He is, on the contrary, a fine instructor.

The commas before and after *on the contrary* [are, are not] _____ necessary.

are

□ Add any necessary punctuation to these sentences.

(a) whole, business

    (a)   *On the whole business is good.*
    (b)   *On the left we can see Baja California.*

□ Add any necessary punctuation to these sentences. Remember that an adverb phrase which is also a connective should have a comma before and after it when it appears in the middle of its sentence.

    (a)   *He made ten mistakes in addition and one in subtraction.*

(b) made, in addition, four

    (b)   *He made in addition four mistakes in multiplication.*

□ Add any comma necessary to these sentences.

(a) cannot, after all,
(b) example, we

    (a)   *We cannot after all please everyone.*
    (b)   *For example we cannot please him.*

REVIEW

Add the necessary punctuation to and remove unnecessary punctuation from the following sentences. Mark correct sentences C.

The comma is not necessary.

□   *In the beginning, he was fine.*

C

□   *However you decide to do it, do it now.*

347

all, he's	□ *After all he's only a baby.*
insist, moreover, that	□ *The men insist moreover that their fringe benefits are inadequate.*

PUNCTUATING INTRODUCTORY VERBAL ELEMENTS

18H   Add any necessary punctuation to the following sentences.

(a) out, she
(b) pleasantly, he

(a)   Everything being laid out she dressed rapidly.
(b)   Smiling pleasantly he hit me in the mouth.

□ Often sentences are introduced by a verbal or a verbal phrase.

Remembering his manners, Henry apologized.

This sentence is introduced by the participial phrase

Remembering his manners

_____.

□ We should always place a comma after introductory verbals and verbal phrases. Add the necessary commas to these sentences.

(a) Grinning, he
(b) auditorium, you

(a)   Grinning he left us standing there.
(b)   To be heard in the rear of the auditorium you must speak loudly.

□ The reason we should always place a comma after introductory verbals and verbal phrases is that the separation between the introductory word or phrase and the main clause is often not clear without the comma.

Leaving Henry waved goodbye.

We have to read this sentence twice before we realize that *Henry* is the [subject, direct object] _____
of the verb *waved*, not the _____ of the
participle *Leaving*.

subject
direct object

□ Supply the necessary comma in this sentence.

Leaving Henry waved goodbye.

Leaving, Henry

□ Punctuate this sentence.

To be certain the scientists checked their figures three times.

certain, the

□ Although we do not ordinarily use a comma after an introductory adverb phrase, we should if it contains a gerund. Add the comma necessary in this sentence.

After questioning the prisoner was returned to his cell.

questioning, the

□ Add the comma necessary to make it clear that *Hughes* is not the subject of this sentence.

In appointing Hughes the supervisor blundered badly.

Hughes, the

□ An introductory absolute phrase—a participial phrase with a subject—should also be set off with a comma from its sentence.

The question coming as it did, Jones was surprised.

is

The comma following *did* [is, is not] _____
necessary.

□ Add the necessary commas to these sentences.

(a) answered, Jones

(b) approached, the

    (a) Having answered Jones sat down.

    (b) The postman having approached the dogs began to bark.

REVIEW

Add the necessary punctuation to the following sentences. Mark correct sentences C.

sure, Ralph

□   *To be sure Ralph decided to look for himself.*

permitting, Senator

□   *The weather permitting Senator Ellis will speak outdoors.*

C

□   *To allow yourself enough time, start by eight.*

speaking, revolutions

□   *Strictly speaking revolutions on college campuses are not new.*

350

NINETEEN

COMMAS WITH ADDED SENTENCE PARTS

PUNCTUATING INTERJECTIONS AND PHRASES OF DIRECT ADDRESS

19A Add any punctuation necessary to these sentences.

(a) *Well, you now, my friend, that*

(b) *No, I*

   (a) *Well you can see now my friend that our troubles have just begun.*

   (b) *No I can't.*

☐ Interjections are words which convey a feeling through sound. *Ouch* and *wow* are examples of strong interjections which we usually punctuate separately with exclamation marks. *Oh, well,* and *indeed* are mild interjections which we sometimes join to sentences.

   Oh, I didn't know.

interjection

This sentence is introduced by the _____ *Oh.*

□ Since interjections derive their expressive force from their sound, they are characteristic of the spoken rather than the written language. Occasionally, however, we do use them in our writing. If quoting a speaker using a strong interjection, we punctuate it separately with an exclamation mark:

"Ouch!"

    "Ouch "

□ A mild interjection used in a sentence is separated from the main clause by a comma. Punctuate this sentence.

Well, you

    Well you can never tell.

□ Add the necessary punctuation to these sentences.

(a) "Hey!"
(b) Indeed, I

    (a)   "Hey "
    (b)   Indeed I was amazed.

□ The words *yes* and *no*, although called adverbs, are a good deal like interjections, and we punctuate them the same way. Add the necessary punctuation to this sentence.

Yes, she

    Yes she can go.

□ Add the punctuation necessary in these sentences.

(a) Oh, is
(b) No, I

    (a)   Oh is she really?
    (b)   No I don't think so.

□ Words of direct address in a sentence—*my friends, ladies and gentlemen, dear,* for instance—are always set off by commas.

    And now, ladies and gentlemen, let me tell you a really funny story.

The commas before and after *ladies and gentlemen* [are, are not]_____ necessary.

are

□ Add necessary commas to these sentences.

    (a)   You are my friends of a lifetime.

(b) are, my friends,

    (b)   You are my friends fine companions for a lifetime.

352

□ Add any necessary punctuation to these sentences.

(b) are, dear, a

(a) You are very dear.

(b) You are dear a sight.

Add punctuation where necessary in the following sentences. Mark correct sentences C.

Indeed, it

□ Indeed it certainly is hot.

going, sir

□ Where are you going sir?

"Gosh!"

□ "Gosh "

PUNCTUATING SHORT CLAUSES OF FEELING OR OPINION

19B Add any necessary punctuation to the following sentences.

(a) are, I hope, the

(a) Here are the stockings which are I hope the ones you ordered.

(b) Here are the stockings which I hope are the ones you ordered.

□ We often include in our sentences short clauses expressing feeling or opinion. *I think, we feel, you hope,* and *he believed* are a few of the more common clauses of this kind.

You have everything you need, I hope.

I hope

Here the writer has added the two-word clause _____ to express his feelings in regard to the idea expressed.

353

□ In most positions within the sentence short clauses expressing feeling and opinion are interrupters and are, therefore, set off with commas.

He has, I think, a good chance.

The commas before and after *I think* [are, are not] _____ necessary.

are

□ The only position in which the short clauses expressing feeling or opinion are not interrupters is directly following a relative pronoun (*who, whom, which,* or *that*).

This is the boat which we feel is the best buy.

Since the clause *we feel* follows the relative pronoun *which,* placing commas before and after it [is, is not] _____ necessary.

is not

□ Add any necessary comma to these sentences.

(a) *is, the creditors feel, overdue*

    (a)   *This is an account which is the creditors feel overdue.*

    (b)   *This is an account which the creditors feel is overdue.*

□ The relative pronouns *whom, which,* and *that* are often unnecessary. If they are missing, we punctuate short clauses of feeling or opinion just as we would if the relative pronouns were expressed.

This is a bargain we think will not be offered again soon.

Here the relative pronoun *which* is omitted after *bargain;* it [is, is not] _____ necessary to place a comma before and after *we think.*

is not

354

□ Add the necessary punctuation to the following sentences. To keep your bearings, mentally add any missing relative pronoun.

(a) That was a question which we believed needed a careful answer.

(b) knows, I imagine,

(b) This is the route he knows I imagine better than any other.

REVIEW

Add necessary punctuation to the following sentences. Mark correct sentences C.

C

□ These are the journal pages the auditors feel need reviewing.

are, we think, several

□ There are we think several important problems remaining to be solved.

C

□ Robert Frost is one of the few poets of his time who we feel will endure.

TWENTY
DASHES, COLONS, AND PARENTHESES

PUNCTUATING APPOSITIVE SERIES

colon dash	**20A** *He demanded only three things, health, wealth, and success.* The comma after *things* should be replaced with a _____ or a _____.

□ A series is any group of three or more words or phrases. We occasionally use a series as an appositive—that is, as an explanatory enumeration following a particular word.

> *There are four cardinal virtues*: *prudence, justice, fortitude, and temperance.*

Here the appositive is a series: *prudence, justice, fortitude, and temperance.* It explains the noun it follows,

virtues _____.

□ An appositive which is not a series is normally set off with a comma.

He had only two shoes, a black oxford and a brown loafer.

Here the appositive following *shoes* is set off by a comma because it enumerates only two things and is, therefore, not a _____.

□ An appositive which is a series should be set off with a colon (:) rather than a comma. Add the necessary colon to this sentence.

He plays three instruments the flute, the oboe, and the piano.

□ *He plays three instruments: the flute, the oboe, and the piano.*

If we substitute a comma for the colon, we can see why a comma would be incorrect following *instruments*.

He plays three instruments, the flute, the oboe, and the piano.

Here *instruments* seems on first reading to be just another part of the series following it. That the three nouns of the series explain *instruments* [is, is not] _____ clear.

□ Although we cannot use a comma to introduce an appositive series, we can use a dash (—) in place of a colon:

He plays three instruments the flute the oboe, and the piano.

□ The difference between a colon and a dash introducing an appositive series is that a dash draws more attention to the series than a colon does.

He brought three kinds of fruit apples, cherries, and peaches.

If we wish to focus attention on the series in this sentence, we will use a _____ following *fruit.* If not, we will use a _____ .

□ Punctuate the series in this sentence to focus attention on it.

dash
colon

We visited three cities in Italy Rome, Venice,
and Florence.

Italy — Rome

□ Punctuate the series in this sentence in a way that does not focus attention on it.

He invited three friends Walt, Mac, and Leo.

friends: Walt

20B Correct the punctuation in this sentence.

courses — math
chemistry — because

This semester I'll be taking only three courses: math, physics and chemistry because I have a part-time job.

□ Since a colon means *as follows,* we use it only if what comes between it and the end of the sentence is part of the enumeration or explanation it introduces.

I have three coins: a nickel, a dime, and a quarter.
I will give you three coins: a nickel, a dime, and a quarter, to perform your trick.

first
second

The colon is correct in the [first, second] _____ sentence but not in the _____ sentence.

358

□ If an appositive series comes within a sentence rather than at the end, we set it off with dashes—that is, we place a dash before and after the series. Punctuate the series in this sentence.

coins — a
quarter — to

> *I will give you three coins a nickel, a dime, and a quarter to perform your trick.*

□ *He owned three cars a Ford, a Chevrolet, and a Plymouth although he himself did not drive.*
He owned three cars a Ford, a Chevrolet, and a Plymouth.

second
first

Although we can use either a colon or a dash after *cars* in the [first, second] _____ sentence, we should use a dash both after *cars* and *Plymouth* in the _____ sentence.

□ Add the necessary punctuation to these sentences, using a dash only where required.

(a) tobacco — in
cigars — its

(a) *Of the three ways of using tobacco in cigarettes, in pipes, and in cigars its use in cigarettes is by far the most dangerous.*

(b) usage: formal

(b) *Some scholars distinguish four levels of language usage formal, standard, colloquial, and substandard.*

REVIEW

Add punctuation needed in the following sentences, using a dash only where necessary. Mark correct sentences C.

aides — speech-writer

□ *Today the President-elect named three new aides speech-writer James Elder, foreign affairs adviser Ralph Briggs, and assistant press secretary Avery Long before departing for a short Christmas vacation.*

Long — before

□ *In homes today we use two important sources of power, natural gas and electricity.*

C

novels: A

☐ *I gave him a copy of each of Hemingway's early novels A Farewell to Arms, The Sun Also Rises, and To Have and Have Not.*

USING COLONS AND DASHES TO EMPHASIZE APPOSITIVES

20C *He had one dream, to live in Paris.*

He had one dream, to live in Paris, and he finally realized it.

dash   colon

dashes

We can substitute either _____ or a _____ for the comma in the first sentence. We can substitute only _____ for the commas in the second.

☐ Appositives following nouns are normally set off with commas.

My mother has only one prized possession, an antique clock.

is

Here the appositive *an antique clock*, which explains the noun *possession*, [is, is not] _____ correctly punctuated with a comma.

☐ If we wish to emphasize an appositive which appears at the end of a sentence, we punctuate it with a colon.

possession: an

My mother has only one prized possession an antique clock.

☐ We can also punctuate an appositive with a dash, giving it even more emphasis.

possession — an

My mother has only one prized possession an antique clock.

360

□   *Some employers insist that their employees have only one object security.*

comma	A _____ after *object* is the normal punctuation.
colon	A _____ will emphasize the appositive *security*; a
dash	_____ will emphasize *security* even more.

□ If an appositive is not the last element in a sentence, we cannot use a colon. We must instead set it off either with commas or with dashes.

    The company had a pact a working agreement with the union.

commas   dashes   We can use either _____ or _____ to set off *a working agreement*; we cannot use a colon after *pact.*

□   *He had one disability a broken arm which kept him out of action.*

    He had one disability a broken arm.

	Depending upon the emphasis we want to give *a broken arm,* we will use either commas or dashes to set it off in
first	the [first, second] _____ sentence. We can use
second	a comma, a colon, or a dash after *disability* in the _____
	sentence.

REVIEW

Add to the following sentences the punctuation needed to give the appositive the kind of emphasis indicated.

□ No emphasis:

fish, trout   *I like one kind of fish trout.*

□ Slight emphasis:

fish: trout   *I like one kind of fish trout.*

fish—trout	□ Strong emphasis: *I like one kind of fish trout.*

USING COLONS TO INTRODUCE EXPLANATORY CLAUSES

succession: the	**20D** Correct the punctuation in this sentence. *These events happened in quick succession; the car stopped, four men climbed out, and the car sped away.*

	□ We often form compound sentences without using con-junctions. You will recall that the clauses in such sen-tences are normally separated by semicolons. *The bank was not open; he was unable to cash the check.*
semicolon	Here, two closely related ideas are separated by a _____ rather than a conjunction.
	□ Occasionally, however, the second independent clause in a compound sentence explains or amplifies the first. *The reason he gave was this: he had not been able to cash the check until the banks had opened.*
is	The second clause in this sentence [is, is not] _____ an explanation of the first.
	□ Since a colon means *as follows,* we use it rather than a semicolon after the introductory clause in a compound sentence if the clause or clauses following it are explana-tions or amplifications. *This much is certain: Henderson was there at the time and could have prevented the explosion.*
is	Since the second independent clause in this sentence is an amplification of the first, the colon [is, is not] _____ correct.

362

□ We should never use a colon to separate clauses of a compound sentence unless the second clause explains or amplifies the first.

It was all too clear the box had in fact been opened.
It was all too clear we needed little additional information.

A colon should be placed after *clear* in the [first, second]

first
second

_____ sentence, a semicolon after *clear* in the

_____ sentence.

□ Add a colon or a semicolon to these sentences.

(a) most: he

(b) most; his

(a) Of all his fine traits, one impresses me most he never says an unkind word about anyone.
(b) Of all his fine traits, one impresses me most his others, however, are certainly worth mentioning.

Add the punctuation necessary in the following sentences.

this: he

□ *His excuse was this he lost the slip of paper on which he had written the phone number.*

fall; in

□ *We planted the trees in the fall in the spring we planted additional bushes for a hedge.*

position: he

□ *This was his position he would vote for the rules change if a majority of the other members favored it.*

PUNCTUATING INTERRUPTERS

me—do
why?—to

20E Correct the punctuation in this sentence without rearranging its parts.

"He asked me, do you know why?, to accompany him."

☐ When speaking, we often interrupt a sentence in the middle to repeat an important point or to change the direction of our thought.

"Will you please bring me — no, not that!"

The break in this sentence shows that some event or thought forced the speaker to stop one sentence abruptly and begin another. The break is clearly marked here with a

dash

_____.

☐ An abrupt shift in grammatical structure should be marked with a dash. Add the necessary dash to this sentence.

her — no

"I'll ask her no, I can't."

☐ If an interruption comes in the middle of a complete sentence, we should place a dash before and after it to set it off:

am — rather
was — going

"I am rather, I was going with her."

☐ Questions or exclamations which interrupt a sentence should be punctuated to show what they are and should be set off with dashes:

there — Ouch! — under

"It hurts right there Ouch under my shoulder blade."

☐ Add the necessary punctuation to this sentence.

Hank — do
him? — who's

"There's Hank do you know him who's rich as Midas."

☐ Although abrupt shifts and interruptions are characteristic of spoken rather than written expression, their occasional use for such specific purposes as emphasis and variety is the mark of mature prose. Add the dashes necessary in this sentence.

opportunity — the
opportunity — to

This is the last opportunity the absolutely last opportunity to offer a realistic plan.

□ Punctuate this sentence correctly.

paused—what
say?—and

The candidate paused what could he say and simply asked if there were any more questions.

Add the necessary punctuation to the following sentences.

local—what
call it?—our

□ "And this is our local what do the students call it our local snake pit."

excited—perhaps
accurate—when

□ She seemed excited perhaps hysterical is more accurate when she learned the good news.

USING PARENTHESES WITH INSERTED INFORMATION AND GUIDES

(a) chart (p. 14) in

(b) society: (1) an
car, (2) a
and (3) an

20F Correct the punctuation in the following sentences.

(a) Keep the chart, p.14, in front of you as you read this chapter.

(b) These are the three most powerful status symbols in our society: 1, an expensive car, 2, a large home, and 3, an important job.

□ Parentheses (( )) are used primarily to set off information not essential in a sentence but interesting or helpful to some readers.

The illustration (p. 434) will help you understand the cost-profit relationship.

Since the page number of the illustration mentioned is not important in this sentence but only added as a help to the reader, it is set off in _____.

parentheses

□   *Tetanus lockjaw is still often fatal.*

should

Since *lockjaw* is added here to give the reader the common name for tetanus, we [should, should not] _____ enclose *lockjaw* in parentheses.

□ If writing about the sugar maple tree, we may wish to include its Latin designation, *Acer saccharum,* to help a reader who is a botanist identify it according to the name with which he is familiar:

(*Acer saccharum*)

The sugar maple _____ *is indigenous to the northeastern United States.*

□ Foreign words, which some readers may not recognize, are often translated in parentheses:

(*which means beet field*)

Beethoven *which means beet field was an honored family name in Holland long before the great composer was born.*

□ Add the necessary parentheses to these sentences.

(a) (*line 4*)

(*a*)   *This quotation was taken from John Donne's sonnet "At the round earth's imagined corners" line 4.*

(b) (*fear of high places*)

(*b*)   *Acrophobia fear of high places is a common neurosis often unrecognized by the sufferer.*

□ The indiscriminate use of parentheses to insert information at random is a mark of poor writing. Commas should generally be used if the information to be set off is related in any way to the sentence's main ideas.

Mr. Miller owner of Miller's Hardware will run for the city council.

commas

Although not essential to the sentence's meaning, the phrase *owner of Miller's Hardware* is related to the central idea of this sentence and should be set off with _____ rather than parentheses.

366

□ If a word or group of words is an interrupter, it should be set off with commas or dashes rather than parentheses. Correct the punctuation in this sentence, using dashes.

Roses—a climbing variety—twined

> *Roses (a climbing variety) twined around the split rail fence.*

□ Only one of the following sentences requires parentheses. Add the necessary punctuation to both.

(a) (food poisoning)

(b) Botulism, a foods, is

> (a) *Botulism food poisoning has caused six deaths in the United States recently.*
> (b) *Botulism a bacillus often found in foods is extremely difficult to trace when large quantities of foods are involved.*

□ Since parentheses show that added material does not belong to a sentence, we always use them to set off numbers used in enumerations.

> *In order to register properly, you must complete the following steps: **(1)** complete the forms provided, **(2)** have your adviser sign your study list, and **(3)** return all forms to the Registrar.*

To show that they do not belong to the sentence but are simply guides to reading, the numbers in this sentence

parentheses

are set off in _____.

□ If letters instead of numbers are enumerating guides, we set them off in parentheses in the same way that we set off numbers. Add the parentheses to this sentence.

(a) one
(b) a
(c) three
(d) a

> *The clerk packed four items: a one dozen eggs, b a carton of milk, c three cans of apple juice, and d a mousetrap.*

□ When using numbers or letters in parentheses as guides in a series, we use commas in the same way that we would if the guides were not there. Add all the necessary punctuation to the following sentence.

(1) to answer the telephone, (2) to greet appointees, and (3) to type

> *A receptionist's duties are these: 1 to answer the telephone 2 to greet appointees and 3 to type occasional letters.*

□ Add all the necessary punctuation to this sentence.

(a) one shotgun, (b) twenty geese, and (c) an

> *The sheriff found the following items in the defendant's car: a one shotgun b twenty geese and c an out-of-date hunting license.*

REVIEW

Add the necessary punctuation to the following sentences.

(chicken cooked in wine)

□ *The French restaurant on Spruce Street serves excellent coq au vin chicken cooked in wine.*

(1) blade assembly, (2) motor shaft, (3) cowl, and (4) handle

□ *Before starting to assemble the mower, identify the following parts: 1 blade assembly 2 motor shaft 3 cowl and 4 handle.*

TWENTY-ONE

PUNCTUATION
OF QUOTATIONS

USING QUOTATION MARKS

21A Add the necessary punctuation to the following sentences.

(a) *shouted "Hey!"*
and

    (a)   *Ed shouted Hey and ducked into the bus.*

(b) *asked*, *"May we*
go?"

    (b)   *Which one of you asked May we go*

□ Any direct quotation of the spoken or written words of others that we include in our own writing should be set off with quotation marks (" ").

He asked me to come.
He asked me, "Will you come?"

We know that "Will you come?" in the second sentence is a direct quotation because it is set off by _____

quotation

marks.

□ Add the punctuation necessary in the following example to show that *China, the giant, is dying* is a direct quotation.

"China dying"

> *China, the giant, is dying, Russell wrote.*

□ The statement which credits a speaker or writer is set off from the quotation by a comma. Add the comma to this sentence.

asked, "Will"

> *The Senator then asked "Will we spend more?"*

□ When the quotation precedes the statement identifying the speaker, the comma comes at the end of the quotation:

now," the

> *"The nation cannot afford to spend more now" the Senator continued.*

□ If a quotation which is a question ends before the sentence does, we place a question mark inside the end quotation marks. Add the question mark here.

ready?" he

> *"Will you be ready " he asked.*

□ If a quotation which is an exclamation ends before the sentence does, we place an exclamation mark inside the end quotation marks. Add the exclamation mark to this sentence.

here!" he

> *"Come here " he cried.*

□ Add the necessary punctuation to the following sentences.

(a) now?" he
(b) now," I

> (a) *"You're leaving now " he asked.*
> (b) *"We're leaving now " I said.*

□ If a quotation which is a simple statement comes at the end of a sentence, one period inside the quotation marks is enough to indicate the end of the quotation and the sentence. Add the period to this sentence.

right."

> *Then he answered, "We're all right "*

□ If an exclamation or a question is quoted at the end of a sentence, the question mark or the exclamation mark inside the quotation marks will indicate the end of both the quotation and the sentence. Add the necessary punctuation to these sentences.

(a) here!"
(b) merger?"

  (a) *He shouted, "Get us out of here "*
  (b) *The reporters then asked, "Will the government allow the merger "*

□ Add the necessary punctuation to these sentences.

(a) can."

(b) tomorrow?"

  (a) *His request was simple: "Please come when you can "*
  (b) *His question was simple: "Can you come tomorrow "*

□ If a quotation which is not a question itself ends a sentence which is a question, the question mark follows the quotation marks. No other punctuation is required. Add the question mark to this sentence.

man"?

  Who said, "Go west, young man"

□ Add the necessary punctuation to these sentences.

(a) impediments"?

(b) ourselves?"

  (a) *What is this line from: "Let me not to the marriage of true minds admit impediments "*
  (b) *Conrad asked, "Why do we lie to ourselves "*

□ If a very short quotation fits easily within the context of a sentence, we do not use commas to set it off. Notice, however, that the quotation marks are used as usual.

  Saying "Very good" at the right time will please the child.

is not

A comma [is, is not] _____ required before and after *"Very good."*

□ If short quotations that fit the context of a sentence are questions or exclamations, we do not set them off with commas; but we do use a question mark or an exclamation where appropriate. Complete the punctuation in these sentences.

(a) Stop!"

(b) you?"

    (a)   *He cried "Stop " as I passed him.*

    (b)   *Bob heard him ask "Where are you " from the darkened building.*

□ Although short quotations that fit easily into the sentence do not need to be set off with commas, we should always set off with commas those quotations which interrupt the sentences to which they belong. Add punctuation to these sentences where necessary.

    (a)   *Repeating "By the way " as often as you do makes your speeches sound carelessly organized.*

(b) way," he
said,"where

    (b)   *"By the way " he said "where were you?"*

21B   Shift, but do not change the punctuation in these sentences where necessary.

(a) buy?";
"Nothing."

    (a)   *I asked, "What did you buy?;" but she answered, "Nothing".*

(b) "Sugarplum":

    (b)   *He remembered only this about "Sugarplum:" she was six feet tall and weighed over two hundred pounds.*

(c) "Amen,"

    (c)   *After whispering "Amen", the devout old woman tottered out of church.*

□ Periods and commas should always be placed inside quotation marks that end a quotation.

"I really think," he said, "that little more can be done."

Here the comma following *think* and the period following

are

done [are, are not] _____ correctly placed.

372

□ Complete the punctuation of this sentence.

roses," the
wedding."

"These are the roses " the messenger announced, "that were ordered for the wedding "

□ Colons and semicolons, unlike periods and commas, should be placed following the quotation marks that end a quotation. Add the necessary punctuation to these sentences.

(a) report": the

(b) Help!"; however

(a) This is what he called his "true report" the prisoner simply opened the cell door and walked away.

(b) We heard a voice faintly crying "Help!" however, we could see nothing in the dark water.

□ Shift the punctuation in these sentences where necessary.

(a) morning," he
week."
(b) no"; but

(a) "I am leaving in the morning", he said, "and I will be in New York City all week".

(b) The Mayor said quietly, "Oh, no;" but his denials were smiled at by those close to him.

REVIEW

Add the necessary punctuation to the following sentences.

Margaret then said,
"I'm leaving now";
however, she stayed
two more hours.

□ Margaret then said I'm leaving now however she stayed two more hours.

Who asked, "Where
did he go?"

□ Who asked Where did he go

He screamed "Ow!"
when I stepped on
his toe.

□ He screamed Ow when I stepped on his toe.

"I am here," he said, "to speak to you about the new assessment rates."	☐ *I am here he said to speak to you about the new assessment rates*

USING SINGLE QUOTATION MARKS, ELLIPSIS MARKS, AND BRACKETS IN QUOTATIONS

21C   Rewrite the entire following statement as a direct quotation, making these changes to it: omit *obove the roar of traffic,* indicating by punctuation the omission; and identify as *Henderson* the person referred to by *His.*

"His [Henderson's] shout of 'Please!' could scarcely be heard . . . ."

His shout of "Please!" could scarely be heard above the roar of traffic.

_____

_____

☐ When quoting a speaker or writer directly, using quotation marks, we must quote verbatim—that is, we must quote word for word, without changing any part of the other person's expression.

> *"While he was commander of the division, the men were quite happy."*

If we wish to use this sentence as a quotation but wish to make it clear that *he* refers to General Lucas, we [can, cannot] _____ substitute *General Lucas* for *he.*

cannot

☐ To clarify a part of a quotation, we can add missing information if we enclose it in brackets ([]). For instance, to make it clear that *he* refers to General Lucas, we add the General's name after *he*, enclosing it in brackets.

he [General Lucas] was

> *"While he _____ was commander of the division, the men were quite happy."*

374

□ Don't confuse brackets, which are square, with parentheses, which are curved. Brackets, not parentheses, are used to enclose information added to quotations without changing the quotation itself.

"The city [Las Vegas] never seems to sleep."

We know that *Las Vegas* is added to this quotation because it is enclosed in _____ .

□ Add the information necessary to show that *it* refers to the Russ Building.

"It _____ is one of the tallest buildings in San Francisco."

□ Quoting verbatim does not mean, of course, that we must quote all of a sentence. However, we cannot simply drop out words or phrases without showing that a part is omitted.

"Interstate bus travel is becoming increasingly popular in the United States."

If we wish to drop *in the United States* when quoting this sentence, we [can, cannot] _____ simply move the period and the quotation marks so that they follow *popular.*

□ If we wish to drop out superfluous words or phrases from a sentence we quote, we show the omission with three spaced dots called ellipsis marks (. . .). Complete the punctuation of this sentence, which now has a part missing. Be sure to include the period which ends the sentence.

"Interstate bus travel is becoming increasingly popular   "

"Patrolman Green ...
witnessed the
holdup."

☐ "Patrolman Green, who was off duty at the time, witnessed the holdup."

Rewrite this quotation, dropping the clause *who was off
duty at the time* and the commas that set it off.

_____

_____

☐ "This new state in the heart of the Pacific Ocean has a
thriving agricultural economy."

Rewrite this quotation, dropping *in the heart of the Pacific
Ocean* and making it clear that the state referred to is
Hawaii.

[Hawaii] ... has a
thriving agricultural
economy

"This new state _____

_____."

☐ One quotation within another is set off with single quotation marks (' ') rather than with the usual double quotation
marks (" ").

"Did you hear him ask, 'Where is the hammer'?"

To show that *Where is the hammer* is a quotation within a
quotation, [single, double] _____ quotation
marks set it off.

single

☐ "That's where the matter stands," the Commissioner
asserted.

If we were to quote this sentence, we would change the
quotation marks it now has and add others:

That's where the matter stands, the Commissioner
asserted.

" 'That's where the
matter stands,' the
Commissioner
asserted."

□   *The farmers in this city reported to an inquiring reporter that their crop yield this year was "middling."*

"The farmers in this city [Omaha] reported ... that their crop yield this year was 'middling'."

Punctuate this statement as a quotation, omitting *to an inquiring reporter* and making it clear that *this city* refers to Omaha.

_____

_____

REVIEW

Make the following sentences quotations, changing them according to the instructions given.

□ Omit *in the beginning.*

" ... Senator Clay found little support for the bill."

In the beginning Senator Clay found little support for the bill.

_____

□ Make it clear that *he* refers to Henry James.

"After living most of his life in England he [Henry James] finally became a British subject before his death."

After living most of his life in England, he finally became a British subject before his death.

_____

_____

□ Omit *called the Sunflower State;* make it clear that *she* refers to Edith Ray. Be sure to indicate that her words are a quotation within a quotation.

" 'Kansas ... ,' she [Edith Ray] said, 'has, in addition to farming enterprises, important aircraft factories located in Wichita.' "

"Kansas, called the Sunflower State," she said, "has, in addition to farming enterprises, important aircraft factories located in Wichita."

_____

_____

377

TWENTY-TWO

QUOTATION MARKS AND ITALICS

PUNCTUATING TITLES

22A Add the necessary punctuation to these sentences. Indicate italics where necessary.

(a) "Hillcrest" Collected Poems

(b) Mourning Becomes Electra The New York Times

(a) E. A. Robinson's poem Hillcrest can be found in his Collected Poems.

(b) The recent revival of Eugene O'Neill's play Mourning Becomes Electra received praise in The New York Times.

□ Italics are slanted letters. Printed in italics, the title of Shakespeare's tragedy looks like this: *Hamlet.* However, since most typewriters cannot print italics, we italicize a word by underlining it: Hamlet.

Shakespeare's Julius Caesar is based chiefly on Plutarch's Lives.

underlined (underscored)

To show that the titles in this sentence would be italicized in a printed book, they are _____.

□ The titles of plays and books are italicized. Indicate the italics in this sentence.

Pamela

Although scorned by many,
Pamela, Richardson's first novel,
has always had a wide audience.

□ The titles of magazines and newspapers are also italicized:

Time   Life
The Wall Street
Journal

My father subscribes to Time, Life,
and The Wall Street Journal.

□ Indicate the italics in these sentences.

(a) Pygmalion
    My Fair Lady

(*a*) Pygmalion, Shaw's fine comedy,
    was made into a musical called
    My Fair Lady.

(b) The Status
    Seekers
    The Atlantic
    Monthly

(*b*) The Status Seekers, Vance Packard's
    appraisal of American society,
    was thoughtfully reviewed in
    The Atlantic Monthly.

□ Titles of poems, short stories, chapters of books, articles in magazines, and columns in newspapers are not italicized but are set off in quotation marks.

"Fissionable Materials" is the
tenth chapter of Gregg's book,
Nuclear Physics.

chapter

book

Here the [chapter, book] _____ title is correctly set off with quotation marks; the _____ title is italicized.

□ Titles of separately published or produced works (books, plays, movies, magazines, and newspapers) are italicized. Titles of works which are part of separately published works (poems, short stories, chapters, articles, and newspaper columns) are set off with _____ marks.

quotation

□ Mark the titles in this sentence.

"Was Darwin
Wrong about
the Human
Brain?"
Harper's

Was Darwin Wrong about the Human Brain?,
Loren Eiseley's article on evolution, was
originally printed in Harper's.

□ Mark the titles in this sentence.

In Our Time
"Big Two-Hearted
River"
"The Three-Day
Blow"

In Our Time, Hemingway's first
published work, contains such stories
as Big Two-Hearted River and The
Three-Day Blow.

□ Although the majority of poems are short enough to be
published as part of a book, Homer's *Iliad* and Milton's
Paradise Lost are among the many poems long enough to
be separately published. As the foregoing sentence shows,

italicize

we _____ the titles of such poems rather than
set them off in quotation marks.

□ Mark the titles in this sentence. The first poem mentioned
is published separately, the second is not.

The Ring and
the Book
"My Last
Duchess"

Robert Browning's The Ring and the Book
is in some respects related to his
My Last Duchess.

□ Mark the titles in this sentence. The first poem mentioned
is not published separately, the second one is.

"Hasty Pudding"
Rape of the Lock

Joel Barlow's Hasty Pudding has the
same mock-heroic tone as Pope's
Rape of the Lock.

(a) "Spelt from Sibyl's Leaves" <u>Poems of Gerard Manley Hopkins</u>	□ Mark the titles in these sentences.
	(a) Spelt from Sibyl's Leaves, one of Gerard Manley Hopkins' more important poems, can be found in Poems of Gerard Manley Hopkins.
(b) "A Hanging" <u>Shooting an Elephant and Other Stories</u>	(b) A Hanging is the most moving essay in George Orwell's Shooting an Elephant and Other Stories.

REVIEW

Mark the titles appropriately in the following sentences.

"The Enormous Radio" <u>The New Yorker</u> <u>The Enormous Radio and Other Stories</u>	□ The Enormous Radio, John Cheever's most popular short story, originally appeared in The New Yorker and then was reprinted in his collection titled The Enormous Radio and Other Stories.
<u>Moby Dick</u> "Loomings"	□ The first chapter of Melville's Moby Dick is called Loomings.

USING ITALICS TO CONTRAST WORDS IN CONTEXT

	22B Italicize where necessary in these sentences.
(a) <u>dux bellorum</u>	(a) One of the earliest written notices of King Arthur refers to him as dux bellorum (general) rather than king.
(b) <u>plastic</u>	(b) The term plastic, now commonly a noun as well as an adjective, refers to material which can be easily shaped or molded.

□ Italics are useful in setting off words or terms spoken about.

> Iron may be found almost anywhere
> in the world.
> <u>Iron</u> may be used as noun, an
> adjective, or a verb.

To show that *Iron* is a word being discussed, not a noun referring to a kind of metal, it is italicized in the [first, second] _____ sentence.

second

□ Our word silly descends from a Middle
English word that described a person
who was prosperous or blessed.

> When I say that she is silly, I do
> not mean that she is either
> prosperous or blessed.

Silly should be italicized in the [first, second] _____ sentence but not in the _____ sentence.

first

second

□ Indicate italics where necessary in the following sentences.

(*a*) Hootenanny

(*a*) Hootenanny was first used in
1950 to describe a gathering
of folk singers.

(*b*) Sophisticated college students
seem to enjoy the handclapping
and folk singing at a hootenanny.

□ Normally we italicize foreign words and phrases to distinguish them from the English words in a sentence.

> We felt that the majority of the
> Mexican people were <u>muy simpatico.</u>

The Spanish phrase *muy simpatico* (very nice) is distinguished in this sentence by being _____.

italicized

□ Many foreign words, such as the French noun *pension* (boarding house), would not be distinguishable from English words identical in spelling but different in meaning. Italicizing such words is often the only way we can show what such words mean. Indicate italics where necessary in this sentence.

pension

Our pension in Rouen was small
but clean.

□ Of course, any foreign word in general use becomes a part of English and is not set off in italics. For instance, the Spanish word *guerrilla* (little war) is now part of English. However, the German word *Weltseele* (worldsoul), although occasionally used by English writers, is not yet part of English. Indicate the necessary italics in these sentences.

(a) Weltseele

(a) For many, Camus' novels are closest
to this age's Weltseele.

(b) The guerrilla fighters moved
down the road behind the
armored car.

□ Both of the following sentences contain borrowed foreign words. Italicize where necessary.

(a) Weltan-
schauung

(a) Philosophers close to the German
tradition often speak casually of
their common Weltanschauung.

(b) arroz con
pollo

(b) Those who dislike Mexican food will
change their minds after tasting
well-cooked arroz con pollo.

Italicize where necessary in the following sentences.

sophisticated

☐ The word *sophisticated* has undergone several important changes in meaning during the last five centuries.

sign
signum

☐ The English noun *sign* comes from the Latin noun *signum*.

Pinus ponderosa

☐ The larger pine trees, particularly the *Pinus ponderosa*, are important sources of lumber for home building.

TWENTY-THREE
APOSTROPHES

PUNCTUATING CONTRACTIONS AND POSSESSIVES

don't children's it's	**23A** Correct the punctuation in this sentence where necessary. *I'd like to play golf, but I dont dare; I have to build a foundation for my childrens' swings today, and its already half past ten.*
not would	□ Certain words are contractions of two words. *Don't* is a contraction of *do* _____ ; *I'd* is a contraction of *I* _____ .
We'd I'll	□ The indication of a contraction is the apostrophe ('). Add the apostrophe to the contractions in this sentence. *We d like to go, but I ll be surprised if we can.*
He's aren't	□ Make contractions of the bracketed words in this sentence. [*He is*] _____ ready, but they [*are not*] _____ .

□ Form a contraction of the bracketed words in this sentence.

It's

[*It is*] _____ *a good idea.*

□ The contraction *it's* has a near twin, the possessive pronoun *its,* which does not have an apostrophe. The apostrophe distinguishes the contraction from the possessive.

It's time for its feeding.

It's

its

The contraction of *it is* in this sentence is _____ ;
the possessive pronoun is _____ .

□ Add the apostrophe necessary in this sentence.

it's still hungry

Its feeding time is over, but its still hungry.

□ *Its* is like *their, his, our* and other forms of pronouns which show possession. These pronoun forms [do, do not]

do not

_____ require apostrophes.

□ Unlike possessive pronouns, possessive nouns are formed by adding an apostrophe and—if the noun is singular— an *s.*

Bob's attitude is good.

Bob

Bob's is the possessive form of the noun _____ .

□ Form the possessive of the nouns in brackets.

Tonight's
Robertson's

[*Tonight*] _____ *paper reports in full* [*Robertson*] _____ *decision on housing.*

□ If a noun is plural and ends in *s,* we form the possessive by adding the apostrophe after the *s: students', teamsters'.*

The professors' position on the matter was clear.

We know by the form of the possessive *professors'* that the position referred to was held by [one, more than one]

more than one

_____ professor.

386

□ *This book discusses the [corporation]* _____
legal problems.

If the legal problems discussed are those of only one corporation, the correct form of the bracketed word is _____. If the problems are those of several, the correct form is _____.

corporation's
corporations'

□ A few plural nouns do not end in *s*. *Children* is the plural of *child*, and _____ is the plural of *man*.

men

□ The possessive ending of plural nouns which do not end in *s* is *'s*, not *s'*. The possessive of the plural noun *children* is *children's*; the possessive of *men* is _____.

men's

□ Add the apostrophe necessary in the following sentence.

The childrens party yesterday was a success.

children's

□ Add the apostrophes necessary in the following sentence.

Mens shirts button on the opposite side from womens blouses.

Men's
women's

REVIEW

Add apostrophes where necessary in the following sentences.

□ *The childrens grades are good.*

children's

□ *I cant give the dog its bath until its warmer outside.*

can't
it's warmer

□ *Id rather not try to sneak in through the players entrance.*

I'd
players'

Charles' *brother-in-law*'s	**23B** Add the necessary punctuation to this sentence. *Charles pearl cuff links were a gift he received for being one of the ushers at his brother-in-laws wedding.*

Phyllis'
Smiths'

□ The possessives of singular nouns ending in *s* (*Charles, Mr. Rogers, series*) do not require an additional *s*. An apostrophe by itself will indicate the possessive form (*Charles', Mr. Rogers', series'*). Add the necessary apostrophes to this sentence.

> *Phyllis watch fell into the Smiths swimming pool.*

□ Some writers prefer to add the *s* with the apostrophe to form the possessives of singular nouns ending in *s* (*Phyllis's, Charles's*). However, the general practice now is to add only the apostrophe to such nouns. Add the apostrophe necessary in this sentence.

Series'

> *The World Series telecasts are beamed from coast to coast.*

□ The possessive of hyphenated compound nouns (*Commander-in-Chief, sister-in-law*) is formed by adding **'s** to the final word whether the compound noun is singular or plural. Notice that the plural of most hyphenated compound nouns is formed by adding *s* to the first word, not the last word, in the compound. Thus the plural of *Commander-in-Chief* is *Commanders-in-Chief;* however, the

Commander-in-
Chief's

possessive of the same compound noun is _____.

□ The possessive form of the singular *sister-in-law* is *sister-in-law*'s; the possessive form of the plural *sisters-in-law*

sisters-in-law's

is _____.

□ Form the possessives of the bracketed nouns to complete this sentence.

brothers-in-law's

bride-to-be's

> The [brothers-in-law] _____
> car broke down on the way to the wedding, but the [bride-
> to-be] _____ knowledge of
> carburetors saved the day.

□ Occasionally we use an entire phrase as a possessive.

> *The man's opinion is lightly regarded.*
> *The man in the street's opinion is lightly regarded.*

man in the street's

In the second sentence the phrase *The* _____
has the same function as the possessive *man's* in the first
sentence.

□   *The man in the street's opinion is lightly regarded.*

This sentence illustrates that to form a phrasal possessive
—a possessive having more than one word—we add 's

last

to the [first, last] _____ word in the phrase.

□ Form a possessive from the bracketed phrase in this
sentence.

The girl in blue's

> [*The girl in blue*] _____
> *hair is attractively cut.*

□ Add the necessary apostrophe to this sentence.

Education's

> *The Board of Educations weekly meeting was postponed
> until Friday.*

Add the necessary punctuation to the following sentences.

Roberts'
brother-in-law's

☐   The Roberts dog bit my brother-in-laws leg.

door's

☐   The man next doors garage burned down yesterday.

sergeant-at-arms'

☐   A sergeant-at-arms duties are few.

TWENTY-FOUR
HYPHENS

HYPHENS WITH COMPOUND MODIFIERS AND NUMBERS

middle-aged
four-by-eight
second-class

24A Place hyphens where necessary in the following sentence.

The middle aged couple sat in their four by eight cabin in the second class section discussing their trip.

□ An important use of the hyphen (-) is to link two or more words that function as a single unit modifying a noun.

The house was built well.
The well-built house was a century old.

In the first sentence the words *built* and *well* function separately. But in the second sentence they combine to modify the noun _____.

house

☐ *The salesman talked fast.*

The fast-talking salesman sold us the car.

In the second sentence the words *fast* and *talking* are joined by a _____ to show that they function as a single unit modifying the noun _____.

hyphen
salesman

☐ *The creature had ten legs.*

The ten legged creature ate the bait.

In the second sentence a hyphen should join the words _____ and _____ that modify together the noun *creature*.

ten   legged

☐ *His hair was cropped short.*

His short cropped hair was bright red.

In the second sentence a hyphen should join the words _____ and _____.

short   cropped

☐ *The high flying plane left vapor trails.*

The plane was flying high above the fog.

A hyphen is needed between *high* and *flying* only in the [first, second] _____ sentence.

first

☐ Place hyphens where necessary in the following sentence.

The well kept secret concerned the sale of a large dry cleaning chain.

well-kept
dry-cleaning

☐ Often two words acting together as the modifier of a noun will involve a spelled-out number. Remember, however, to join with a hyphen only those words acting as a group modifier of a noun.

The building has only three stories.
The three story building will be torn down.

A hyphen after *three* is needed only in the [first, second] _____ sentence.

second

	□ *His performance was second rate.* *He gave a second rate performance.*
second	A hyphen after *second* is needed only in the [first, second] _____ sentence.
	□ Place hyphens where needed here.
second-class	*He always travels first class, but only second class tickets were available.*
	□ A group modifier requiring hyphens may have more than two words.
	A fly-by-night company did the roofing.
company	Here a group modifier consisting of three words, *fly-by-night*, modifies the noun _____.
	□ *It was a flash-in-the-pan venture.*
flash-in-the- pan	In this sentence the noun *venture* has a group modifier consisting of four words, _____.
	□ Place hyphens where necessary in this sentence.
off-the-shoulders	*She wore an off the shoulders blouse.*
	□ Place hyphens where necessary in this sentence.
under-the-counter	*Careful customers avoid under the counter sales.*

	24B Place hyphens where necessary in the following sentence.
twenty-four one-quarter	*The package contained four hundred and fifty nails, twenty four wood screws, and ten one quarter plates.*

	□ Hyphens are often used in compound numbers, those having more than one word when spelled out. For instance,
is not is	*seventy* [is, is not] _____ a compound number, while *seventy-six* [is, is not] _____.

□ All compound numbers below one hundred are normally joined by hyphens; those above are not.

The twenty four salesmen sold over four thousand cameras.

In this sentence a hyphen is needed only between the words _____ and _____.

twenty four

□ A hyphen is needed in *twenty-four* because it is a compound number below _____.

one hundred

□ Place hyphens where needed in this sentence.

Two hundred homes were built on the thirty seven acres.

thirty-seven

□ Place hyphens where needed in this sentence.

Eighty two members voted for the tax measure; four hundred and fifty voted against it.

Eighty-two

□ Since fractions are compound numbers below one hundred, they also are generally hyphenated.

The radius is three quarters of an inch.

In this sentence a hyphen is needed between _____ and _____.

three
quarters

□ *One fourth of the team left.*

Here a hyphen is needed between _____ and _____.

one
fourth

□ Place hyphens where needed here.

Three eights was the inside diameter of all thirty two lengths of conduit.

Three-eights
thirty-two

□ Remember, only compound numbers below one hundred need hyphens. Place hyphens where needed here.

One third of one hundred and five is thirty five.

One-third
thirty-five

394

Three-fourths *twenty-five*	☐ Place hyphens where needed here. *Three fourths of the two hundred boats here were built* *more than twenty five years ago.*

REVIEW

Place hyphens where needed here.

off-the-cuff	☐ *The retired admiral had several pointed off the cuff remarks to make.*
Twenty-four *thirty-five* *fifty-nine*	☐ *Twenty four and thirty five is fifty nine.*
seventy-five *second-rate*	☐ *At least half of the seventy five homes were built with second rate fixtures.*
over-the-counter	☐ *All over the counter sales were tallied before the close of the market.*
second-mortgage *lower-income*	☐ *Second mortgage costs were said to be the reason for the reduction in the building of lower income dwellings.*

HYPHENS DIVIDING WORDS

re-/bate-/ment *vest-/ment* *photo-/graph*	**24C** Which of the following words can be divided by a hyphen at the end of a line of writing? Show where each can be divided. *adore* *through* *rebatement* *vestment* *thorny* *photograph*

□ The hyphen (-) is a punctuation mark we use to show the connection between word parts.

The new urban redevelop-
ment project is completed.

Here parts of the word *redevelopment* appear on different lines. The sign showing that *redevelop* is not a complete word is the _____ following it.

hyphen

□ *Shares of the new consoli-*
dated stock are on the market.

consolidated

Here the word _____ is divided by a hyphen.

□ If we divide words at the end of a line, we should divide between syllables. For instance, the word *keepsake* has two syllables, _____ and _____.

keep   sake

□ The word *prepayment*, which has three syllables, can be divided at one of two places, between *pre* and *payment* or between _____ and _____.

prepay   ment

□ *Plans for expanding the wareho-*
use are going forward.

is not

In this example, *warehouse* [is, is not] _____ properly divided.

□ *Warehouse* should be divided between its two syllables, _____ and _____.

ware   house

can
cannot

□ We [can, cannot] _____ divide *frontage* at the end of a line, but we [can, cannot] _____ divide *round*.

□ *Four of the ten managers were bro-*
ught to Cleveland for a retrain-
ing program.

The word in this sentence which should not be divided is

brought

_____.

□ If a word has a syllable of a single letter at the beginning or end, we should not divide the word so that the single letter appears by itself.

The twins were not really a-
lone in their grief.

should not

Alone in this sentence [should, should not] _____ be divided as it is.

□   *The counterman prepared a froth-*
    y milkshake for the entire foot-
    ball team.

The word that should not be divided as it is in this sentence

frothy

is _____.

□ To divide a word with hyphens, then, we divide only between syllables; but we do not separate a syllable of a single letter from the rest of the word. Thus, we can divide *adoring*

dor   ing

a   dor

between the syllables _____ and _____ but not between the syllables _____ and _____.

rub

ber   ber   y

□ We can divide *rubbery* between the syllables _____ and _____ but not between the syllables _____ and _____.

REVIEW

□ Show with hyphens where, if possible, we can divide the following words at the end of a line. Note that we can divide some of the words in more than one place.

thru-/way

dis-/burse-/ment

ex-/ten-/sive

wick-/ed-/ness

form-/less-/ly

alive	*extensive*
thruway	*wickedness*
disbursement	*formlessly*

TWENTY-FIVE
CAPITALIZATION

CAPITALIZING FIRST WORDS IN SENTENCES AND QUOTATIONS

"A

25A Capitalize the appropriate words in this sentence.

"a sudden squall," he reported, "threw us off our bearings."

□ We capitalize the first word of every sentence.

the three of us went together.

The

In this sentence we should capitalize the word _____.

□ If a sentence contains a quotation, we capitalize the first word in it also. Capitalize the appropriate words in this sentence.

He
"Wait

he said, "wait a minute."

398

□ If a quoted sentence is broken in the middle, we do not capitalize the first word after the break.

> *"Where were you," the boy asked, "when the fire broke out?"*

should not

In this sentence *when* [should, should not] _____ be capitalized.

□ Capitalize where necessary in this sentence.

"There

> *"there they were," he said, "looking as though nothing had happened."*

□ If a break in a quotation comes between two sentences, the word beginning the new quoted sentence is, of course, capitalized. Make the necessary changes in this sentence.

"Hey!"
"Come

> *"hey!" he shouted, "come see our new home!"*

REVIEW

Capitalize the appropriate words in the following sentences.

To
"Yes
Swell!"

□ *to this she replied, "yes, I'd love to go"; and all I could think to say was "swell!"*

"There

□ *"there we were," he said, "fifty miles west of Acapulco, without a breeze stirring and without a drop of fuel."*

CAPITALIZING PROPER NAMES

(a) *There*
   Sergeant Burns
(b) *The Renaissance*
   Christian
   Middle Ages

25B Capitalize where necessary in these sentences.

(a) *there is no other sergeant like sergeant burns.*

(b) *the renaissance, breaking in abruptly on the christian traditions of the middle ages, created an upheaval which still lasts.*

□ Proper names are the names of individual persons, places, or things. Such names are always capitalized.

The man gave Frank and Bob a ride.

Frank and *Bob* are capitalized in this sentence because they are _____ names.

proper

□ The names of specific places—cities, states, nations—are also proper names. Capitalize the appropriate words in this sentence.

Duluth, Minnesota

We visited duluth, minnesota, last spring.

□ The names of geographical areas are proper names if they refer to specific locations rather than directions. Thus we capitalize *south* in *the South* but not in *south of Detroit*. Capitalize the appropriate words in the following sentence.

Central United States

Flying west, we were soon over the central united states.

□ The names of specific oceans, mountains, lakes, rivers, and similar geographical features are also proper names. Capitalize the appropriate words in this sentence.

Sierra Nevada
Mountains
Rocky Mountains

The sierra nevada mountains are west of the rocky mountains.

□ Capitalize the appropriate words in this sentence.

Minnesota
Mississippi River
Gulf of Mexico
New Orleans

Running south from its origins in minnesota, the mississippi river divides the continent, emptying finally into the gulf of mexico below new orleans.

400

☐ The names of particular historical epochs and events—the Renaissance, the Enlightenment, World War II—are proper names. Capitalize the appropriate words in this sentence.

> The boer war established britain's claims in south africa.

Boer War
Britain's
South Africa

☐ Capitalize the appropriate words in this sentence.

> The so-called reconstruction period following the civil war had a profound effect on the history of the south.

Reconstruction
Period
Civil War   South

☐ The names of the days of the week and the months of the year are proper names. The names of the seasons (*spring, summer, autumn,* and *winter*) are not. Capitalize the appropriate words in this sentence.

> Last spring—on sunday, may 4, to be exact—I was promoted to my present position.

Sunday, May 4

☐ Words not usually capitalized—lieutenant, bridge, university—are capitalized if they are part of a proper name. Capitalize the appropriate words in this sentence.

> A professor, who was not identified, secretly nominated professor blake for the position.

Professor Blake

☐ Capitalize the appropriate words in this sentence.

> In looking over the various school bulletins, Ed decided that the university of california offered the best courses in his field of any university in the west.

University of
California
West

☐ Adjectives based upon proper names are normally capitalized: *Christian* (*Christ*), *Roman* (*Rome*), *Asian* (*Asia*). Capitalize the appropriate words in this sentence.

> His knowledge of english poetry—particularly the poetry of the renaissance—made him the most popular lecturer at the university of indiana.

English
Renaissance
University of Indiana

☐ Capitalize the appropriate words in this sentence.

Professor Flynn
California
Depression

When professor flynn moved west to california, he did not realize that the cost of living there had gone up since the depression.

☐ Capitalize the appropriate words in this sentence.

Far East
Marines
Korean War

Henry toured the far east in less than favorable circumstances; he was one of the many marines shipped there during the korean war.

REVIEW

Capitalize the appropriate words in the following sentences.

Senator Bundy's
Pacific Coast

☐ *The other senators applauded senator bundy's appeal for greater conservation efforts along the pacific coast.*

May
Italian Alps

☐ *In may of last year we visited the italian alps.*

Great Depression

☐ *The great depression is misnamed because it was relatively mild when compared with previous depressions.*

CAPITALIZING WORDS IN TITLES

Someone's
Kitchen
Dinah

25C Capitalize the appropriate words in this sentence.

Do you know the music to "someone's in the kitchen with dinah"?

402

☐ The first word of a title—whether of a book, play, short story, poem, song, movie, or other publication or work of art—is always capitalized. The other words in the titles are also capitalized, except for articles (*a, an, the*) prepositions (*for, by, to, with,* etc.), and coordinating conjunctions (*and, but, or, nor*). Capitalize the appropriate words in the title in this sentence.

"The Idea of Order at Key West"

Wallace Stevens' poem "the idea of order at key west" is unusual in its imagery.

☐ Capitalize the appropriate words of the title in this sentence.

"A Sense of Movement"

Russell Blair's article on modern music, "a sense of movement," is a useful guide to some of the important contemporary composers.

☐ Capitalize the appropriate words of the title in this sentence.

"The Bride Comes to Yellow Sky"

Although Stephen Crane was an Easterner, his short stories of the West, particularly "the bride comes to yellow sky," have a strikingly authentic quality.

REVIEW

Capitalize the appropriate words in the following sentences.

La Gioconda
The Mona Lisa

☐ *Da Vinci's la gioconda is a painting better known in this country as the mona lisa.*

"Black Is the Color of My True Love's Hair"

☐ *An almost forgotten folk song is the traditional "black is the color of my true love's hair."*

"In the Back of the Mind of My Father"

☐ *One of James Roberts' most unusual short stories is called "in the back of the mind of my father."*

INDEX